To Sea in Haste

E
N S
W

Halifax

To Sea

Boston

FLORIDA

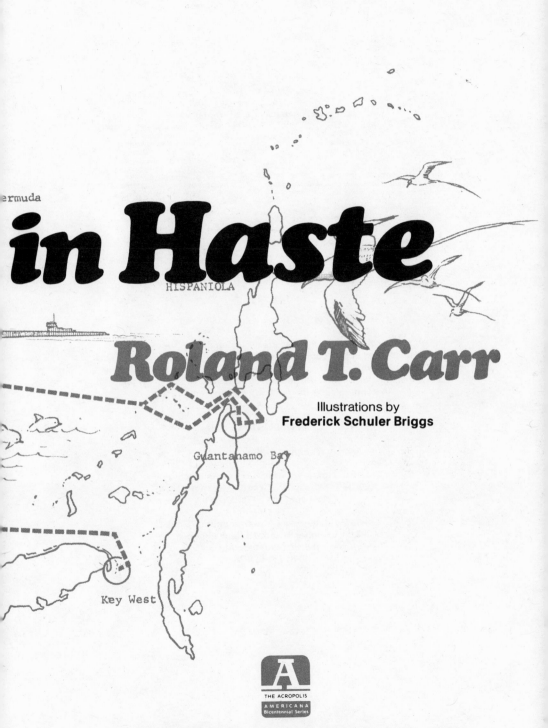

in Haste

Roland T. Carr

Illustrations by
Frederick Schuler Briggs

ACROPOLIS BOOKS LTD. ● WASHINGTON, D.C. 20009

THE ACROPOLIS AMERICANA/BICENTENNIAL SERIES

To Sea in HASTE
Discover USA '76
Entertaining In the White House
The Inaugural Address
Washington Walked Here
Presidents On Wheels
An Apology for Printers
The Jefferson Drafts of the Declaration of Independence
Grant The Soldier
Lee
The Gentleman from Ohio. An Introduction to Garfield
An Eye for An Eye
The American Film Heritage
To Be A Congressman
Dear Congressman Howard:
Liberal Leader in the House
Yarborough of Texas

The Life and Accomplishments of Herbert Hoover
Washington III
Rhetoric of Revolution
Violence In America
Inside America
O Say Can You See
Nine Black Poets
An Anthology of Verse by American Negroes
A Galaxy of Black Writing
Divided We Stand
Appalachian Dawn
Entries from Oxford
The North Carolina Adventure
From Bussing to Bugging
The Encyclopedia of Howard Hughes Jokes
The Kidner Report
Senator Sam Ervin's Stories

Handbook of Humor by Famous Politicians

ACROPOLIS BOOKS LTD.
Colortone Building, 2400 17th St., N.W.
Washington, D.C. 20009

Printed in the United States of America by
COLORTONE PRESS, Creative Graphics Inc.
Washington, D.C. 20009

Library of Congress Catalog Number 75-13944
International Standard Book Number
0-87491-240-0 (cloth)
0-87491-020-X

To Lorraine, my lovely wife of twenty-five years, who first heard from a tea leaf reader at 42nd Street and Fifth Avenue, circa 1960, that this book might be published; and to Dr. Alec Horwitz, surgeon extraordinary, miracle worker, who performed the patchwork on my reincarnation in December, 1963, assisted by my longtime personal physician, Dr. Israel Kessler; and to Isabel, successor to my high school and college teachers, for her skilled editorial advice and assistance, and to her late, beloved husband, Colonel James Mangum, for his timely encouragement.

Thankfully and affectionately,
RTC
May 8, 1975

Acknowledgments

The splendid cooperation of my former fellow officers of the HASTE in the development of this volume is most gratefully acknowledged. Skipper George R. Boyce, Jr.; roommates Tom Cooney and Chuck Turner; and our own inimitable medic, Dr. Raymond Hofstra, were of immense assistance. George Dunbar and Charles Pangle also contributed via long and helpful correspondence over protracted periods.

Special acknowledgment is made of the encouragement and helpfulness of Vice Admiral K.K. Cowart, USCG(Ret.), and the charming Mrs. Cowart (who shares with me a special secret about our birth dates); and of Commander Hugh A. Doyle, USCGR(Ret.), close friend and confidant since our days at Ellis Island Receiving Station in 1944-45; and to our former superior and Finance Officer at #42 Broadway, Commander Garland Sponburgh, USCG (Ret.). Helpful cheers and boosts have emanated from our special SPAR shipmate at Ellis Island, Lieutenant Dina S. Fleischer of Richmond, Virginia.

A profound word of thanks is hereby included for the timely and generous assistance of the Director of Naval History, Vice Admiral Edwin B. Hooper, USN(Ret.), and to the skilled and courteous members of the staff of Operational Archives Branch: Dr. Dean C. Allard, head of the branch, and historians Mrs. Kathleen M. Lloyd and Mrs. Nina F. Statum.

I cannot close without mentioning the faithful and tireless efforts of my longtime secretary and assistant, Mrs. Maria B. Ruhe, who contributed many hours of her own time and weekends typing the many copies of the manuscript and struggling with the additions, changes, and revisions, etc. A further word of thanks is due Miss Alice B. Manning for her initial assistance and helpful encouragement.

Foreword

TO SEA IN HASTE is the story of a small World War II warship that was engaged in anti-submarine and convoy activities in the Eastern Sea Frontier of the United States — a frontier that extended roughly from Halifax to Florida and Cuba.

The story is based on a diary kept by the author under difficult conditions, the most important being that it was against regulations. This regulation hinged on the fundamentally sound theory that such material might fall into enemy hands and thus furnish information on the movement of ships and men. Nevertheless, the author had an overriding impulse to leave behind some record of his thoughts and feelings for a son, only four months old at the time, should the events of war take his father permanently out of his life.

The shipboard diary entries, which began awkwardly and apprehensively, picked up in style and content as the author, a banker transplanted by the advent of World War II into this strange new milieu, learned in an astonishingly short time to accustom himself to the ship and the sea, and began to find moments of beauty, heroism, pathos and humor in the day-to-day activities around him.

TO SEA IN HASTE is not fiction. It is a true story. The ships, the characters, the events—all are real. THE U.S. COAST GUARD IN WORLD WAR II reports that between March and June of 1963 the U.S. Coast Guard furnished 850 personnel for manning eight corvettes that were being transferred to the United States from Canada via Lend-lease in reverse. No other mention of these ships, or even their names, appears in this volume. Therefore, this account, which revolves around the activities aboard and surrounding the corvette USS HASTE and involves her sister ships, USS ALACRITY and USS INTENSITY, and at times other corvettes and converted yachts, as well as smaller escorts such as PC's and SC's, is a genuine and heretofore undisclosed microcosm of the naval history of WORLD WAR II.

The story of the HASTE has been broadened to include post war research into declassified material, including U.S. Sea Frontier Diaries and related records and captured German War documents, which reveal the devastating submarine activities which preceded the arrival of the HASTE, as well as those which continued to take place in and around the waters through which she sailed.

Also incorporated is the author's chronicle of his hectic and sometimes humorous "90-day wonder indoctrination" at Curtis Bay, Maryland in early 1942.

To those shipmates whose names do not find mention here, humblest apologies. The omission is related to the general problem of keeping notes on a small, crowded and constantly moving vessel, plus the further complication of keeping them as small and compact as possible. Then, too, there was the additional problem of trying to catch up in good weather, for the lack of notes in bad weather.

Despite the deficiencies of this account, it is hoped it will bring back many memories and perhaps a few nostalgic chuckles to all those who sailed from Boston and Staten Island, suffered their shakedown tribulations in Bermuda, and put in at Key West and Guantanamo.

We hope, too, that this narrative may find some small medium of identification by all those men and women who served in the Coast Guard in those hectic and often heroic days, and who, like us, were inspired or intimidated — or just plain awed — by the fearsome motto of that gallant service: "You have to go out, but you don't have to come back."

1

> Boast not thyself of to-
> morrow; for thou knowest
> not what a day may bring
> forth.
>
> Proverbs 27:1

IT WAS FOOLISH IN THE Spring of '43 even in Miami to regard anything as permanent or stable. On the other hand, it was folly to let oneself dwell upon the instability. World War II—like all wars—was obviously not being run for the convenience of any of us who were so unwittingly involved in it, and there was little we could do but take it as it came. Nevertheless, there had been a sickening suddenness to my orders for sea duty.

During those eleven months while I had been stationed in Miami there had been very little news, or any sort of communication from former friends and banking associates in Washington. As far as the home front was concerned, everyone in the bank was far too busy with an "overload of work" to bother with those of us who had gone into the Service. They had their own problems, and evidently regarded us as being wrapped in some sort of splendid isolation, completely removed from them for the present and sufficient unto ourselves.

There also seemed to be a general assumption that I was "set" for the duration. Burks Summers, a prominent Washington businessman and client with whom I had struck up a friendship during the banking conventions at White Sulphur Springs, was one of the few people who took the trouble to write me. In a letter of January 20, 1943, he mentioned that he had heard from Vice President Bisselle, my former boss at the Bank, that "you like your work and are probably as comfortably situated as you can be for the duration."

It was a pleasantly optimistic view which I had never really permitted myself to share. With a keeping-my-fingers-crossed attitude, I frequently told myself and others that I couldn't believe I had enlisted to reap all the benefits of that lush and fascinating Florida background. In spite of this rationalization, my new assignment coming so suddenly took me completely by surprise, and was much more rugged than anything I had expected. To add to my first sense of shock, my orders seemed portentously ambiguous.

I was to report to Boston, where The Coast Guard District Office would direct me to my ship. When Personnel called me, they sounded a bit apologetic about not being able to tell me what sort of ship I was to sail on. "All we know—it's the *PG-92*," I was told. "That's a Patrol Gunboat, of course, and most of them are converted yachts; but we've looked through everything we have and we just don't seem to be able to find this one."

There was little in that to reassure me or answer the dozen questions which were of deep concern to me at the moment. So I made a hasty call to a fellow alumnus of my Pay Clerk training class at Curtis Bay, who was stationed at Headquarters in Washington.

He listened sympathetically to my problem and said, "Hold on and I'll see what I can find out here." When he came back to the phone he was chuckling in what seemed to me a rather macabre manner. "Remember the K75 at Curtis Bay? Well, you're in luck, boy. This is a corvette—one of the eight we're taking over from Canada. Call me if I can be of any help."

It didn't seem to me that anyone or anything could be of help at that moment. The K75! Ah, yes, I remembered her, indeed! I could still see the small English sailor who had given us a personally-conducted tour of her at Curtis Bay—could still hear the Cockney voice explaining the "good points" which had been so hard for us to detect.

So there I was—the second-oldest member of the class who had started in "boot camp" back there at Curtis Bay, Maryland, near Baltimore, and with a son not yet four months old—now about to go to sea on what to our class at Curtis Bay seemed a classic example of every undesirable feature a ship could possess.

I was appalled. As a matter of fact, if I had been willing to admit it, even to myself, I was more than appalled—I was scared as hell. The inspiring Coast Guard motto, "Semper Paratus," fell somewhat short of getting through to me during the first impact of my orders. The Coast Guard might indeed be "Always Ready," but at that moment—quite frankly—I was not.

I had gone to sea on a freighter with no experience and very little realization of what I was getting into; but I had been younger then, and hungry for adventure. This was different. This was no temporary, self-propelled enterprise. The stakes were higher. And with only training in pay and supply work, no background of gunnery, of navigation, of engineering or communication, my new assignment seemed little less than suicidal.

My low spirits were not lifted when my new boss in Miami, Commander A. A. Strain, who had come off the *Wakefield*, decided to throw a farewell dinner for me.

The *Wakefield* had been the passenger liner *Manhattan* before the outbreak of World War II, but had been taken by the Navy for troop-carrying and renamed. After numerous trips across the Atlantic, and having voyaged to Colombo and Bombay and Capetown, she had burned while at sea off Halifax on September 5, 1942. She was subsequently towed to the Boston Navy Yard for reconditioning and was finally re-commissioned in April 1944. But, in the meantime, Commander Strain never tired of telling of the hazards of the *Wakefield* voyage, which ended with the fire and the abandonment of the ship. He was really a very decent sort, but extremely single-minded and inclined to plow full steam ahead. Then, too, he had the condescending manner which all men coming in from sea duty displayed—consciously or unconsciously—toward those who had not yet been out.

Over cordials the night of my farewell dinner, he speculated on where my "battle station" might be. I felt at that time that I couldn't care less, and I wished he would drop the subject, but he didn't. "You'll probably be on the bridge," he decided, "at fire control or damage control." He stared at me speculatively then as though weighing the effect of his words and whether or not I'd be able to measure up to what lay ahead. My face must have remained mercifully blank, because he continued, "You know when you 'fight your ship' everybody has an assignment, and it's what you do at your post that makes or breaks your ship."

Strain will remain in my memory as a good officer with a most considerate and attractive wife, and it was nice of them to plan a sendoff for me—but never have I been happier to have a supper party behind me.

After these goodbyes, Dee and I and Junior and my mother started the trek that would bring me to Boston and the unknown, and would leave them behind in Washington. At least I had ten days' leave en route which would afford time to settle them in Washington and to take a proper farewell.

Under ordinary circumstances, that sudden move undoubtedly would have proved to be a hardship; but, while it naturally presented problems, moves of Service people during the war had become more or less routine and were characterized by speed and efficiency. We shipped what we couldn't pack, and in the '41 Ford convertible—and with Junior in his bassinet in the back seat with my mother—we pulled away from the Blue Ocean Apartments. We crossed the 71st Street Causeway, with its vista of blue water and palms against a cloud-flecked sky, and turned into U.S. 1 leading North.

During the three day drive, beginning with the long stretches of highway along the Florida coast, I was reflecting on how I came to get into the Coast Guard in the first place. I began to recall some of the strangely unrelated and extraordinary things that occurred during our basic training at Curtis Bay, the Coast Guard's own "Navy Yard" near Baltimore, where I took the training that made me a Pay Clerk—a warrant officer ranking just above the highest enlisted ratings.

There was plenty of time on that trip back to Washington for a recapitulation and re-evaluation of all that had happened to me so far, which seemed a far better mental exercise than trying to contemplate what the future held in store.

The Coast Guard had taken me at face value, and after the door presumably had been closed. I had sought admission to the Officer Training schools of several other services, but because of my age—thirty-four—I was deemed to be "over the hill" for such training.

I had already been informed that the Coast Guard class for pay officers had been closed when I ran into Admiral Waesche, Commandant of the Coast Guard, in the bank one day when he was calling on our Chairman, Robert V. Fleming. Surprisingly he told me, "We're looking for some men with practical experience," and suggested that I talk with Admiral Frank J. Gorman, the head of Finance and Supply.

And so it happened that on an April day in 1942, with the suddenly unloved cherry trees, which had been a gift of the Mayor of Tokyo back in 1910, in mocking full-bloom beside the newly completed Jefferson Memorial, I called at headquarters building, next to the Bureau of Engraving, to talk to Admiral Gorman.

I found him a pleasant person with an easy manner, who was sympathetic toward my cause, but told me it was hopeless—the class was closed. However, he showed a polite interest and asked me if I had ever had any sea experience. I told him that in 1936 I had taken leave from the bank and worked my way to Europe as a deck hand on the freighter *Black Condor*, and it was then I saw the doors to the Pay Clerk class reopen. He picked up the telephone and said to someone on the other end, "I've got another good man here. I think we had better expand that class a little."

It seemed a tremendously lucky break, especially when the "expansion" subsequently was able to include two long-time good friends from the bank, Harry Bergmann and Frank Gibbons, who signed up and became fellow Coast Guardsmen and classmates.

The swearing-in ceremony for the three of us took place at the old Southern Railway Building on Pennsylvania Avenue, in that same month of April, 1942. Far down that grand thoroughfare the Capitol was agleam atop its misty hill when we dutifully reported that morning, carrying the suitcases that would be used to return our "civvies" back home for the duration. We were to enlist as Yeomen, Second Class; this meant we would be somewhat lowly enlisted Petty Officers until we succeeded in passing the Pay Clerk course.

The formalities had been gratifyingly impressive with the flag, the oaths and the Bible; and the two Chiefs who performed the ritual had seemed to be men both knowledgeable and considerate.

When it was over, one of them said, "I'll drive them over," and told us to meet him at the pickup truck out front.

When we looked into the back of the truck we discovered that its only seating arrangement consisted of a number of unpainted boards fitted crosswise into the side paneling. They had all slid back to the rear and now formed a solid table-like surface.

"Arrange the boards," the Chief barked at us, as he came out and went around to climb into the front seat. We hastily and

15

clumsily clambered in and started pushing the boards forward, and barely managed to sit down before the truck lurched into the Avenue, and we started on our journey toward Baltimore and Curtis Bay and into the service of our country!

Curtis Bay and Curtis Creek, on the southwest side of the Patapsco River, somewhat northwest of Fort Carroll, were the approaches to large coal and oil wharves, several industrial plants at South Baltimore, and to the Coast Guard depot at Arundel Cove. The Coast Guard base was situated at the mouth of the small bay that narrowed into the creek.

The Yard, as it was called, was on one side of the creek, and on the other was the newly established Training Station. A concrete span connected the two. On our way to and from the clothing locker of the training station where some of us had been employed temporarily as clerks and cleanup men, we used to pause to lean against the bridge-railing and stare back at the hum of activities in the yard or harbor. It was the only chance we had to get a view of the other side of the vessels docked there.

One of them, coincidentally, had arrived at about the same time my class had, and she furnished our first contact with the real war going on outside our harbors. She was a small, blue-gray, grimy looking warship carrying the markings K-75, an English corvette, the first we had ever seen. Already some of her gun mountings had been stripped off for replacement by heavier weapons and her bridge was being reinforced with extra armament. She was a veteran, the only genuine one in the harbor and a source of fascination to us as green enlistees in the Pay Clerk class.

There were other ships in the harbor that attracted our attention from time to time as we moved around for our indoctrination. We were sent, a few at a time, into the different departments and offices to pick up what we could in the way of information from people sometimes reluctant or too busy to take the time to instruct us, or who occasionally knew little more than we did. Our rating of Yeoman Second Class, required and entitled us to wear an arm patch showing a quill and a white stripe above the Coast Guard shield; a rating which seemed comparable to a corporal's rank in the Army, and did not get us much attention from our informal instructors.

At the clothing locker we worked for a Warrant Officer named Mintz who was younger than most of us, but who had a year's serv-

16

ice in the Coast Guard. In the supply and commissary sections, his counterpart was a Warrant Officer named Chaiken (these two officers alternated at times in all three sections) and both of them tried hard to make up for the deficiencies of their staffs and to impart to us as much knowledge-in-a-hurry as possible.

In the pay office our instructor was the veteran Coast Guard finance officer, Lt. Commander Luther Cartright, who was a storehouse of all there was to know about pay and finance regulations. He was a sandy-haired North Carolinian with a boisterous manner and an impish grin who delighted in regaling his "bankers and insurance men" with his inexhaustible store of ribald anecdotes. He gave us confidence and status by his blustery acknowledgment of our presence, and he told us, "Don't worry; you'll do all right."

A career Academy officer, Commander Arrington, had been put in general charge of our class. He lectured us at the end of each afternoon in a hastily set up classroom in the gymnasium, trying to relate our practical experience, gathered during the day, to the hard complexity of regulations. But even Commander Arrington, we discovered, had had little experience as a lecturer—he looked as if he would have preferred sea duty any day to facing the befuddled crowd of embryo pay and supply officers with which he was confronted.

The corvette continued to be the focal point of much of our interest and curiosity. She was sitting now under the bow of the former American liner *City of Chattanooga,* and although she looked as though she could be loaded on the liner's forward deck, the *Chattanooga* looked helpless by comparison, despite the gun mountings workmen were erecting high up on her hurricane deck. The "Choo-choo," as she had inevitably been dubbed, had just been fumigated, and she was plastered with signs warning of "Deadly Poison."

On May first, appropriately enough, a tender named *Mayflower* had come in, heavy and ugly and resembling a ferry boat. She had been a buoy tender, but since most buoys, lights, and other aids to navigation had been beached, she herself was being converted to the armed class.

Four lightships were sitting out in the harbor. They were fire engine red and their names were painted in mammoth white letters across their sides: *Frying Pan, Chesapeake, Five Fathoms,* and *Relief.* They seemed lost and dismayed at being dragged in from their separate shoals and anchored up here in this dirty harbor so ingloriously. Rumor had it that, still anchored, they would be converted to training purposes.

Early in May a short, thick-set English sailor accommodatingly took us abord the corvette. It seemed to me that her most notable feature was the fact that utility superseded all idea of comfort or appearance. Although she was exactly a year old, there was not a spot aboard her that suggested the least newness. She might have been sailing for twenty years, judging from her appearance. Her bridge-house and cabins were a hodgepodge of seemingly unrelated equipment which looked as though it had been installed piecemeal with absolutely no regard for order. So many additions and changes had been made that she seemed a monument of patchwork.

With a Cockney accent so thick we could barely understand it, our British friend explained the corvette's good points, at least by his calculations. We were continually ducking to escape not only "doorways" but ceilings. It seemed to us an explanation for the small fellows making up the crew, because it seemed certain that any tall, or even average height man, would soon have knots on his head.

While we were aboard we asked our diminutive guide about conditions on convoy duty. He told us that during their last trip the convoy had taken nineteen days, and that during that time there had been some contact with the enemy throughout. There was practically no sleep for any of them during the entire period.

He also told us that the crew were being sent up to the Blue Ridge Mountains for a week, but we assumed he meant down in Virginia and was simply turned around in his directions. Then a few days later we saw a purchase order go through for transportation for them to Birdsboro, Pennsylvania!

I went home on a weekend pass, and when I got back Bergfeld who was from the bank next door to my own at 15th Street and Pennsylvania Avenue, told me, "We saw the wardroom of the corvette—it's below the waterline! Can you imagine eating down there with all those subs around?" Young Chatfield-Taylor, whose father was Undersecretary of Commerce at the time, and a socially prominent economic advisor, broke in, "God! I've had claustrophobia ever since I saw the place!"

Gene Crewson, son of an insurance executive—a pleasant, but

very ample young man—was especially disserviced by our sailor uniforms and had already been dubbed by some of the sailors working near us as "Gruesome Crewson." Now, the very thought of the corvette made him shake his head. "After you've served on one of those things, I guess you're ready for Birdsboro," he said.

We joked about the corvette and fervently hoped we would never see service on one. It seemed unlikely, since the British ship carried only about sixty men and six line officers, and did not include a finance and supply officer.

The top brass at Curtis Bay had originally been a little undecided as to where to quarter our class of roughly thirty men. They apparently thought that, as officer trainees, we should not be sent over with the "boots" in the training station. However, the regular barracks were already overcrowded, and as a result we had been billeted, goldfish fashion, in a line of bunks that ran down one side of the new recreation hall. All our gear had to be stored in a duffle bag that hung from a hook at the head of each of our bunks. When we returned from work at five in the evening and fell down exhausted on our bunks, we were serenaded by the band, just formed, which practiced punctually five nights a week from five to six—in the recreation hall. The leader played a trumpet, and we thought he blew it with extra relish and volume in our direction. But nature being what it is, we learned to fall asleep in the midst of a stirring, discordant, and loud rendition of *Semper Paratus,* which, of course, was the *pièce de résistance* of this hastily assembled group of alleged musicians.

After supper there was another distraction—the player piano, which was pumped full blast by one enthusiast after another right up until lights out at ten o'clock, more often than not to the accompaniment of a group of choristers. *Dear Mom* was a great favorite on the contraption.

At a time when we had passed a little over two months in this noise and confusion, continuing the learning process as best we could, and receiving occasional respite in the form of a weekend pass, or a night out at one of Baltimore's famous "hot spots," we were shaken by a strange happening. The player piano wouldn't play. Reason: the key part of its mechanism commonly referred to as "the guts" had disappeared. Dire glances were cast in our direction, but we knew nothing. A wonderful quiet reigned and we wrote an extra number of letters home.

Then one day Commander Arrington called a sudden and surprise inspection of our clothing and gear. The purpose, it was announced, was to determine that we had everything we were supposed to have been issued, and that each piece was properly stenciled with our names and service numbers.

The inspection went fairly uneventfully, with a few exceptions and admonitions, right down to my bunk. Commander Arrington looked over my display, picked up one of my sailor caps and inquired, "Is that ink?" and when I answered that it was, he said, "Make it heavier than that," and tossed it back. It was at the next bunk to mine that the fireworks happened.

He found nothing wrong with the fellow's gear, but for some reason he turned up his spring mattress. There, wired to the bottom of it, was the "guts" of the player piano!

The poor guy, who was shy anyway, gulped, turned purple, gasped, and finally sputtered, "Sir, honest to God—I didn't—believe me—." To put an end to his misery and embarrassment, to the confusion and consternation of the rest of us, and to Commander Arrington's own barely concealed mirth, that good officer turned his head and yelled a loud, "Tenshun!" Then he said to an aide, "Finish up and make a report on that," and headed for the nearest exit outside of which, we were sure, he had roared with laughter.

The next night we had piano music again.

Early in June we observed on our early morning inspection that the corvette's camouflaging had been completed and she was a very personable ship. She was evidently wearing her summer colors, light blue and green against a predominantly white background, and we speculated as to whether she was going north or south. A thin white stream of smoke came from the side of her funnel, indicating some sort of activity below deck, but she hadn't moved from her berth.

Two destroyers flying the Colombian flag came in. They were former British destroyers, and from their flush decks they appeared to be the vintage of World War I. The sailors aboard them wore uniforms identical with those of the British, except for their cap ribbons, and we decided that the uniforms, too, had probably come from England.

20

The ships appeared to be in good order and were bigger and smarter-looking than the corvette, which looked like a small, heavily loaded trawler by comparison. We figured the South American ships must have come in for anti-aircraft guns, since they did not seem to carry any at all, although each ship had eight torpedo tubes.

By the middle of June the corvette was gone. We had grown accustomed to her, and one day there was just a space in her berth—and we missed her. Actually, we had done very little talking to the English sailors during their stay. They were fed up with being ashore and as anxious as we to get on with the war.

But we soon had other things on our minds. An admiral and his party came through the Yard for inspection a couple of days later and took exception to our billeting in the recreation hall. "I don't care where you put 'em," he was reported to have said. "Just get them out of there."

Consequently, the following evening we found ourselves moving to the top deck of the regular barracks, a place that was intended only for storage space. The rafters came down low at the sides like a tent and almost touched our noses. Air was at a premium, coming meagerly through little round windows, one on each side, like those in an attic. We had to stand on tiptoe to see over the sills and then we only got a distant view of the grounds.

There was a coil of heavy rope attached under each window with a newly lettered sign saying "In case of fire." We could imagine trying to crawl through those windows in a hurry and trying to hang on to the rope. Some of us, we felt sure, especially Crewson, couldn't get through the windows.

The only entrance to the place was a ladder from the second deck that led straight up to an open hatch. We had to climb up there one rung at a time, hauling our bedding and sea bags on our backs.

We stretched out in exhaustion and resignation on our bunks and decided we would simply have to make the best of it. It turned out that Gibbons drew a cricket that was lodged in the roof insulation somewhere just above his bunk. It started its concert at 7:55 by our watches, though it was barely dark outside, and sounded as loud as a sewing machine. Gibbons also discovered he had above his bunk the one blue light bulb that would burn all night.

"Some people get everything," somebody muttered.

The move to the garret brought us an unexpected champion.

The stocky but wiry little commander of the Yard, Captain Reinburg, had opposed the move in the first place and only consented to it on a temporary basis.

"They've been around here for almost three months," he was later quoted as having said. "So give them their exams and get them the hell outa here. They're not going to learn a lot more till they get on the job anyway. And on my responsibility, they're not gonna stay up in that damned airspace."

By June 28th, the news was good. Bergmann, Gibbons and I would be on our way to Miami as Warrant Officers around the first or second week in July. We had passed the final test. Actually several of us, not having done too well on our first test, had passed a second one. Four of our classmates had failed and were informed they would be held over temporarily. None of us knew what that meant, but we would have had to be a hell of a lot more self-centered than we really were if we had not keenly suffered with our less fortunate companions.

There was a little ceremony in Captain Reinburg's office in which he said to us, "Gentlemen, you are being appointed into a service that has a reputation for performing miracles with practically nothing." That both relaxed and delighted us, and provoked a few chuckles and scattered applause. "You may be called upon," he went on, "to continue that tradition in the performance of your duties." The rest was congratulations, general observations, advice and good wishes that got a little hazy because most of us were trying to record his opening statement in our minds. Then the new officers of the United States Coast Guard Reserve were dismissed.

On July 4, 1942, after I had come back home to Washington, and was dressed for the first time in my Warrant Officer's "whites" with the gold braided shoulder boards and the gold cap insignia, Dee said, "I'm going to take you down to Galesville to the dance and show you off." And she did.

Sometime later, on a shadowy, breeze-filled pier on West River, near Annapolis, Dee told me, "Now you look like yourself."

Mellow and happy, proud of my uniform, Curtis Bay a thing of the past, and Miami an encouraging prospect for the future, I raised my glass in a toast and said, "Here's to you, dear, and God bless Admiral Gorman and Captain Reinburg."

And so it came to pass that eleven months after that toast on

West River, after spending a lush winter in Miami as Assistant Pay Officer for the U.S. Coast Guard at 7th Naval District Headquarters, I found myself enroute to the unknown PG 92, a Canadian cousin of our old friend, curiosity catcher, and "horror ship," the K75 at Curtis Bay.

So far as I knew at the time I was the only member of our class reporting to a corvette, although I later learned that several others received similar orders shortly thereafter.

I had left my friend Gibbons still serving as Supply Officer at the Conversion and Maintenance Division, located in a lush grove of coconut palms on the banks of the brown Miami River. C & M ("Coconuts and Monkeys," as it had been christened by its own people), was engaged in converting small private yachts into picket boats for duty along the swamps and canals and keys of southern Florida, hunting subs, spies and evidence of sabotage. Bergmann had been sent to San Juan, Puerto Rico, as a supply officer.

I had been over every detail I could recall of the K75 (We learned later she was *HMS Celandine*, of the flower class, and named for a plant of the poppy family) and had finally decided that despite our reactions, which were those of rank novices, it appeared that the men and the ship itself had survived in good shape their first year at sea, and perhaps there was no reason to assume that we on the PG-92 might not do the same, it being generally assumed that our tours of sea duty would also be for one year.

> "If any
> Count on two days, or any more
> to come,
> He is a fool; for a man has
> no morrow,
> Till with good luck he has got
> through today."
>
> *Trachiniae*
> Sophocles [496-406 B.C.]

BEFORE I LEFT WASHINGTON FOR Boston, there was another "farewell party" in my honor. This one was a gathering of my family. Tom Worford, who was married to my mother's cousin Sue, and who was one of my favorite members of the family, had been in the Navy as a young man and I remember saying to him in a moment of sentimentality during the evening, "Don't worry about me, Tom. I have lived to be thirty-five. I have won a few small honors and have been elected an officer of my Bank. I have been married and have a son. That's more than many men are given in a lifetime, and from here on in I don't feel that I can be robbed."

The more I said it, the more I believed it. Suddenly it was a speech, and it was my immediate, much-needed and hastily-assembled philosophy. It had taken a bit of doing, but it had evolved, and I felt better for having gotten it off my chest and straightened out my own thinking in the process. Looking back, it sounds a little sticky— but that's the way things were in those days. We all dramatize ourselves a little—especially in a moment of crisis—and it isn't a bad thing. It takes some of the sting out of reality.

I heard my mother say to someone, "Roland will be alright once he gets started." And somehow, in spite of my age, and all of the wisdom and philosophy I had supposedly picked up with the years and was still working on, it was oddly reassuring to hear her say it; and inwardly I thanked her for her confidence in me and her instinctive understanding—for I felt the same way now. It had always been like that. All I needed was to get started—and from there on in, I'd make it on my own.

I suppose we are all frightened of the unknown, but once we can confront it, measure it, and determine our chances, our normal confidence, hard-won courage, resignation, or pride, reasserts itself and we turn to whatever individual faith or philosophy we possess to meet what lies ahead.

One of the saddest moments of that party was the farewell to my older brother Franklin, with his crippled right hand and artificial right leg. (Frank's hand was paralyzed from brain damage at birth; he lost his right leg to bone cancer at 16). We said very little. Extending that withered hand, Frank told me huskily, "Take care of yourself, Butch." "I will," I answered. I was almost sure that what Frank was thinking was, "I wish I could go in your place." And for my part, remembering all that my brother had gone through, and his courage in the face of it, I determined that whatever I could do would be for both of us. It didn't have to be said. We looked at each other, grinned shakily, and that was that.

By June 10, 1943, I was in Boston. "I don't really know much about what I'm going to do," I wrote. "I got into Boston at twelve forty-five last night. Took a cab to the Statler and had to sit in the lobby for an hour until they found a room for me. This morning called the Coast Guard to find out how to get to their location. I took down some directions and then walked over there, hoping to learn a little something about Boston on the way. So far it seems neither good nor bad—it's just a town." May the shades of the Adamses, the Cabots, the Lowells—and even the Kennedys and Fitzgeralds—forgive me! My only excuse was that I had a lot on my mind, and Boston was just the first link in all that was to come.

The Coast Guard was expecting me and had me on the list of the *USS Haste*, which is the name of the PG-92. "She will carry seven or eight officers besides me," I noted in my diary. "The personnel office here knew about my promotion, and I took my physical and passed. As soon as a recommendation comes through from Miami (by dispatch—probably tomorrow), I'll be sworn in as a j.g. (lieutenant junior grade)."

In the meantime, I had been handed an official communication from the Coast Guard Headquarters in Washington which read:

TO: Pay Clerk Roland T. Carr, USCGR

VIA: Prospective Commanding Officer, *USS Haste* (PG-92)

SUBJ: Special Disbursing Agent: Designation as

1. You are hereby designated special disbursing agent for the *USS Haste* (PG-92). Disbursing symbol 55-269 is assigned you in connection with these duties.

2. HQ is ordering an emergency supply of 200 checks which will be delivered in the near future. Regular supply of checks will be ordered by you in accordance with instructions contained in Finance Circular No. 12-42, 21 January 1942.

3. $200,000 is being credited to your account.

H.C. Nussear

By direction

It seemed a somewhat unusual way to go to sea—with 200 checks and $200,000 to draw on, but it had a nice, reasonably-permanent connotation which I found pleasantly reassuring. Certainly they wouldn't want me to sink with all that money!

I was anxious to see the *Haste*, but although she was right there in Boston there was no opportunity for even a glimpse of her that day. Other officers who would be aboard her or on sister ships were reporting in just as I was, and one of the ensigns turned out to be a fellow I used to pay down in Miami. He introduced me to some of the others; and as usual speculations and rumors were rampant. Someone said we would take over the *Haste* on the 15th. Another said even if we did, we would still be in Boston several weeks. Somebody advanced the opinion that our home port would be New York instead of Boston.

The most interesting thing I heard was that we might run south to Key West, Trinidad, and then to Dakar—which would have been wonderful, since my younger Brother Paul was stationed at Trinidad at that time. However, I wasn't counting on anything until I heard something from the Skipper. He arrived late that day, and it was probable that we would all be called in the following day for a conference. The consensus was that we would have to work like hell the week following.

Ensign Adams, another ensign named Mullins, and I rounded out the day by finding a room that would cost us six dollars a week each. Since that was what I had paid to stay one night at the Statler, it was obvious why I considered the move a good one.

At a later date, I wrote a brief impression in my notebook of that temporary abode at 135 Beacon Street. "In Boston we lived in an old residence on Beacon Street near the Common. The 'Common' evidently received its name from the fact that the common man might practice freedom of speech there, because there was always a crackpot on a bench pouring out a tirade against something or other. But the park was a wonderful place, green and spacious, with magnificent old trees and several duck ponds the size of small lakes.

"We used to stop there on the way home from the shipyard, and the peacefulness and quiet were a genuine boon after the hustle and bustle we had been through. We had two entire Sundays off, and I passed both days lounging under the trees, reading, sleeping, writing home, or making notes in my diary. The weather was delightful. June in Boston had all the virtues of spring a little farther south.

"The old residence with its tall gilt mirrors, ornate chandeliers, twisting staircases, reminded me of my childhood home in southwest Washington. The landlady was a kindly soul and proud of the number of Service men who stopped there. Her rooming house was on the 'recommended' list at Coast Guard Headquarters. She was careful to remind us to read the Bible and to say a prayer when we needed it—which she tactfully implied might be oftener than we realized. Undoubtedly she was a good—or at least a restraining—influence on all of those fellows who were living their last days ashore for a good many months.

"It was here that I had my first contacts with Turner, the Westerner, who was to be our Gunnery Officer; and Adams, the Southerner, who was to be our Sound and Communications Officer. . . ."

They were all there at the first conference when we had our initial "staff meeting" with our Skipper, Commander George Rowland Boyce, Jr., formerly skipper of the *Calypso*, convoying out of Norfolk. His seagoing eyes roved over us and, as he gave us the opening briefing, and the usual politic, "We're all going to be in this together and we've got to work as a team" climax, I knew he was just wondering how much of an efficient, integrated whole he would be able to make out of what he was being given to work with.

How would we fit together, I wondered. We came from varying professions and walks of life. We had little in common but the war. I was a banker, with eleven months experience as a pay officer. Some of the others had undoubtedly sprung from occupations equally illogical for manning a patrol gunboat. Turner, Adams, and I were hitting it off all right. The others were unknown quantities for the moment. There was Ramsay, the Executive Officer, an MIT graduate and two striper off the *Duane*; Pangle, the Engineer Officer; Stolzer, the Assistant Engineer Officer, there was Janes, Dunbar— and there would be others, including Dr. Raymond Hofstra, the young, short and rotund Public Health doctor; and Cooney, the tall, handsome young veteran of the Greenland Patrol—who, for one reason or another, were not at this first conference. And then, of course, there was the *USS Haste*—PG92—the greatest imponderable of all.

3

"The destiny of mankind is not decided by material computation. When great causes are on the move in the world . . . we learn that we are spirits, not animals, and that something is going on in space and time, and beyond space and time, which, whether we like it or not, spells duty . . ."

Winston Churchill,
*Radio broadcast to
America on receiving the Honorary
Degree of Doctor of Laws from the
University of Rochester, New York,
June 16, 1941.*

THE GRAVITY OF THE SITUATION which eventually resulted in my orders for duty aboard the *Haste* was as little realized by some of us in the service as it was by the general public. Most of us who were stationed in Miami—and elsewhere—had to guess at what was happening. The background leading up to my orders for sea duty was, on the whole, gathered long afterward. At the time the events were taking place, the majority of us who were on duty in our various capacities were practically as uninformed as the rest of the population. Like Will Rogers, all we knew was what we read in the papers. At least that was almost all we knew; whatever items of "privileged" information we may have picked up were usually of little importance.

We knew, naturally, about the training center that had been set up in Miami, Florida, on April 8, 1942, two months before we had arrived. This school was to instruct officers and men in how to handle PC's, SC's, and other anti-submarine craft, and was operated on a seven-day-week basis. Despite indignant protests from the Miami Chamber of Commerce, the school expanded over several piers of the waterfront, and into about ten hotels on Biscayne Boulevard.

Close relations were maintained with shipyards at Miami where the half-finished craft, "completed" by private builders, could be fitted for sea duty. About four-fifths of the student officers were from indoctrination school. The remainder were experienced officers untrained in handling destroyer escorts. In this Miami subchaser school, 360 officers and 1,374 enlisted men were trained for fourteen different Allied navies in 1942-43.

Although the number of ships at sea increased encouragingly, there was still a shortage of escort vessels to protect them. Troop convoys took the pick and increasing proportion of the larger types. The 173-foot steel-hulled patrol craft (PC) and the 110-foot wooden-hulled subchaser (SC) were being turned out in fair quantities, but the PC's were of limited use and the SC's were of no use at all to transocean convoys. They were, of course, useful in the interlocking coastal convoy system, where they could be mixed with converted yachts, minesweepers and small Coast Guard cutters.

The Combined Chiefs of Staff estimated in January, 1943, that 566 escort vessels of 200-foot length or over would be needed that year in the Atlantic. Deficiencies were said to be greatest along the East Coast of the United States.

In March, 1943, officers and nucleus crews of two Canadian corvettes assigned to the United States Coast Guard were sent to Quebec for precommissioning details. In June, at the time I received my orders, the Coast Guard was furnishing 850 personnel for manning these and six other corvettes. That month the Chief of Naval Operations had directed the Coast Guard to assemble and train officers and crews for thirty destroyer escorts (DE's) to be manned by the Coast Guard. Some of these vessels were 305 feet long, had agile maneuverability, accurate fire power, and especially designed anti-submarine weapons.

Our corvettes, classified as patrol gunboats (PG's) were 207 feet long, and an adaptation of the old fishing trawlers of England, with their deep holds and sea-keeping qualities; for our needs they were scaled to a size large enough to mount guns, depth charges, and anti-submarine gear, and to carry the men to operate them and the engines and fuel to sustain long voyages. They did not have to be fast because they were designed to escort the slower kind of convoy, the kind that made ten knots average during calm weather. Although they were considered among the most seaworthy ships in the world, fairly bouncing over the waves and seldom sustaining storm damage, this buoyancy made them most uncomfortable and a severe strain on their crews.

Some of this I had heard on my brief visits aboard the K-75; the rest I would have to learn in the course of time. I know that we were all aware that the situation must have been serious or we would not have been ordered to sea duty. How serious, we could only guess. I would probably have been even more disturbed about my chances of survival in the role of an unskilled member of a destroyer escort in troubled seas if I could have read the careful notations that were then going into the Secret and Confidential War Diary of Eastern Sea Frontier for the month of June, 1943.

Very early in the morning of the first day of that month, the same day we left Miami to begin our three-day drive back to Washington, D.C., the Texas Oil Company's 9,000-ton tanker *SS Montana,* was steaming up the seaward end of the swept channel approach to Norfolk. Her cargo, intended for NOB Iceland, had been loaded at Bayport, Texas, and consisted of 3,881 barrels of white unleaded gas, 38,229 barrels of 100-octane aviation gas, 54,000 barrels of 80-octane gas and 3,765 barrels of kerosene. She had been convoyed all the way to Norfolk by *USS Palmer,* a high speed minesweeper, converted from the old four-stacker DD-161.

Halfway up the swept channel, the captain of the *USS Palmer* became concerned about the erratic course the *Montana* had been steering, which had been crowding the center-buoys on her port side. This channel could be navigated only with difficulty, even under ideal conditions, because it was complicated by five jogs, or elbows. At 0407 hours, the Captain of the *Palmer* said over the telephone between ships:

"When you are abeam of buoy, change course to two-five-two, and watch out for ship on your port side."

Until that time no one aboard the *Montana* had sighted any vessel, but suddenly they saw it in the darkness—already very near and on a course which would take her past close aboard. Suddenly, it seemed to those on the bridge of the tanker, the freighter altered course violently, so that she was on collision course to *Montana.* "Hard right" was ordered, but it was too late.

The approaching freighter was *SS John Morgan,* loaded with munition material and outward bound on the first leg of a voyage that should have taken her through the Panama Canal, then across the Pacific to the Persian Gulf.

She had loaded her lend-lease cargo at Pier 27N in Philadelphia. Included in what the Eastern Sea Frontier's recorder termed her "martian assortment" were 424 drums of glycerine, two cylinders of nitrogen, eighty-three cases of sulphuric acid, 790 tons of isoalkylate and 400 tons of toluene. Topping those off were tires, petroleum products and foodstuffs below; trucks, tanks and planes on deck. Having completed her loading, she had cleared Philadelphia and proceeded down the bay; then, apparently, through the Chesapeake and Delaware Canal; thence to Norfolk, arriving May 29, 1943. Her master had attended a convoy conference in the Norfolk Routing Office at eleven-thirty on the morning of May 31 and had received instructions for sailing that night, so that the ship could join the New York-Key West convoy NK-544 at sea off the Virginia Capes the following morning. The escort vessel who would precede her down the channel was the U.S. Coast Guard Cutter *Antietam*.

The ships had gotten underway shortly after midnight and all went well as they passed through the harbor nets and started down the first leg of the swept channel, leaving all channel buoys to port. Later, as the cutter proceeded on the westward leg of the jog toward buoy "Peter," the sound watch picked up the propellor noises of USS *Palmer* on the sound gear, and a challenge was given with a light. The two escorts passed each other without incident in the thousand-yard-wide channel, each leaving buoy "Peter" to port. Then the cutter lookouts sighted SS *Montana* about one mile astern of the destroyer. Having passed at a safe distance, the Commanding Officer of the cutter looked back at SS *John Morgan* about a half mile astern of *Antietam* and saw that the courses of the freighter and the tanker were converging. Closer and closer they came until the crunching sound of metal on metal could be heard across the water. Sparks flew as the bow of SS *John Morgan* plowed into the port side of *Montana* just forward of the bridge.

The Commanding Officer of the *Palmer* saw the sparks and heard the dull crunching sound through the darkness. He logged the collision at 0409 hours, and noticed that fire immediately broke out on the surface of the water. At 0412 hours, there was a terrific explosion, but the Commanding Officer of the destroyer could not tell, because of smoke obscuring the area, in which ship it occurred.

U.S.S. HASTE, PG 92, taken from blimp. August 1943.

Lt. JG Roland Carr, February 1944.

Staff of the Haste.

Standing, left to right: HOFSTRA. Medical; CARR. Pay and Supply; DUNBAR. Welfare and Assistant Gunnery; COONEY. Navigation; TURNER. Gunnery; JANES. Communications; STOLZER. Assistant Engineering. Sitting: RAMSAY. Exec.: BOYCE. Captain; PANGLE, Chief Engineer.

Sister ship USS Intensity, 3G-93.

From crow's nest looking forward toward number 1 3-inch gun.

Courtesy James Ramsay and Photo-Arts, Cupertino, California

Looking aft toward covered number 2 3-inch gun and depth charge racks; stack in foreground partially hides ensign.

Tough and ugly, April 1944.

Chuck Turner, gunnery officer, leans against number 2 3-incher.

Practicing with a "tame sub"
in the Caribbean.

Sister ship Alacrity, PG-87,
comes alongside at sundown.

Label from our
favorite beer, Hatuey.

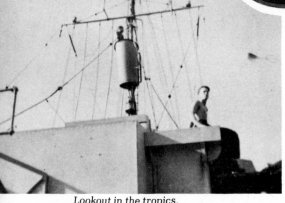

Lookout in the tropics.

PC 619 off Capa Maisi, Cuba.

We put Doc Hofstra aboard a merchantman.

Some members of the Haste crew at Bermuda anchorage. Three DE's in background.

Intensity lays a smokescreen.

Mr. Ramsay, our second skipper, in tropics.

We take aboard a case of acute appendicitis.

Those on the destroyer felt the heat and the blast of the concussion, and falling and burning fragments showered the surface of the sea. The destroyer turned back toward the scene of the disaster. The fire, burning furiously, was spreading around the tanker; at 0420 hours, the Commanding Officer of the destroyer noticed that the freighter had disappeared; nobody aboard his ship had seen her after the explosion.

The Commanding Officer of the cutter saw the *Morgan* before the freighter sank. The initial explosion blew all the glass out of the *Antietam's* pilot house and showered the cutter with debris. The cutter altered course and escaped from the fury southward, returning as soon as possible to attempt rescue. At the time of the explosion, the captain had seen both vessels clearly—the tanker bright in the blaze of burning gasoline; the freighter a dark shape silhouetted against the flame. Afterward, no sign of the freighter could be found. She had apparently disintegrated with the explosion and the hull had sunk.

The desperate crew of the *Montana* managed to release several life rafts and eventually sixty-five survivors from the tanker were rescued. Not one regular member of the crew of the freighter survived, and only two members of the armed guard gun crew, who jumped off the stern of the *Morgan* as the ships collided, were saved. Rescue vessels also picked up thirty-seven dead bodies. From a combined complement of 151 men, therefore, eighty-four perished and sixty-seven survived. No personnel survived who were close and competent witnesses of either vessel and the record of precisely what happened, and why, was lost in the murky, flame-seared darkness of the channel.

Exactly ten days later (the very day I reported for duty in Boston, June 10) the Eastern Sea Frontier suffered another atrocious incident, as revealed by its Secret War Diary.

The 10,000-ton tanker, *SS Esso Gettysburg*, enroute from Port Arthur, Texas, to Philadelphia carrying a cargo of more than 120,000 barrels of West Texas crude oil, had reached a position southeast of Jacksonville, Florida, on the morning of June 10, 1943.

Having a speed of better than sixteen knots, she was routed independently and had proceeded without trouble through the Gulf of Mexico from June 6 to June 8, when she received a coded message from Commander, Gulf Sea Frontier: "Proceed with caution, possible submarine vicinity Dry Tortugas." During the next twenty-four hours, however, no submarine was sighted by those aboard the tanker.

The morning of the tenth, coverage had been afforded by the blimp K-75, but squalls and electric storms, a special hazard for this type of craft, had apparently driven the blimp in, for she headed back toward shore shortly after noon. After an hour of squalls, the weather cleared, the sea was smooth with a southwest wind, force two, and enormous white clouds drifted in the typically blue tropical sky.

At 1400 hours there was a violent explosion in the hull on the port side, between the midships house and mainmast. Geysers of oil from her ruptured Number Six and Seven tanks spouted one hundred feet in the air, matched by another column of water. Before either had time to settle, a second explosion and a second geyser occurred on the port side near the engine room. The entire electric system was knocked out and the ship was unable to get off an SOS.

Almost immediately an explosion blew four enormous ventilators from the after deck house higher than the mainmast and fire developed at once. Flames spread rapidly and very soon enveloped the midships house. Immediate aid was impossible since there was no ship or plane in the vicinity. Desperate but futile attempts were made to release lifeboats; rafts were consumed by the burning oil spread outward on the surface of the water. The ship was turned into a death trap for at least fifty-seven of her complement.

Suddenly the vessel started to turn her nose into the air, then her whole bow lifted and water started coming over the midships house. All the remaining men along the deck jumped into the water and swam into the wind, the flames creeping at their heels. They swam far out and gathered into groups to help support those who had no life jackets and to protect each other from the sharks that began to circle them.

Suddenly and unbelievably, the survivors saw a lifeboat drifting toward them out of the holocaust, scorched and smoking but whole. Some of the stronger survivors swam to the boat but found it so hot they had to soak her down with water before climbing in. A dead body was there ahead of them, charred beyond recognition. After they bailed her out, they tore boards from the inside of the boat and used them as paddles. They headed for their shipmates as rapidly as possible but found a pitifully small total—fifteen, including themselves.

The tanker settled slowly until she was submerged except for her bow, which rose fifteen or twenty feet above the surface and drifted with the Gulf Stream current. Gradually the fires subsided and the survivors searched for several hours hoping to find others who might be swimming or clinging to wreckage. They stayed in the area during the night and by morning the fire had burned itself out, leaving only debris and an oil slick.

Quite by accident, on the morning of June 11, a B-25 escorting the transport *George Washington* sighted the lifeboat and diverted the ship for the rescue.

"This sinking," wrote one historian, "was sadly reminiscent of the massacre of 1942."*

So that was June 1943—and gathered there in Boston were the anomalous components of the *USS Haste*, who must somehow be welded into one of those units who could stand between Doenitz and more "*Esso Gettysburg's*" and face up to those other cruel hazards of the sea as exemplified by the murderous collision of *John Morgan* and *Montana*.

By June 12th I was jotting down, "Finished my special jobs at Headquarters. . . . Went to the tailor's to get my blue uniform. The braid for the sleeves cost $7.10. Putting it on cost $3.25. They surely do soak us for that stuff."

I had discovered the Officers' Club, which had taken over a magnificent old mansion across the street from the park. I found out that for ninety-five cents they served a meal that elsewhere would have cost approximately $2.50. Dinner was served in the mansion's ornate dining room with its high ceiling, massive chandeliers, and huge fireplace. Saturday night turned out to be reservation night. There was a string orchestra, many of the officers were accompanied by their wives or dates, and it was all very pleasant. I ate at a stag table, and pondered how different it was being a j.g.

*The German Navy, by keeping an average of a dozen U-boats constantly in the Eastern Sea Frontier, relieving them every two weeks and refueling them from tanker submarines stationed 300 miles east of Bermuda, pulled off one of the greatest merchant-ship massacres of history during the first four months of 1942. Samuel Eliot Morison, *History of the United States Naval Operations in World War II*, Volume 10, *Atlantic Battle Won, May 1943-May 1945*, Boston: Atlantic Monthly-Little, Brown, 1956.

"I'm evidently one of the lucky ones. They have slowed down the promotion rate of Ensign to j.g. and the Club was crowded with Ensigns, most of whom turned out to have been in the service longer than I have. The j.g.'s in this town seem to be scarce. Last night a husky-voiced matron, one of the sponsors, insisted on eating with the 'two handsome officers in white.' She called me 'Lieutenant' in practically every sentence. At first it was hard to realize she meant me—but after a bit, I began to rather like the sound of it."

However, there were many more pressing matters to absorb me than the momentarily pleasant sound of a new title. An additional item on the same date observed, "I worked out a lot of problems at Headquarters today, and things are in a little better shape. I found out that I am to carry $25,000 in cash aboard ship."

By June 17th, I was writing with a decided note of grumpiness, which seemed more than justified at that time. "I am tired, disgusted and lonely. It seems to me that it is a funny war, and only a few of us are fighting it. I missed my 'sea trial' today because it was more important for me to go over to the big Navy Yard to get our supplies."

The other officers told me that the *Haste* was a "sweet running thing," but I had spent the entire morning, and part of the afternoon, checking over our supplies; and the rest of the afternoon I had spent supervising the loading of them on two big trailer trucks. I had about 200 invoices—but that was not the half of it.

Indignantly I noted, "At 4:30 with the loading platform still full of heavy material those damned patriots up here walked off the job, and we had to load the rest of the stuff ourselves—I and three little sailors who had been working all day."

After cursing every man in the office who was within cursing distance, I had finally taken off my coat and started hauling the stuff myself. The truck driver couldn't help us because he was a union man and not allowed to do any loading. We had three heavy coils of cables among the stuff.

There were a few more notes to be added to my trials and tribulations of the day. "A Navy captain came by, and when he saw me laboring and sweating to get the job done he told me approvingly, 'That's the right spirit, Lieutenant,' but I was too damned mad to answer him. At seven o'clock we finished piling it aboard—anywhere, for the night—and then I got a ride back to the boarding-house in a truck. My khakis are filthy, but I don't give a damn. I decided to wear them until they stood up in the corner, and were as dirty as the work clothes I had worn aboard the *Condor* as a workaway in 1936.

"We took over the ship officially at 4:00 today, and one of my roommates, Ensign Adams, is standing night duty. We may move aboard Sunday, but at present the ship is so cluttered up there's no place to live aboard."

By Sunday we were aboard and on June 21 I wrote, "Except for about five minutes this morning I haven't been off the ship today. Have been busy trying to get our two offices in shape. The ship already had a little office where all the personnel records, correspondence, etc., are kept. It contains a couple of desks and typewriters. But for a pay office we took over a clothing locker and installed some shelves and desks, and bit by bit my Pay Office is emerging. It's only about six feet long by four feet wide, but it'll be all right for my storekeeper to work in.

"My safe came aboard last night weighing 1,200 pounds, and we nearly had to rebuild the ship to find a place for it. Needless to say it would not go into my office, even when we took the door off the hinges. Finally we found a place for it in a corridor beside the galley. It's a good step from my office, but it was the best we could do. We are certainly running into difficulties trying to get organized.

"I slept very well in my bunk—surprisingly so, considering it was my first night. Tomorrow the ship is going 'outside' for a trial, but I will have to miss the trip because I've got to go to District Headquarters to see about getting our crew paid. So far the Skipper has not asked me to do a single job in the line—meaning that I'm concentrating on pay and supply and not having to bother with watches, etc. I hope the arrangement continues.

"We're awfully hot and tired tonight, and Ensign Turner (the former forester) and I are going up to the canteen inside the Navy Yard here, for a couple of beers and a change of scenery. . . ."

It was hot as the proverbial hinges down in the ship, we were already discovering, and whenever we could we felt we had to get out for some fresh air. I was feeling dirty and hard-working, and for a couple of days I had been aware of another feeling that was like an old nightmare returning. There was once again the grim realization that "sea duty" meant facing up to the fact that "out there," death lurked just beneath the surface.

This mood of temporary perturbation was evoked by a newspaper account of the sinking of the *Escanaba*—and it had hit three of us in the same way at the same time.

It had been the Friday before when Turner, Adams and I had gone out on the town. We had been working hard and we felt we deserved a bit of night life—and we were not sure how much freedom of movement we would have when we finally took our permanent quarters aboard ship.

We found our way to a nightclub with the promising label "The Latin Quarter," where we saw a fair and not very spicy floor show, resisted temptation when several girls spoke to us, and ended up by drinking too much in the course of virtuously "stagging it."

When we came out of the Latin Quarter, a newsboy out in front was shouting over and over like some dire refrain, "Coast Guard cutter torpedoed with loss of fifty-eight!" We bought a paper, crowded together to read the headlines, then bought two more and found a store window which gave us enough light to read the highlights of the story. When we had come out of the nightclub we had been a little inebriated, but as we read the details of the sinking of the *Escanaba* we were suddenly cold sober.

"The Coast Guard cutter *Escanaba*, skippered by a Newtonville man and including ten other greater Boston men in its complement of at least sixty officers and men, sank almost immediately after an explosion of undetermined cause while on convoy in the North Atlantic.

". . . The time and place of the disaster was not announced. Only two enlisted men survived when the 718-ton vessel was sundered amidships by an explosion that Navy officials said could be a torpedo, a mine, or some internal mishap. The *Escanaba* sank so quickly its crew had no time to send out disaster signals. . . . Skipper of the 165-foot vessel, which distinguished itself earlier this year by rescuing 133 men from a torpedoed ship in the North Atlantic, was Lieutenant Commander Carl Uno Peterson . . ."

Navy records after the war furnished a more complete story of the *Escanaba*. Although the newspapers featured the story as an "Extra" that night of June 19 when we read about it, the actual sinking had occurred on June 13 when a task unit, consisting of *Mojave* (flag), *Tampa*, *Escanaba*, *Raritan*, *Storis*, and *Algonquin*, was escorting Convoy GS-24 from Narsarssuak, Greenland, to St. Johns, Newfoundland. At 0510 hours, observers on board *Storis*, the vessel nearest *Escanaba* at the time, saw a cloud of dense black and yellow smoke and flame billowing upward from that cutter. No explosion had been heard by those aboard the escort vessels and no signals had been either seen or heard. Yet the 165-foot *Escanaba* had blown up and she sank within three minutes, leaving only small bits of wreckage afloat. She sank so quickly that there was no time to send out signals. *Raritan* and *Storis* searched the area and picked up two enlisted men, but the rest of the crew of 103—instead of the much smaller number reported in the newspaper account—including the commanding officer, Lieutenant Commander Carl Uno Peterson, USCG, were lost. The survivors, Malvin Baldwin, DM2c, USCG, and Raymond F. O'Malley, S1c, USCG, had no idea what caused the explosion. The fate of the *Escanaba* could have been due to a mine, torpedo, or internal explosion of magazines or depth charges. On the basis of slim evidence, a torpedo seems the most probable cause of the disaster.*

Whatever brought about the sinking of the *Escanaba*, the result was the same, and three fellow Coast Guardsmen, who were about to face their own baptism in convoy duty, were considerably shaken by the tragedy.

Standing there in the dim light of the store window, we slowly folded our papers. Adams was the first to recover. He flashed his usual broad grin—perhaps a little forced at the moment—but cheering, nevertheless. "Well," he mused, "You know the old Coast Guard saying—we *have* to go out, but we don't have to come back."

That was it for a moment, and then Turner, the quiet, sound Coloradan, suggested, "Maybe we shouldn't talk about this in front of the kids." We knew he meant the fellows in the crew. We knew, too, that we would just as soon not talk about it ourselves, or even think about it for that matter, at least not right then.

We walked to the curb and hailed a cab, when normally we would have headed for the subway. We didn't talk much on the way back to the boarding house, and it was many months before the name *Escanaba* was mentioned aboard the *Haste*.

U.S. Coast Guard in World War II by Malcolm F. Willoughby, Lt. USCGR(T) U.S. Naval Institution, Annapolis, Md.

4

> "Everything that enlarges
> the sphere of human
> powers, that shows man
> he can do what he thought
> he could not do, is
> valuable."
>
> *Life of Johnson*
> James Boswell [1740-1795]

THE WEATHER HAD CHANGED DRASTICALLY, and I was finding that June in Boston could be equally—and unpredictably—hot as June in Washington.

My little pay office on the crew deck was, like everything else down in the ship, as hot as Hades. It was about half the size of the closet in our small apartment back in Washington. We had one porthole, but it was high up, and the air seemed to give up trying to get through it. It was easy to see that the ship would be very uncomfortable in a hot climate. The decks, the bulkheads, everything proved hot—or at least warm—to the touch, but we determined to make the converted clothing locker that now formed our minuscule pay office serve its purpose.

My storekeeper was about twenty-five, rather shy, but hardworking and willing. He had a picture of his girl on one of the shelves. She was nice looking, and the picture, a colored photograph in a small leather frame, was a pleasant touch.

In spite of our good intentions to "make do," at the Skipper's instigation we eventually gave up on the clothing locker, and a pay office was created around a vacant section of the mess deck near the galley. Some yard workmen came aboard and built a special frame of heavy steel to hold the safe, welding it into the frame against the side of the ship. "This has to be done right," the Skipper had said, "because if that safe ever gets loose, it can go right through the side of the ship."

48

Finally the workmen constructed a metal framework around the space that was to be the "office," fashioned a door, and covered the whole thing with rugged metal webbing. Inside, in addition to the safe, was a small desk, a table, two chairs, an adding machine, a typewriter, and a file cabinet. And that was the pay office—"The finest," we averred, "in the whole corvette fleet."

On June 23 I wrote, "We went 'outside' today, and this time I went along. For some peculiar reason I felt a little queasy in the stomach. There was very little wind and we did nothing more than roll a little, but these small battle wagons have a sickening heavy roll that does something to you. I'm not sure at this time just how it's going to be.

"A big convoy was making up, and we passed a long line of freighters and tankers going out to their rendezvous. We went out through the submarine nets which are stretched across the harbor entrance, and then threaded our way back through the mine fields until we got inside. Then we just turned and twisted and maneuvered here and there, testing things out. I enjoyed it—but, as I've already noted, I felt a damned uncomfortable sensation.

"I understand that I'm already entitled to wear the little ribbon for the American zone of operations—just for going outside the submarine nets. As the Captain put it, the war begins on the other side of them. We carried all our guns ready for action and had our sound gear going."

The next day I noted, "I was feeling much better today and I don't believe the roll and kick of this tub will bother me if I'm feeling this good when we finally go out on regular duty.

"We have fairly good meals aboard, and if ever we get this scow in order I think it will be pretty good. Right now it's a helluva mess. A lot of equipment has been dumped aboard and we can't find half of it. Some of our crew have still not shown up, as well as a couple of our officers, but I think that by the time we get out of Boston we'll be pretty well fixed for any contingency."

The following day we shifted ship to Lockwood Basin in Boston, where we reportedly were to undergo some process to help protect the ship from magnetic mines—a subject I preferred not to think about. However, I couldn't help overhearing a couple of wardroom conversations in which the terms "deperming" and "degausing" were used, and I gathered that one or both of them involved a charge of electricity which would be sent through the *Haste.* Our wrist watches and certain of the ship's gear would have to be removed beforehand, but it was said that the procedure entailed no danger to the crew. As a matter of fact, those aboard would be unaware that the processes were taking place, as far as any physical reaction was concerned.

Captain Boyce later indicated that "deperming" was the process of reducing or eliminating the permanent magnetism in a ship's hull, which is introduced he said, "by the welding, riveting, and pounding on the steel members during construction."

In Lockwood Basin coils of wire were wound around the hull and given high voltage shots, which would counteract or change the magnetism acquired during construction.

"On the other hand," Captain Boyce explained, especially for my edification, "'degausing' is the system consisting of fore and aft and athwartship coils installed in the hull and charged by the ship's generators with an appropriate current to compensate for the residual magnetism.

"Theoretically," he said, "all the magnetism of a ship can be cancelled out so that she can pass over the most sensitive magnetic mine without actuating it. In the *Calypso* I know that many times we sailed safely over magnetic mines that blew up other ships behind us. This was especially true around Norfolk where, after Pearl Harbor, the Germans sowed a large number of mines.

"I feel certain," he added reassuringly, "that the same system will be beneficial to the *Haste.*"

We hoped so. At the moment, I, at least, was happy to dismiss the whole subject.

The next day I recorded, with a faint touch of pride, "From four to seven Lieutenant Carr took over the ship. All the combat officers, including the Skipper and the Exec, went to an 'attack school,' and the Lieut. was left aboard as Officer of the Deck, or O. D.

"I guess—and hope—I looked the part. I know I felt it. We have to wear a forty-five automatic pistol strapped to our waist, and in addition I wore a knife in a sheath, which I bought for wearing aboard after I found that most of the officers have them. It wasn't a pleasant thought, but they said the knives might prove helpful in cutting free of shrouds or wreckage in case of an explosion.

"The O.D. has absolute control of the ship when so designated, and no one can come aboard or go ashore without his permission. It was hot as the devil topside, so I exercised my authority by ordering the officers' steward to bring me up some lemonade. Some stuff, I thought.

"I am working damned hard. This job is really keeping me going. The worst part of it is getting back and forth to the places in and around Boston where I have to go for supplies. We still haven't taken the pay accounts aboard. We are stalling around while the crew collects and is tried out, and while we keep taking aboard equipment and supplies. Meanwhile, both officers and crew are attending lectures and courses of various kinds; and between time we take the *Haste* out for short trips. The one today shaped up fine. She handles like an automobile coming into dock."

Friday's entry reported, "I'm in my little hot office again, right off the galley, and the perspiration is dripping off me. I can look up through the open port and see the mast and part of the after platform of the *Intensity*, which is tied up alongside of us. She is inboard from us, and we have to climb across her decks to go ashore. They have a ten-foot tide here, and last night, when I went ashore to mail a letter, the gangplank was at nearly a 90-degree angle. But I seem to be getting a little more agile about decks again.

"We are tied up over in East Boston, the worst part of town, and, if ever there was a depressing waterfront view, this is it. The water is dirty, the houses are dirty, the streets are dirty, and—as usual—it's hot as hell. We'll be here for six days without leaving the dock, and living aboard now is no fun. But like lots of other things, it's just something to be gotten through . . ."

A lot of the work I was doing was physical, and the heat didn't make it any easier. It seemed that Boston was determined to give us a good hot blast-off. The *Boston Herald* of June 29, 1943, announced, "Boston sweltered yesterday in sultry weather with the mercury reaching a peak of 95 degrees, but the weather bureau predicted showers and thunderstorms this morning would clear the air for a considerably cooler afternoon. Record of 97 for June 28 was in 1901." It added, "Five deaths, three of them men who collapsed at work, were attributed to the heat."

That Friday morning there had been a conference in the wardroom. The top officials of the Yard were gathered there with the top officers of the *Haste*, and I was present as Supply Officer. We had gone over all the phases of the ship's equipment, engines, guns, sound equipment, mess equipment, and all the rest of it, and I had been able to answer more questions than I had expected concerning the amount of this or that we had on board. "Fortunately the Commander of the Yard asked just the right questions," I added to my account of the day. "For example, the Commander said, 'What do you have in the way of fire-fighting equipment?' and the Captain sort of turned to me, and I was able to say, 'We have nine hydrants, sir, American-type. The British type were taken off at the other Yard.' Then he asked, 'What about sprinkler nozzles?' and I answered, 'We are allowed five, sir, but we have none aboard. A requisition has been submitted for our allowance and we expect to receive them soon.' So I guess I've learned a little something about the ship, and will know a lot more before I come off here."

And so, the *Haste* and I were adjusting to each other. We might not always be compatible, but we were stuck with each other and would try to make the best of it.

5

> "Too busied with the
> crowded hour to fear to
> live or die."
>
> *Nature*
> Ralph Waldo Emerson
> (1803-1883)

June 30, 1943

WE ANCHORED OFF PROVINCETOWN AT eight-thirty tonight. The afterglow in the sky threw the old town into quaint relief as we came in. A few fishing craft were in the harbor.

In the comparative quiet, the gulls called and the wind sang as it cut streaks across the water. Then our starboard anchor ripped the silence, the chain twisting and writhing across the deck like a live thing. "How's she tending?" they yelled from the bridge. And we let out to thirty fathoms.

We fired everything aboard today, from machine guns to depth charges. It was my baptism, of course. And, in a sense, it was the ship's. We broke up a lot of equipment.

My battle station is in the chartroom, just aft of the wheelhouse. All I have to do is to report readings on the "fathometer" which records the depth of the ocean by electric impulses, and is fairly important in attack tactics over a submarine. When I opened the after door of the chartroom, I could see the whole after-section of the ship, and, inasmuch as the forward part of it opens into the wheelhouse, I have a view of almost the whole ship. The bridge is right over us. The flash of the number one three-incher on the forward deck filled the wheelhouse and overflowed into the chartroom. I was concentrating on the men huddled around the gun, particularly on the pointer and the trainer who rub shoulders with it. The explosion rocked my vision and jarred me loose from my concentration. Never once could I hold onto an unbroken sight of them.

The explosion of the gun is pretty terrific. It's a quick, sharp blast that "runs up your pants-legs," as one fellow put it. I held my ears because nearly everyone else had cotton and I missed getting some. When the first blast came, I involuntarily stepped back a pace and stepped on someone behind me. It turned out to be the Chief Engineer, one of our senior officers, an old-timer in the service who said he just didn't like the noise.

Next we fired the twenty millimeter machine guns off the sides—two at a time. One was located almost over my head on the bridge platform, the other in a side turret amidships. I had grown bolder and stood out on deck without holding my ears to watch the twin streams of bullets streak away into the distance, interspersed with tracer shells that shone like live coals streaming out. The performance was repeated on the other side.

The first depth charge caught me by surprise. The detonation was an awesome *arumphhh!* that threw up geysers of mud and water. The *Haste* shuddered as though she had been smacked on the after plates with a giant mallet, and almost simultaneously the second depth charge went off on the other quarter. Those things seem to shake the structure of the earth. You can almost feel the sea bottom vibrate.

The final performance was firing the "hedgehog," an ingenious arrangement on the forward deck for shooting twenty-four depth charges of smaller weight at one time. They make a high trajectory, like a long fly in a baseball game. All twenty-four are shot off at different intervals, but the time lapse is so brief we saw the pattern of the twenty-four of them in the air long before they wrote their splash upon the water.

A checkup after the final firing showed we had broken the barometer, the fathometer, the dials in the engine anunciator, and most of the electric bulbs around the bridge. It's a good thing we're going back to Boston tomorrow.

July 2, 1943

We just got in from our sea jaunt, and everything went very well. I'm still rolling around the deck, although the ship is tied up securely—but other than that I can report no ill effects. I seem to be a pretty good sailor. Several of the men were seasick, one or two violently, but aside from a headache below decks I felt pretty good.

A series of fogs came over us yesterday morning, and we were held up until about ten o'clock to begin some more speed trials. We also had gun drill and fire drill. I was in charge of one-third of the crew at Quarters. This is when all the men on the ship not absolutely needed at their posts are required to fall in for muster. My men muster on the after deck and I call the roll and report to the O.D. any stragglers, sick, et cetera. That's about the only piece of work I do with the crew as a whole; and I enjoy it. Yesterday I was standing back in the middle of the deck, not even holding on to balance myself from the pitching, and several of the crew had to ask permission to fall out and get to the rail. It made me feel gratifyingly tough.

The sun came out later in the day and it was pretty nice sailing. I had to stay below in my office most of the time, however, and only got topside spasmodically. At lunchtime I climbed up on the bridge (we have an open bridge) and took the glasses and looked around. Each officer has at his disposal a pair of binoculars. I seldom use mine, but they're there if I want them. Last night after supper I was up on the forward gun deck with the gun crew. The water was calm, except for a billowy swell, and the sunset colors were reflected across it. Once we saw a huge shark, possibly twelve feet long, but nothing else but the little fishing boats and our sister ship, the *Intensity*, which trailed off our stern. Our Skipper is senior so we stay first in line. The *Intensity* seems to be our inevitable partner in everything.

We ran up and down the ocean through the night, between Cape Ann and Cape Cod. I worked in my office until about ten-thirty, then went topside again. It was so dark and effectively blacked-out, I could see nothing at all for five or ten minutes. I just hung on to one of the shrouds until my eyes became a little accustomed to things. When I came down again, the crescent moon was hanging low over the water. I slept very well, considering the fact that we picked up a headwind early this morning. At six o'clock, I was knocked out of my bunk by the general alarm for battle stations. I was in pajamas, and I had one helluva time getting on trousers, shoes, life jacket, cap, and getting up the hatch. There was bedlam aboard, with half-dressed sailors running in all directions. It was a fake, of course, and when I met the Exec he said he had been up since midnight and he couldn't see why everyone else shouldn't be. Nevertheless, despite the discomfort of the thing, it's excellent practice, and no doubt we shall have more of it.

This evening I climbed up on the bridge again as we came into Boston Harbor, and looked over the shipping with my glasses. It makes me feel kind of "salty" to be coming in and have everybody on the docks and ships we pass stare at us though we're coming in off convoy. These corvettes attract a lot of attention. They've been publicized highly for their work in the North Atlantic, and even though our ships are new, and haven't been in actual combat, we still get the benefit of the good name of the type.

July 3, 1943

With a whole city off there under the sky, I go down this dark pier and down into the interior of my ship to sleep. It sometimes seems an incredible thing.

If someone should ask me how a city-dwelling landlubber can find sleep down there below those steel decks, I couldn't answer. I only know that each man seems to carry within him the alchemy that produces sleep out of his surroundings.

On my right as I move along is the purple shape of a destroyer, dark except for dim lights on her bridge. Across the gap between this pier and the next is the long bulk of the heavy cruiser *Boston*, sleek panther of a fighting ship. The two corvettes are behind the destroyer, ours on the outside. They look small and innocuous by comparison, but we have a respected lineage. "Mongoose"—snake-killer—I like to call the corvette.

Off to my left, two piers away, in a chartreuse brilliance is the rejuvenated hull of the *Wakefield*, the color deriving from the green anti-corrosive paint that is used in this war because of the scarcity of red lead. Arc lights are strewn around her, and the blue flashes of acetylene torches play upon the scene. The poundings and hammerings never cease, but there is little evidence of progress about the giant hulk.

This is the gangway. I must cross our sister ship to get to the *Haste*. The man on watch stirs and salutes me, not knowing who I am, but trusting my uniform. Workmen are walking about on both ships. Something is being done on the bridge. There is no gangplank between the ships. I step through a space in the railing. To the man on watch in the *Haste* I mumble "Back aboard," and he reaches for the log book.

I enter the doorway amidships. Immediately a ladder leads down. I go down sideways as I have learned to do, my head bent back. My feet touch the main deck, and in the half-darkness I stop to lean over the drinking fountain. Another ladder leads below. I descend again swinging my weight down the last two steps from a bar above. The officers' wardroom is in front of me; my room is to the right. The wardroom is deserted. I come back and enter my room. The ventilators are going and some air is fighting its way through. I turn on the electric fan.

Mechanically I undress, piling my clothes on a chair, which was a thing I always hated to do. But there is nowhere to hang them. The small locker is taken up with what uniforms I have. Both my bunkmates are apparently staying out late. I turn down the covers and slip backwards into my bunk. The light goes out by a switch near my bed. I turn it off and lie there listening to the breathing of the ventilators. Sometimes they stop and silence settles down, and the dank air begins to accumulate in the room.

Vaguely I wonder how far below the water line I am. Not that it makes any difference. I must sleep here anyway.

July 4, 1943

Created our own fireworks this evening. We were night-firing about ten miles outside the gate.

First we fired three star shells over the target. The timing, angle, and placement were perfect, and they floated down-ward dripping their perfect whiteness against the night. The raft was silhouetted and we opened up with both three-inchers. The yellow explosive flashes and orange tracers carried on and finished the pyrotechnics.

But in the din and excitement we had forgotten it was Independence Day.

July 5, 1943

Well, here it is Saturday afternoon and we're tied up in the harbor at Boston. One of our biggest and most modern fighting units (a carrier) is across from us, and they have a loudspeaker high up on one of their turrets from which they are broadcasting popular recordings. The sound is so loud it fills this whole section of the harbor. I was out on deck a moment ago reflecting on what a curious mixture it makes, music and gun turrets, this ugly, smoky harbor filled with begrimed ships and buildings and the smooth rhythms they have been playing floating over it all. I guess it made me just a little bit sad, and particularly since some of the records were by Glenn Miller, whose music has always been one of my favorites. Now it seems part of another world.

We're here in a state of confusion. From the first minute we hit the dock, workmen have been swarming over us, dragging electric wires with them, and strewing tools and materials in all directions. Last night they were welding and riveting most of the night. It got so bad down below I climbed on the bridge once where I could get somewhat out of the noise and the glare, and just stayed up there trying to be quieter than I had been below. At least it was halfway dark, and the racket and the cursing came up there only faintly.

There's no sense in thinking of how good it would be to get back to a normal life. All semblance of regularity has gone out of our lives. By "ours" I mean the lives of the officers aboard. We belong to the ship in a sense. We do whatever is demanded, at whatever hour and in whatever manner. We tried to establish something of a routine when we went out for our trials, but we had barely made a start when we were back in here. In a way I'll be glad to get out again.

Speaking of our present confusion, our three ships, *Haste*, *Intensity* and *Alacrity* have done so badly in our trials that the roguish wits in our crew have corrupted our proud English names to *Waste, Insanity* and *Laxity!*

At supper the Skipper was telling us what it is like at Guantanamo, as though the New York to Guantanamo run was all set. One of the officers was complaining that there wasn't much to see at the lower end of the run, and "absolutely no women." At that point, the Skipper interjected, "Well, so long as we have New York on one end of the run, we still can't complain."

We are going outside again Monday for three days, but we'll be back again Thursday and Friday, and we'll shove off Saturday for down below.

July 6, 1943

Last night we sat too long in a night club called the "Seven Seas" watching the dancers and looking at the very mild floor show and drinking. Later we went to a place in Scollay Square where a tassel dancer named Sally Keith put on an incredible "twirling exhibition, fore and aft" that had to be seen to be believed. "Gowd sive the flippin' king," said a little Limey Chief Petty Officer near us, "What a contribution to the war effort!"

July 7, 1943

Things are not quite so good today. We had some personnel troubles last night; two of the five or six men who jumped ship were returned by the Shore Patrol, and tonight we have them in leg irons. Since we have no brig, this is the only way we can keep them aboard until sailing time. It is a little depressing.

We're still on the same schedule—sailing Saturday in the morning for a three-week shakedown in Bermuda. Anticipations are that we won't get much time ashore in Bermuda because we've a lot to do to build this ship into a unified command.

A good number of our boys are raw and absolutely untrained in anything pertaining to a ship. (I should talk!) However, we've finally started to work up some enthusiasm, and have formed the nucleus of our permanent and working organization.

We have some excellent men in key positions, and our officers are tops. Our Skipper, as I have already explained, was master of the *Calypso,* a Coast Guard cutter that has been doing southern convoy work out of Norfolk since we entered the war. He's calm, and he instills confidence in all of us. The Exec, Ramsay, despite being somewhat young, is a cool, clearthinking, exceedingly well-turned-out graduate of MIT, with a positive genius for anything mechanical. He's a Reserve, but he's very highly regarded by the old-time Naval officers around here.

Our new j.g., Cooney, from the Greenland Patrol is only twenty-three, six feet two, with a Columbia College background, and perfectly tempered by his eight months' experience aboard the Coast Guard cutter *Modoc.* He's shaping up into a number one officer, and the Skipper has already made him his assistant navigator. The Exec has been doing the navigating.

It isn't surprising that I feel a lot of confidence in the officers around me. We also have some excellent chiefs aboard, and some experienced and reliable petty officers among the enlisted men. Some of our gunners have just come in from long periods in the North Atlantic. Around these experienced and key men it will be our job to build a working crew.

As the Skipper remarked philosophically, "We'll probably go from chaos to confusion, to organized confusion, before we really shake down."

July 8, 1943

Every time I think I'm getting used to the ship, something happens to shake loose my new-found sense of security.

Today, while we were still tied to the dock, Turner and I were relaxing in our bunks. Since I was too comfortably at ease to bother to look around the corner myself, I asked Turner the cause of a commotion outside our room. It sounded as though they were lowering something with chains and tackle from the hatch above. There was a great deal of clanking and many shouted commands and admonitions.

"They are loading the magazine," Turner told me, and naturally I was trapped into the next query, "Where is it?" Grinning, Turner replied, "Right under your bunk," obviously enjoying himself.

Then I remembered that my thoughtful roommates, when we moved aboard, had said to me, "Since you're the senior man, why don't you pick the bunk you like?" Surprised and pleased at their consideration, I had chosen the one nearest the door which had no second bunk above it. And so, knowing the damned thing was right under there, they had let me make the fateful choice, which absolved them from whatever the future had in store.

Now, seeing signs of consternation on my face, Turner's grin broadened as he added in his best navalese, "Don't worry, Carr. If a 'fish' comes through the 'skin' of the ship, it won't make any difference whether we're six feet one way or the other." And that was it. Since there was nothing else to do, I immediately adopted that philosophy as my own.

July 9, 1943

This is my last night in Boston, apparently. I was uptown this evening at the District Office, and I looked at the old State House, hovering in the shadows, with just a bit more interest.

I haven't really seen this town; I've just been here. The whole of Boston has just been a Navy Yard for our ships so far as I'm concerned. The things I will remember most are the parks, and the churches, and my short stay among the row of old houses on Beacon

Street, where the correct building material is plain red brick, and where new buildings are considered extremely regrettable, though occasionally necessary. Beyond that, Boston is just a place where I caught the ship.

Famous names and historic memories have been all around me, but once again—as it was on my workaway trip to Europe, aboard the *Condor*—there has been little time to savor them as I would have liked to do. As interested as I have always been in history, I am at the moment too busily involved in our part of it to be able to enjoy the relics and memories of the past.

And so, if all goes as planned, we'll be on our way tomorrow, loaded to the gunnels with supplies and materiél and green personnel. I have 102 men in my payroll now including twelve officers. Our ship is carrying twice as many officers and fifty percent more crewmen than the K-75 at Curtis Bay. I realize that the British manpower resources were spread pretty thin at the time. Also we are trying to train officers and crews in a hurry for whatever future phases of the war may develop.

I was mad as hell tonight over the laundry situation. Wednesday a laundry truck came down here with a foreign driver, and with sign language and an occasional intelligible word he guaranteed to have our laundry back by tonight. It came all right, but *how* it came back was something else. It looks as though the stuff was thrown into a community tub, pressed out dirty, wrapped up and sent back. I sent a white cap-cover, and it came back with grease all over it from somebody's dungarees. My khaki pants just had all the dirt ironed into them, and the same thing was true of a khaki shirt. Just one more thing to make life more complicated. We're hoping for better luck in Bermuda.

I don't know how I feel about going out again. A little numb perhaps—because it is becoming more and more for real. However, things have gotten into such a muddle here at the dock, we're all anxious to get away, mostly on the basis that things could get no worse.

Outside of our few recalcitrants, I still think we've got a crew the *Haste* can be proud of. I hope we, in turn, will be equally proud of the *Haste*. We'll be able to tell more about how we stack up during this Bermuda shakedown. At any rate, the past month, since I left Washington on June 9, has certainly been packed with learning for me.

6

"If the Bermudas let you pass,
you must beware of Hatteras."

Two Years Before the Mast
Richard Henry Dana (1815-1882)

July 10, 1943

SHOVED OFF FOR BERMUDA THIS MORNING. When we went through the submarine nets at the entrace to Boston Harbor, the Skipper turned to me and said, "Mr. Carr, we're in the war now."

For the first two hours I was expecting a submarine to turn up under every wave.

July 11, 1943

What a cruise this would be in a world at peace—and in a different kind of ship! The perfect weather and the absence of any enemy contacts reminded us of the message we received just prior to sailing. The three corvettes, *Haste*, *Intensity*, and *Alacrity*, were to have sailed in company from Boston. *Alacrity* had problems which required her to delay. Our message, amending the sailing orders, read in part, *"Haste and Intensity sail without Alacrity."* Made it sound like a leisurely vacation cruise!

However, have heard from many sources that when we reach Bermuda any illusions of a cruise will be shot to hell. They say the training we get will be intensive and rugged.

[NOTE. It was! A little background I gathered later from official sources, gives more of an overall view of the situation than I was able to furnish at the time I was actually going through the experience.

The DD-DE Shakedown Task Force at Bermuda was commanded by Captain James L. Holloway, Jr. (father of the present Chief of Naval Operations, Admiral James L. Holloway, III), who "broke his pennant" in *Hamul*, mother ship of the group on April 13,

1943, only three months lacking one day ahead of our arrival on July 12. *Hamul* had been accompanied by the destroyer escort *Andres*, fourth of that class to be commissioned.

The program was based on Captain Holloway's assumption that his business was to take care of repairs, logistics, and mechanical readjustments, while the commanding officers of the ships could concentrate on training their crews. And they didn't have to hunt the crews with shore patrol parties—the ships anchored in the bay near the mother ship or tied up alongside her. The debilitating effects of marking time in port were left back home and shore leave was practically nil. Movies, a PX, a Post Office and other nominal recreational amenities were provided on *Hamul* (a *real* mother ship).

The weather and the scenery were ideal and the crews had the time, sobriety, and physical well-being to make the most of it and concentrate on learning their jobs. They certainly cursed the setup, but it worked.

The course was well rounded and covered practically everything: practicing with a "tame" U.S. sub, firing on towed targets, night battle practice, refueling from a tanker, and special instructions in communications and radar. Although streamlined to finish in four weeks, the course gave us an opportunity to use every piece of our equipment and was an efficient indoctrination for our fledgling crews.

Even before we arrived, the course had been hailed with such enthusiasm that the Navy Department decided to make it available to all new destroyers as well as DE's and our PG's. For that purpose, another mother ship, *Altair*, was scheduled to be sent to Bermuda.

This was a brilliant effort on the part of the Navy and one for which we owed much thanks to our good friends, the British, and to the Bermudans themselves, who put up with our boisterous intrusion and sometimes unskilled comings and goings in their island paradise with elegant humor, helpfulness, and tolerance.

There were variations in the program, of course, and it could not possibly cover every contingency we would face; but, as my diary entries for the period show, it was an effective taste of the real thing.]

July 12, 1943

Arrived at Bermuda today.

At the moment the sunset is painting the clouds over this beautiful harbor and the water has changed from an aquamarine to a deeper shade of green.

At noon Cooney and I were on the bridge while the other officers were below having lunch. The day was sparkling, with a blue sea, blue sky, and foam-tipped waves. A strange breed of birds was circling our masts—slender, white birds with long, feathery tails. One of the oldtimers in the crew had told us they were "bos'n birds" because the tail resembles a marlin spike or fid, used by bos'ns for splicing, hence the name "bos'n bird." We weren't sure he was correct, but we were having an exciting time examining them through the glasses.

The *Intensity* was a quarter of a mile away from us and we were dipping along uneventfully, expecting to hit Bermuda at about four in the afternoon. Suddenly Cooney, with his Greenland patrol experience and sharpened eye, exclaimed, "There's a ship!" and pointed to a smudge under a cloud along the horizon. Before I could get the glasses in focus, he jumped to the voice tube and yelled down to the wardroom, "Land ho, dead ahead!" and a moment later was telling the quartermaster to log the fact that land had been sighted.

When we finally collected ourselves, the Captain and the Exec and all the officers were on the bridge, and everybody was staring through whatever glasses were available. Bit by bit their composite observations indicated that we were actually off Bermuda, though how we got four hours ahead of schedule nobody at that moment could explain. A hasty consultation with the Skipper of the *Intensity* brought the decision to veer off slightly to the east while our navigators checked their figures.

Finally they discovered what had happened. By some quirk, both officers had made an error of one degree in their calculations (sixty miles), and since we traveled at about fifteen knots per hour that put us almost exactly four hours ahead of their reckonings. Both Execs, who supposedly checked the figures, are Reserve officers. I couldn't help wondering what the situation might have been if we had run up on Bermuda at night, with all aids to navigation blacked out and with our cantankerous Canadian radar inoperative, as it so frequently is. Such, I guess, is an example of what can happen when Reserve officers get to fooling around with the sea.

We had turned back toward the islands and our Skippers had decided to go on in, despite the discrepancy in our estimated time of arrival, which we had flashed ahead to the naval commander there. By that time the outlines had become clearer. We could spot a lighthouse, several wireless towers, and one or two planes circling over the hills. An hour later, as we approached Bermuda, we saw a pilot boat coming out, and very soon we stood by to receive our pilot for the tricky run in through the reefs. After he had come aboard, the pilot, without any hesitation, had called for standard speed ahead and took us up the tortuous channel that ran beside the islands, the *Intensity* following a little distance astern of us.

Soon we came to a more populous locality, and numerous small houses in pastel shades dotted the hillsides. There appeared to be very few large trees, but only a consistent growth of low, scrubby pines. The houses looked solid and neat, and the whole place had a well-kept appearance. Shortly, the entrance to a large bay opened ahead of us, guarded on either side by ancient looking fortresses.

Inside, we located through the glasses a mammoth supply ship and a score or more of DE's at anchor. After all, this was the DE shakedown range, and we were really out of our class. The Skipper said they didn't know what else to do with us, so we were ordered down here for a performance test and some drilling in firing, convoying, and fueling.

The supply ship signaled us the number of our anchorage and the pilot put us alongside the buoy. We were also told that we would be joining the drills in the morning, and the Skippers of both ships were ordered to come over to the supply ship in small boats to pick up their instructions. Thus we found out there would be no liberty tonight.

For the first time the thought has come to us that getting ashore here might not be so easy after all. On the way down we had visions of pulling up alongside a dock and stepping off onto the fabled soil of Bermuda, but now here we are, sitting out here in the middle of the bay, in company with dozens of other ships. As far as we can see around the bay there is no sign of a town. Hamilton, someone told us, was around a bend and out of sight. The establishment along the shore is a newly constructed air base.

But the sunset is colorful, the sights all new, and we have buried our apprehensions in the reassurance that we will be here for several weeks. Much can happen in that time.

July 13, 1943

Bad day today. Out at six in the morning for firing. This is going to be no picnic. Exhausting routine, but we need it. Maneuvers that would have been simple for more experienced crews have often been complicated for the *Haste,* and our trial runs before we came here indicated that the three things we have to combat are the enemy, the ocean, and our own inefficiency. We may not be able to do much about the first two, but this training should do much toward alleviating the last.

We haven't been ashore yet. Most of the day we lay alongside the big supply ship and stewed in the foul fumes from her galley and engine room. She towered high above us and was to windward; hence we got nothing but the odors and the heat.

Moved back to our anchorage this afternoon and just sat there in the sun. This crate heats up like a frying pan. When I work in my office, perspiration pours off me like water. These ships are definitely *not* built for this climate.

At four o'clock we had swimming call. First, however, we set up a shark patrol, with men with rifles on the bridge and the afterdeck, and a look-out in the crow's nest. While this may not be absolutely necessary in Bermuda waters, it is a routine we have to learn for swimming elsewhere.

The crew went over the side like a pack of seals into the limpid water. When I came out in a pair of swim trunks, Ramsay, the Exec, called me up to the bridge. "A couple of enlisted men just went off here, Carr, so I guess we can do the same." I didn't know whether it was a dare or an order, but Ramsay, with a grin, climbed over the rail and dove in.

It wasn't much of a dive—he simply pushed off as he started to fall. I hadn't made that kind of a dive in a long time, not since I was a kid and practiced from a high-diving platform anchored in the Severn River at Herald Harbor, near Annapolis.

The height from the bridge must have been twenty-four or thirty feet or more, but there was nothing else I could do but take a try at it. Without looking down, except a hasty glance to make sure the spot was clear, I made something between a jackknife and a swan dive. It was a pretty good dive, although my legs went over too far and burned a little.

Found the water lukewarm and brackish, and remembering the shark patrol I took several energetic strokes to the rope ladder that had been lowered. Struggling up, I tried to keep from turning toward the ship. Scraping my knees in the process and burning my feet on the deck, I decided it hadn't been worth it.

After I had dressed, I climbed up to the bridge for a breath of air and any possible breeze that might be around; and from there, looking at the stern of the ship I saw a spectacle that amazed me. Several members of the crew had brought their mattresses topside and stretched them out on the depth charge racks, where they were happily lolling about or dozing. After only a few short weeks of instruction in the use of those cans of high explosives, they were able to relax right on top of them! What a testimonial to the adaptability of the human being!

We had one funny incident last night. It was impossible to sleep below decks, so at about midnight I followed the lead of some of the other officers and opened up a canvas cot on the deck. The temperature up there was delightfully cool with a breeze blowing out of a clear, moonlit sky. For a long time I watched the stars and an occasional drifting cloud and thought about home, finally falling into a sound sleep, my shoes and cap beside me on the deck.

Not many minutes had passed, it seemed, when suddenly the weather did an abrupt about-face and rain was coming down hard. I grabbed shoes and cap and headed for shelter. The other officers came from all directions, most of them soaked to the skin. Turner, my ex-forester roommate, had set up his cot on the quarter deck near the entrance to the deckhouse. Being accustomed to outdoor sleeping he merely pulled the blanket up over his head and, still sound asleep, lay there for an unbelievably long time with the rain pelting down. Suddenly his cot seemed to explode as he came to and realized he was lying in several inches of water in the midst of a downpour. By that time we were all standing nearby, under shelter, watching and laughing.

We went below for coffee and didn't turn in again until nearly three o'clock. Not much sleep.

July 14, 1943

Another bad day today. Our engines broke down this morning and we were unable to sail on schedule. Most of the afternoon we spent alongside the supply ship while the masterminds probed and sweated. We're still here tonight in a noisy, smelly, confusing muddle. We may also be here tomorrow.

We managed to get ashore last night, but the experience was disappointing. We got a hop from our ship to the supply ship (her name is the *Hamul*—she's named for one of the stars), and then had to wait an hour for another hop to town. "To town" takes another forty minutes by whaleboat, thus making the one-way trip nearly two hours. I can see quite plainly that there will be little of that done under these circumstances. Nearly all the establishments were closed when we arrived and we had only a few hours before the departure of the last boat coming back.

The night was exquisite, which seemed to make everything worse. We found a little hotel terrace on a cliffside, with a long sloping landscape running down to an enclosed bay. A million night-things were singing a drowsy cacophony. Loudest night-things I ever heard. I was told that most of the volume was created by tree frogs, for which Bermuda is famous. A Negro orchestra was playing surprisingly good music under a vine-covered arbor. Our table was in a corner and before us was a vista of the water down below.

The liquor went to my head and made me homesick. I looked around and felt more mournful every minute. The tall hedges in the shadows turned out to be oleanders. Periwinkles were blooming a few feet away in a flower-bed. Big, white periwinklés like Dee and I used to know in Florida. I remember carrying her a bouquet of them to Jackson Memorial Hospital when the baby was born on February 28. A few palms were scattered around and some Australian pines. Nostalgic memories piled up.

Only about half a dozen couples occupied the dance floor. The rest of us were stag. Five of us occupied our table, just sitting and drinking, glad to feel the good, cold liquid on our tongues. Ice-water aboard is almost nonexistent.

Finally we ran down the terrace and missed our boat back to the fleet-landing. Cooney fell and smeared his new uniform with grass stains. We had to wait half an hour for another boat.

Finally the little ferry came chugging out of the distance and we headed back toward the fleet landing at Hamilton, where we caught the last whaleboat out to our 'home on the waves.'

July 16, 1943

Time seems absolutely to stand still now. We've been broken down every day so far. Today we came out again on schedule, but something has gone wrong and we're headed back again.

The hard part about it is that we've got a certain amount of trials to go through, exclusive of the days when our engines are out of order. That means that the four days we've been here so far are totally lost, and we've still got a three-week schedule to complete after we get started. So it appears that getting back to the States has already been pushed back into the first week of August.

There is one compensating factor. While we're in this neighborhood, we're taking a minimum of chances and the real war for us hasn't begun. There's enough air protection around here to keep out almost anything, and we're almost as safe as though we were testing on the Great Lakes.

The worst thing we have to fight is heat. Characteristically I don't suffer much from that element—but down here it has been terrific. The steel plates of these warships pick up the heat of the sun, until by the middle of the afternoon they're nothing but floating frying pans. The heat from the decks penetrates the leather soles of our shoes if we stand for any length of time in one spot. Below decks it is almost unbearable. And it doesn't cool off very much at night, because what the sun doesn't heat up the engines do. Consequently, this damned crate stays red-hot most of the time. Cooney was sick yesterday from the heat, and two other officers were bothered by it today.

Went ashore again last night with Turner and another ensign. We hired a carriage for a dollar apiece and drove around for an hour in the fading daylight.

All the shops were closed again, but we located a shop that sells Wedgwood china and I have in mind purchasing some additional items down here. Naturally I'll also pick up some perfume.

Several poinciana trees were flaming in the purple twilight and I pointed them out to my companions. The same trees were in bloom when I left Florida. Later we had a couple of drinks on a terrace overlooking the main street, then dragged ourselves back to the officers' boat at eleven o'clock.

Haven't yet received a letter from home. No one seems to know a damned thing about our mail and we haven't gotten a letter aboard. I've been mailing letters pretty regularly via air mail, but I can't buy any more stamps and will have to resort to the franking arrangement. We get scattered news reports indicating the war is going well in Europe.

I saw a bookstore in town and, as usual, I'm going to buy a book. I guess I'll have to fall back pretty heavily on books. There's not another damned thing to do.

July 17, 1943

Just came down from sitting on one of the mooring bits and watching the moon's reflection across the bay. The mailboat came back from the supply ship tonight, and when the letters were distributed I didn't receive any, though I suppose Dee has written. We've gotten only a trickle of mail. The rest of it must be sitting in some accursed post office somewhere.

We were out all day today, from five in the morning until six tonight. Throughout those thirteen hours we practiced sighting and firing until my eyes felt as though they would fall out of my head. The weather was delightful, with big white combers running under the bow and the flying fish going away in schools. But the noonday sun was deadly. After six or eight hours the strain became apparent in back and leg and neck muscles. We were glad to get in again, even if it meant only staying aboard and a swim over the side.

It hazed over around eight o'clock, which is when we have officers' swimming call, but I went in anyway and swam for awhile. Dove twice off the side—about twelve feet, I think. The water wasn't invigorating and finally I crawled up the ladder and got out.

Even our radio has gone out, so that we can get nothing from the States. It would help some if we could hear something that people back home might be listening to, but the only thing we can get are the British programs that are broadcast down here and which we do not particularly enjoy.

A dull Saturday night.

July 18, 1943

We're still moored where we were last night, sitting out here in our separateness passing the Sabbath.

I have a certain definite number of places to go aboard ship, and I've visited them all a number of times today. And when I get through with the routine I start all over again.

Here's what my Sunday has been like. I slept until eight, went up to the officers' washroom, shaved, and took a shower. It was not like the showers I used to take at home, but it was a shower and felt delicious after eight hours in the stinking hull of this trap. Then I dressed in shorts and rubber sandals and went in to breakfast. No Sunday paper! No one will ever know how longingly I sat on deck this morning, looking at the blue-green water and thinking about Sunday morning at home in the apartment, reading the papers in my blue chair!

For two hours this afternoon I sat on deck and read *Mission to Moscow*, a long, dull, and very unliterary book, but containing a host of information on our times. Then I went up to the forward deck and paced back and forth in the wind and sun for half an hour to get some exercise.

Climbed up on the bridge this afternoon and started searching the shore through the glasses and a long spyglass we have aboard. Checked the contour of the horizon against a big chart we have of this place, and finally concluded that I was fairly familiar with the lay of the land, was tired of it all anyway, so came down and wrote a letter.

We're scheduled to have long, arduous drills this week, including some night runs. We'll be in for a full day on Friday, and the Exec has already appointed me a one-man purchasing commission to go ashore that day and buy whatever presents all of us have listed. I hope nothing interferes with it.

July 19, 1943

Today we practiced refueling beside a tanker. This was a tough job—both exciting and dangerous. We simulated combat refueling and ran at fifteen knots, which would make us at least a difficult target for an enemy.

We were in line behind some DE's and awaited our turn to come in and take the hoses. The tanker looked·enormous and we seemed to shrink as we edged over toward her. Chief Spillane, an experienced chief coxswain, had the wheel as we bore in toward the tanker's expectant, talon-like hose riggings, ready to reach out for us. I saw the perspiration dripping from the chief's face as he fought the wheel and struggled to keep us in the right position, at the same time battling the wind, the current, the downdraft from the big ship, and the pull from her bow eddies. Eventually we took the hoses, coupled, and took on some fuel—and then were ordered away with a "well done." Searched the shoreline as we came in this evening. Saw a grotto on one of the points, with a cloud of gulls and tropic birds circling in and out.

July 24, 1943

Yesterday was the first time we have been in port for three days. We were out on an extended exercise that carried us a good long way into the Atlantic. We had night battle practice both nights and got very little sleep. I was chief gun observer on the bridge, and I can remember standing up there sleepily at three o'clock in the morning trying to keep awake until the firing started. Then I had to keep my eyes trained down the beam of the searchlight to watch our three-inch shells on the target; all the while the concussion was bouncing the deck of the bridge and nearly knocking the glasses out of my hand. The first night we fired star-shells and the effect was very beautiful, even if uncomfortable. I guess I'll be somewhat of a veteran pretty soon.

Our sailing time swings back and forth between three weeks and four weeks from the time we got here. It'll probably be about the fifth or sixth [of August], meaning the States a couple of days later. After that, it's anybody's guess!

I went ashore yesterday during the day. I was commissioned to make a lot of purchases for the other officers. I bought about two hundred dollars' worth of stuff for them. For myself I bought eight teacups and saucers and eight bread and butter plates in Wedgwood's "Patrician" pattern, which I think is what we have at home. I bought perfume, too, and a wonderful book on Bermuda with lots of photos and maps. It cost three dollars, but I felt it would be a memorable addition to our little library back home, with the name of the Oxford Book Shop, where I purchased it, stamped inside.

Came back aboard last night loaded down and a little mellow from drinking beer in a subterranean joint called "The Quarry." It's actually a long flight of stairs down into the earth and is dug out of the solid coral rock. The coolness seems to come right out of the rocks and is really the only place down here I've found that is actually cool. The place was almost deserted but I sat in there and just drank beer for about two hours. Did a lot of thinking.

I've been censoring some of the crew's mail and they write the damnedest letters! Just repeat the same silly phrases over and over again, and I got to wondering if mine sounded as bad!

July 25, 1943

Hit the jackpot on mail today! Got four letters and went down to my little bunk and stretched out to read them. It was wonderful to hear from home. I read them a couple of times.

The *Hamul* is our post office, of course, since we are not permitted to buy stamps or mail letters ashore. Upon my first inquiry I found out that the *Hamul* post office was "fresh out" of airmail stamps and was awaiting another shipment. That went on for about a week, and only today, coincident with receiving the four letters, did I finally manage to buy some airmail stamps.

Our whole routine here revolves around the big ship. She is our only source of food and supplies, canteen articles, laundry service, and entertainment. Movies are shown almost every night on a large screen rigged up on her quarter-deck. Last week I saw "The Constant Nymph," with Charles Boyer, Joan Fontaine and Alexis Smith.

In the evening when we come in to our anchorage, all communication is carried on by blinker lights and a flotilla of little motor whaleboats which shuffle back and forth between the supply ship and her brood.

The fresh water tanks became polluted with salt water last night, and until two o'clock this afternoon there was not a drop aboard to drink. It was almost like being in an open lifeboat. I kept thinking about how good it was to go to the refrigerator at home and get out a cold bottle of beer or Coke, or the iced tea which was always on hand. I sent over to the supply ship this afternoon to try and get a couple of bottles of something to drink, and I'm hoping it comes soon. The drinking water still has a trace of salt in it, but it's gradually going out.

Took a swim a couple of hours ago off the side of the ship. Water very good today, almost cool. The salt water here is very buoyant. It will hold you up easily for floating. Swam all the way around the ship and looked her over from a fish-eye view. She's pretty small compared to the other craft moored near her, but she's been giving a mighty good performance in formation with them.

July 26, 1943

Firing all day today. The Coast Guard did itself proud.

We were at the end of a line of eight ships. Ahead of us were six Navy ships. We were seventh, *Intensity* was eighth and last. Perhaps that was the way they rated us.

The Navy ships were bigger and had more guns. We looked a little like weak sisters, very much out of our class. A plane towing a "sleeve"—which is a target looking like a huge sleeve torn out of somebody's coat—comes down the line of ships and each vessel in turn has a chance to fire fifteen shots at the target as it goes by. They started up front with the first of the six Navy ships.

Well, what happened sounds almost incredible. The plane pulled the sleeve past all six Navy ships, and it was still going strong and showing no signs of damage from the black clusters of smoke around it—and then the *Haste* opened up. After five shots from each gun, the red sleeve started down, all shot to pieces from one of our guns. The other CG ship behind us never got a shot. Congratulations came through from the flagship up the line.

An hour later the plane came down again with the second sleeve and the Navy ship two in front of us got it. We never fired a shot. Then, an hour later, the procedure was reversed because the last CG ship (the *Intensity*, behind us) hadn't yet fired a shot. The plane went by and then came the target, a white sleeve this time. The CG behind us opened up and didn't do very well. Then we opened again. After exactly twelve shots, down came target number two. Not one of the Navy ships got a shot. When we reported it, the flagship said, "Take it a little easy, Coast Guard; we're trying to play, too!" We only had three shots left for the fourth and last sleeve, and they came so close it wasn't funny. The sleeve ran the whole gauntlet of the eight ships without damage. I was up on the flying bridge throughout as chief gun observer again, giving the deflections, which means noting whether we were shooting ahead or behind the target. I really didn't do much, but I was right in there pitching. When the second target came down, the crew yelled so loud you could have heard them a mile. Reminded me of a touchdown at a football game.

At any rate, this has been the *Haste's* best moment in this shakedown. We can only hope that the same spirit and skill and luck will remain with us in the days ahead.

July 27, 1943

More firing today, confused and not so good. Planes were diving on us, our crew was hot and tired, the angles were bad, and we just didn't do much. This ends our firing, and I'm glad. We've been through a lot, and I'm just beginning to realize how nerve-wracking it has been. Sometimes I was on the bridge for five hours at a stretch, straining to see the targets and then bracing for the thunderous vibration of the guns. No place to sit down in between. Just stand and lean against the roll of the ship and wait for the next action.

We were late getting in last night. Harbor all cluttered up when we arrived. Anchor went over in the dark. Load of supplies came alongside and we didn't finish loading them until almost ten. Had to wait an hour to take a shower. Stood under the salt water for a long time, then turned in. Kept the light on quite awhile reading my new book on Bermuda and learned that "The British Colony of Bermuda perpetuates the name of its Spanish discoverer, Juan de Bermudez. The exact date of the discovery is unknown, but it was certainly less than two decades after Columbus' first voyage. . . ." What they are saying is that it was before 1512. Wonder what Bermudez would think if he could see us anchored out here in this naval base.

This is a helluva life. Same food, day after day, salt water in the drinking fountains half the time; and always the ship is hot and smelly. In the evenings I climb up on the flying bridge when we come to anchor, with just my shorts and sandals and stand up there getting "blown out." The air is cool and clean and that's almost the only place we can feel it.

A few more days of submarine practice, and I believe we can go home. Hope so.

July 28, 1943

We're running toward the friendly land again. I don't know why I say "friendly," except that the little white houses on the hillsides always mark the end of our day's work and they seem to extend a welcome to us.

From far out we steer toward a point of land and a lighthouse.

Then we turn and run parallel to the shore for an hour to get in. We pass arcs of sand beach, high cliffs, grottoes carved by the surf, and behind them all an inexhaustible variety of houses, white and pink, fitted into the sloping landscape. On the jutting promontories are the remains of old forts. I always turn the glasses on the shore as we pass and try to fit the sights into the history I've been reading.

We will anchor out again tonight as we did last night, and the night before, and all the other nights. We only see the shore and feel what it must be like to be resting over there, watching ourselves come in. Then we drop the "hook" in the harbor and settle down into our own patch of silence and silvery water. In the morning it's the same sights again as we go out. We never get to belong to the land; we're one of a series of wraiths that come and go with the daylight.

I noted yesterday we were all through firing. We were—with our guns. Today we fired all our depth-charge equipment, and the "booms" were equally tremendous in a different way. Was on the bridge for four hours and helped time the flight of our forward "hedgehog." I'm getting pretty good on split-second timing while explosions are splitting the air all around me and rocking the ship. I always get the figures down somehow.

Awfully glad to get in again. The sun and salt air are beating us down a bit. After four or five hours in the middle of the day standing on the bridge in the wind, our heads are swimming. Took my shirt off today and I ought to be getting tanned. The sun is so intense, however, that the sunburn continues to peel right off.

Out of a clear sky tonight at dinner the Captain said, "By this time next week we may be in New York." I almost dropped my fork trying to maintain an outward calm. No one is supposed to express any desire or anxiety about getting home. We all want to, but being the officers, we're not supposed to appear that way. So somebody just tried to say calmly, "Is that so, Captain?" and the reply was, "Yes, that's the way it looks." I certainly hope it's true.

I have no idea how much leave I can get in New York. I'm going to try to get at least three days. If we stay there any length of time, I may be able to sneak home another weekend.

July 29, 1943

We're headed in again. The land is off the port side and something about the scene is reminiscent of the cliffs of England along the Channel. Another day gone. They can't go too quickly.

We were practicing laying down a smoke screen today. I was astonished at the thick, heavy clouds of vapor we and the *Intensity* were able to produce that went billowing out into the breeze and hanging above the wavetops to screen a DE that was running a parallel course about a mile away. We actually obscured the vessel from sight completely. It reminded me of the account of the sinking of the *Bismarck* back in 1941 when English destroyers were laying down a similar screen so their sister ships could dart through and let loose torpedoes at the Nazi monster ship.

Most of the time, however, we worry about not making smoke. As Captain Boyce had explained it, visibility at sea in a clear atmosphere during daylight, is a direct proportion of the sum of the height of the eye of the observer, plus the height above water of the object. Since the height of eye above water for a submarine is very small and, when running at periscope depth is practically zero, the height of the object determines the distance at which it can be seen. The gist of it was, as he had emphasized, that a smoke plume from a ship would have to be only equal to the height of the vessel to double the visible distance.

As to what to do about it, he had told us that it was a matter of keeping a finely tuned, efficient combustion of fuel oil and guarding against any sudden increase in the mixture which might put out heavy smoke. "A light grey haze from the stack is considered optimum," he had concluded.

In policing the situation, I had learned, it is the duty of the officer of the deck to watch his own stack and instantly report to the engine room if anybody is goofing. He also watches the stacks of the merchant ships and reports smoke to the commodore by voice radio.

We blow our exhaust tubes at night to eliminate the day's accumulation of soot. This is done only in the darkest hours, after getting permission of the OD, and is accompanied by a loud roar and clouds of blackness and occasionally sparks.

Under normal operating procedures, therefore, smoke during the day is *verboten*, like garbage, which is also dumped at night, and only with permission.

The going home next week gets more definite. We received a copy of a dispatch releasing us and our sister ship on Monday. The only point not yet cleared up is whether we'll leave at once or wait around this neighborhood to join a convoy. But, at any rate, we're going—*and soon.*

July 30, 1943

From the flying bridge today I was watching the flying fish. That sounds a little silly. Everybody else was concentrating on a submarine (ours) that was playing games with us, but I was fed up with this business temporarily and took to watching the flying fish through my glasses, and trying to hold them in the lenses until they hit the water again. The long-tailed tropic birds, which are also called bos'n birds (which I mentioned seeing when we first arrived) were flying around. Since the first sighting of them, I have found their name in my book.

However, I was rudely brought back to the game we were playing with the sub by the events that occurred in the next few minutes.

Our practice consisted of picking the sub up on our sound gear, making a run in on him and, at the right time, dropping a marker and sending out underwater code. The sub would fire a slug of compressed air and, if it came near our marker, it was called a kill.

Turner had the conn, when, off about a thousand yards, the sub fired a red smoke bomb. Inasmuch as they had been using green bombs to mark their position, the Captain said the sub was probably getting ready to surface. To check, he called the Officer in Tactical Command, who answered, "No, he is just showing you where he is. Continue with your run."

So we bore in as ordered. We all saw it at about the same instant the lookouts yelled, "Periscope dead ahead!" It was cutting the water less than a hundred yards ahead of our keel. He *was* surfacing! Even as we looked, it bore off slightly to starboard as Turner gave, "Left full rudder."

We held our breaths, waiting for the seemingly inevitable crunch of our keel into the sub. It never came. The sub made an emergency dive. We had been retrieved from tragedy. We got the hell out of there and so did the sub, and the OTC looked as foolish as the devil.

Plans are still the same.

Must stop and censor some of the crew's mail before we get back into port. It's quite an experience. You can certainly pick up pointers on life in general from reading their lurid correspondence. It's surprising how many of them write identical letters to different feminine addressees.

August 1, 1943

We're hoping to shove off tomorrow. We have all had quite enough of this place. It's been miserably hot, and they have worked us pretty damned hard. Bermuda is beautiful, but what we have mostly gotten to see of it was from well out in the harbor or on a 110 AATC range, under the glare of the hot sun with the gun crews, all of us learning to shoot fast and straight.

Hate to admit that I haven't felt too well for the last day or so. It's the heat or some of the questionable food we've been eating, or both.

Last night all the DE's had to have convoy escorting practice. The good old *Haste* was the convoy because all of her sub-detecting gear was out of order, so we had a nice protective screen of about a dozen DE's. Along about midnight somebody started shooting star-shells over us. Come to find out, a couple of mine sweepers had penetrated the "tight and alert" DE screen and had taken us for a sub. The DE's will never live that down, and the brass hats will probably never hear about it. We have had fun with our playmates, the DE's, and our rivalry is a friendly one.

Our time in New York has already been cut to one week. I rather expected that. But the thought of getting back at all helps out a lot, since at the moment I'm beginning to hate this smelly, filthy little trap. At night, when we have to black out by closing every porthole and hatch, the decks down below become what we call "the black hole of Calcutta."

August 2, 1943

Today, before heading for home and our first assignment, we had our military inspection.

The Captain had his doubts about how we would show up—and well he might! "But," he said, "Everybody tear around full of pep and act like you know what you're doing, whether you do or not."

As it turned out, this was good advice. The inspecting board knew a lot less than we did, so we really made an impression on them and received an excellent rating. We were classed as a first-class fighting ship.

We are not sure we can live up to this somewhat optimistic appraisal of our merits—but, at any rate, we're going to try.

Periscope dead ahead!

> "Of what thickness are
> the boards of this ship?"
> —"They are fully two
> inches thick," replied the
> pilot.—"Merciful God,"
> said Panurge, "We are
> continually within two
> inches of death."
>
> *Pantagruel*
> Francois Rabelais
> (1495-1553)

August 5, 1943
(Returning from Bermuda shakedown)

TODAY WAS PAYDAY, AND LAST night at eight-thirty I was busily preparing for it in the pay office. Chief Curtis, the Commissary Steward, stuck his head into the office and said, "Well, it looks kinda bad. We're headin' right back where we came from."

I couldn't believe it, and I expressed my incredulity by asserting that we were probably only zigzagging. "No we aren't," he insisted. "I was in the wheelhouse when the order came for full right rudder." That was enough for me to shut up the office and investigate.

The ship had just been blacked out and the interior was lit by the eerie light of red bulbs. At the foot of the ladder leading down from the cabin, I ran straight into Adams, the Communications Officer, who exclaimed in his Southern drawl, "Well, boy, we're in it now! We just had orders to search for a submarine." In response to some quick questions he added that the Commander, Eastern Sea Frontier, had radioed that a plane had been fired on by a sub earlier in the evening, at a spot within fifty miles of our present location. We were to conduct an all-night search.

Adams went on down the ladder leading below, and for no reason at all I headed up toward the deck. It was a relief to step outside. Surprisingly it was not yet dark, although the hour was close to nine. There was no one in sight and nothing to indicate any unusual activity on our decks. Trailing us on the port side was the *Intensity*, diffusing her usual froth of foam. I continued up the ladder to the bridge.

Ensign Dunbar had the deck and the Captain leaned nonchalantly, as usual, against the wind guard. I arrived just as Dunbar was giving instructions to the coxswain of the watch. "Have you got some good men on the number one gun?" he wanted to know. "The best on the ship," the coxswain told him. "Well, tell 'em to keep an extra lookout tonight. We've had reports that there may be a sub in the vicinity." That seemed to be about it. The coxswain said, "Yes, sir," and went about his business.

Dunbar was nervous, and he staggered about the center of the bridge with the motion of the ship. He had the worst time of any of us in keeping his balance up there. He had been a teacher at a boys' school in Connecticut before he entered the service, and even in uniform he had an Ivy League look.

Dunbar was changing courses in accordance with our zigzag plan. "Right five degrees rudder," he called down the tube.

I walked up beside the bridge platform and started searching the darkening horizon through the glasses. The Captain leaned over and said, "Well, this may be it." There was the sound of somewhat pleased anticipation in his voice, and I looked up and said, "Is that so, sir?" He shook his head, and the smile on his face matched the tone of his voice. "It's almost too good to be true. Probably just another needle in a haystack." Then he explained what a triumph it would be if we could make contact tonight. "We'll be in the center of the search area at eleven-thirty," he added.

We must have talked for about fifteen minutes when the TBS (telephone between ships) in the little shack under the cowl of the bridge started buzzing, indicating that the *Intensity* was calling us. The Captain backed in and picked up the phone. Before he said a word, Mr. Dunbar agitatedly called over, "Oh, sir, I forgot to give the 'zig'—I should have changed course a couple of minutes ago."

The three of us glanced across the bridge, and there, almost rubbing elbows with us was the *Intensity*, looming up out of the ascending darkness. Her captain's voice sounded over the TBS, "I don't mind you coming close, but this seems a little crowded. We changed course a couple of minutes ago in accordance with the plan."

"You are absolutely right," our Captain responded. "We are correcting immediately."

Captain Boyce's voice had retained its characteristic conversational evenness. You couldn't have heard him ten feet away. I remembered that time during the Bermuda shakedown when the Commander of the flotilla had chided us for being out of line after a turn. Ahead of us was a jumble of ships at all angles—some even at right angles to the intended line. "The line is indistinct," the Captain had told the Commander, with the same casualness that seemed never to desert him.

Now he reached for his glasses and started searching the horizon ahead. I walked over to the starboard wing and did the same. I could see very little. The horizon was becoming more and more indistinct. Remembering the instructions for night searching, I started looking just above it. To test the glasses, I walked over to the other side of the bridge and trained them on the indistinct blur that was the *Intensity.* She came out clearly even to the foam at her bow. I decided the glasses deserved the appellation "night glasses."

For a long time I stood there, leaning against the guard rail of the twenty-millimeter machine gun, while the stars became brighter and the phosphorus began to gleam in the water. Periodically I would search my angle of the sea. At ten o'clock I went below to secure the rest of my gear before returning to my vigil. Very carefully I put a couple of pictures of my wife and baby in my inside pocket. Then I gathered up life belt, knife, and jacket, and went topside again.

Nothing happened during the night. Nothing happened until this morning at ten o'clock and then a lot of things happened. The *Intensity* broke down—burned out a bearing and sent word over that she would be several hours in making repairs. She was dead in the water and, since we were still in the center of the danger area, we started making slow circles around her, meanwhile radioing for permission to come in, towing *Intensity* if need be.

We were bragging a little, as we always did, about being the better ship, and that proved calamitous because, incredible as it seemed, about an hour later word came up from our engine room that the top had dropped off one of the crossheads, and we would have to be shut down until it was found, or another one manufactured. There we were like ducks on a pond—two "killer ships" fresh from our shakedown, and neither one of us could have dropped a can!

We speculated on the chance of a plane finding us, but it hardly seemed likely. Somebody said we were safe enough anyway, be-cause if a sub saw us, it wouldn't believe what it was seeing. It would think we were decoys. The day was brilliant, and we tossed lightly in the mild swell and looked out with frustration and forebod-ing at the sparkling sea.

In the midst of this confusion—and perhaps not even realizing that any state of confusion existed—Smith, the messboy, appeared in his white coat and said softly, "Lunch is served, sir." Captain Boyce, still maintaining a pleasant and unruffled appearance, de-spite what must have been a very galling situation to endure, calmly announced, "Gentlemen, I think we might as well go down and have some lunch. Mr. Pangle tells me he will need a couple of hours to make repairs."

How I envied Cooney and Adams, who had the bridge, and who grinned maliciously as we followed the skipper down the ladder!

The absence of Pangle, Cooney, and Adams caused a shuffling of seating arrangements in accordance with seniority, and I ended up at the left of the Captain's chair, seated on the leather-covered bench that ran fore and aft along the outside bulkhead. Our heading was north, and the thought occurred to me that the whole width of the Atlantic Ocean, with whatever might be out there, was at my back.

If the Skipper was perturbed, it was not apparent from his affable conversation, and I joined in as best as I could when it seemed my turn. But it was the Skipper, probably anticipating some of our uneasiness, who took the lead by saying, "We get into some tricky situations out here. One of the trickiest I ever saw was on the *Modoc* in 1941, when we found ourselves between the *Bismarck* and the British." He contined with an absorbing narration of how at dusk, while on weather patrol in the North Atlantic, the *Modoc* had spotted the giant apparition of the *Bismarck*, Hitler's mightiest bat-tleship, to her southwest, and the vauge shapes of several smaller ships on the northeast quarter. A group of torpedo planes had come suddenly out of the mist and circled the *Modoc*, then continued in the direction of the big German ship. "There was heavy anti-aircraft fire, and a flash that appeared to be a bomb hit," Boyce said. "We tried to get out of there in a hurry, but every time we changed position the other ships seemed to make reciprocal changes, and for a half hour or so we really sweated it out!"

Our interested questions brought forth the amazing fact that this had happened on the same day that the *Bismarck* had blown England's largest, most powerful battle cruiser, the *Hood*, out of the water and we became so absorbed that before we realized it, we had finished coffee and were starting topside again. The Skipper's story had served its purpose.

Shortly after we returned to the bridge, a plane appeared from the land side and, at almost the same instant, the engine room gave us one-third ahead. How good the plane looked coming in low and friendly—a big PBY, which agreed to screen us during repairs.

Two hours later the *Intensity* phoned that she could get under way. We thanked the plane, and those two valiant "killers," *Haste* and *Intensity*, started once again for New York on radio orders just received, their tails—figuratively—far between their legs and their first "mission" far from accomplished.

August 6, 1943

Received word tonight that the *Plymouth*, a converted yacht manned by the Navy, was torpedoed at four o'clock yesterday afternoon, at a spot about seventy-five miles from where we broke down. She went down in four minutes with the loss of half her crew.

That was close!

[NOTE. It was much closer than we realized. Kapitanleutnant Hans Hornkohl of *U-566*, a U-boat commander to be reckoned with, was having a time for himself sowing mines off the Lower Middle Ground inside the Virginia Capes on the nights of July 30 and 31, 1943, and then setting out after bigger game.

Reports gathered long after the war, and research of naval diaries and official chronicles, reveal that Hornkohl set off an air-surface hunt which showed up Eastern Sea Frontier in an untypical and embarrassingly weak position. A Martin Mariner out of Norfolk first sighted the submarine on the evening of August 2, 1943, 260 miles east of Cape Henry. The plane made a run on the target and released flares which failed to function, but the pilot observed a long, narrow wake. As the plane approached the wake, two bursts of fire and tracer shells were fired from the scarcely visible vessel.

The plane withdrew, returned later and conducted expanding box search without further contact.

Eastern Sea Frontier's "Enemy Action and Distress Diary" for August 3, 1943, a yellowing, one-and-a-quarter page document on file in the Operational Archives Branch of Navy History Division, describes the foregoing contact in detail and then contains the optimistic sentence, *"Haste* (PG) and *Intensity* (PG) directed to area."

There we were, in the middle of the action, and I will always remember the pleased anticipation with which our veteran Skipper, Commander Boyce, commented that the situation was "too good to be true," and the resultant small shiver that ran down my neophyte spine. There followed, of course, the ignoble breakdown of our cantankerous engines and the probably exasperated orders from Eastern Sea Frontier for its two brand new gunboats to proceed forthwith to their base.

Meanwhile, Hornkohl and *U-566* remained busy and invulnerable in the vicinity, and it was sheer luck that we had no direct contact with him as we scurried on our way back to New York.

The *USS Plymouth,* Hornkohl's next target, was the former luxury yacht *Alva,* owned by W. K. Vanderbilt and purchased by the Navy in 1942. She had been converted to an armed escort vessel and was assigned primarily to the New York-Key West run. Her Commanding Officer, Lieutenant Ormsby M. Mitchel, Jr., USNR, was a graduate of the Submarine Chaser Training School at Miami. He first came aboard the *Plymouth* as Executive Officer. In July, 1943, he relieved his Commanding Officer, who had been detached from duty aboard the *Plymouth,* and, as the new skipper, had made one round trip between New York and Key West.

USS Plymouth departed from the Section Base at Staten Island (which was to be our own base) at approximately 1025 hours on August 4, as a unit of TU 02.9.10 which included *USCGC Pandora* (escort commander), *USCGC Calypso* (which, very coincidentally our Skipper, Commander Boyce, had formerly commanded) and a newly built tug, destined for the British Fleet, *HMFT-22* (His Majesty's Fleet Tug-22). The latter was manned by a British crew and was in command of a retired British Admiral, Hon. Sir H. Meade-Featherstonhaugh, who had returned as a Royal Navy Reserve Officer with the rank of Lieutenant, to serve in bringing American-built ships from the United States to the British fleet. His destination was the West Indies, and the presence of the tug as a part of the escort was merely a coincidence.

The convoy proceeded southward without incident until the afternoon of August 5, when their position was about ninety miles due east of Elizabeth City. USS Plymouth had been searching wide on the starboard bow of the convoy when at 1535 hours her echo-ranging watch reported a contact, bearing 100 degrees true, range 1200 yards, ship's head 150 degrees true. Full left rudder was ordered, the Commanding Officer notified, depth charge watch and ready guns on standby. While the rudder was still hard left, target 900 yards, Plymouth suffered a violent underwater explosion abaft the bridge on the port side, and in the vicinity of her port deep tank, containing diesel fuel. The force of the explosion rolled the ship to starboard, then she listed heavily to port and immediately started to go down by the head. The entire port side forward of amidships was in flames. Word was immediately passed to set all depth charges on "safe."

The initial damage of the explosion was very serious. Many officers and men in the forward part of the vessel were instantly killed or were trapped by flames. The Commanding Officer who had reached the bridge, was thrown violently against a bulkhead and sustained serious injuries, including dislocation of the left knee. Nevertheless he remained at his post during the two remaining minutes before the ship sank. When driven from the bridge by flames, Lt. Mitchel threw himself down to the well deck because the ladders had been carried away by the explosion. In spite of his painful injuries, he insisted on being supported so that he could continue to supervise the "abandon ship" routine.

Several lifeboats were cut away and many who had been on the upper decks went over the side. Lt. Mitchel remained aboard his ship until she sank; indeed, he went down with the ship, but was miraculously brought to the surface by his life preserver. When a raft was brought alongside he pointed to others in greater need of assistance, and only reluctantly he finally agreed to be taken aboard. Later it was found that his injuries were so severe that it was necessary to amputate his left leg above the knee.

There were instances of heroism among officers and men. The Engineer Officer, Ensign R. Keltch, had already assisted several crew members to safety when he entered the engine room to search for others and was trapped there. Soundman McGinty attempted to rescue a man trapped in the flaming armory, and was himself trapped there when the ship went down. Three other men saw shipmates without life preservers and presented their own, then were lost themselves after reentering the life jacket compartment.

The Escort Commander aboard *USCGC Pandora* ordered *Calypso* to take charge of rescue operations and she closed the scene of the disaster, which was now marked by the struggling survivors in the water and a small amount of debris. Overhead a PBM was circling the spot and dropping life rafts and life jackets. The British tug was also closing the scene to assist in rescue operations. The Commanding Officer of *Calypso* carefully picked his way through the survivors to reach those in most desperate need. One of *Calypso's* officers asked permission to launch a small pulling boat to pick up survivors who had drifted downwind. Permission was granted and a voluntary crew launched the small boat with great skill and determination in the rising seas which threatened at times to swamp her. The little boat was of great assistance in picking up strays and in towing back life rafts.

Inevitably, sharks appeared in the vicinity of the struggling survivors and two men on *Calypso* were stationed by 30-calibre machine guns to fire salvos in attempts to drive them off. The two gunmen had an unenviable dilemma in trying to shoot the thrashing sharks but spare their comrades.

In the midst of all this activity, the tug had been working closer to *Calypso* while hauling survivors from the water. Because of the heavy seas, the Commanding Officer of *Calypso* feared the two vessels might collide and crush survivors between them, and in the excitement he shouted to the Commanding Officer of the tug:

"Get that goddam tug out of there!"

The former Admiral took his orders from the SOPA (senior officer present afloat) like a gentleman, saluted and answered:

"Aye, aye, Sir."

A short time later the former Admiral was observed at the oars of a lifeboat which had been put over the side of the tug. His assistance was subsequently described as "of inestimable help."

Although the PBM plane reported all survivors spotted had been picked up, the final accounting indicated the heavy loss caused by the explosion, fire and the quick sinking: four officers and eighty-seven crew lost; eight officers and eighty-four crew saved. Three survivors died enroute to Norfolk.

Unfortunately the adventures and destructive power of Kapitanleutnant Hornkohl and U-566 were by no means finished. He had made no radio report since August 1, but on the night of August 6 he brazenly used his radio three times to send the same message to Berlin on three different frequencies. Direction Finder stations recorded the times of sending at 2158 hours, 2208 hours, and at 2309 hours; the "fix" was given as within twenty-five miles of a point about 250 miles east of Cape Charles. An elaborate search mission was projected for the next day consisting of eleven bombers accompanied by a blimp.

At 0720 hours, August 7, 1943, a Ventura pilot from Floyd Bennett Field picked up a radar target at fourteen miles while flying at 3500 feet. The pilot was Lieutenant (jg) F. C. Cross, USNR, and his co-pilot was J. T. Aylward, Jr., USNR. Back in the after cabin were three enlisted men—a radioman, a machinist's mate, and an ordinanceman. The pilot immediately prepared for a depth bomb attack while gaining speed in his homing descent. At about six miles he sighted the sub fully surfaced, and immediately broadcast the sighting on 3000 Kc's Voice. When he had flown within one-and-a-half miles of the sub, air speed 250 knots, he opened fire with his bow guns. The fire was returned from the deck of the sub and one of the first bursts hit the starboard engine of the plane. The direct hit not only stopped the engine but also mortally wounded the pilot and seriously wounded the co-pilot. The pilot continued the attack and all four depth bombs were dropped in a stick across the bow of the submarine.

There was no chance to circle back to see the effect on the sub. However, it is quite possible that the depth bombs were released late and exploded forward of the sub without doing serious damage. The plane was losing altitude steadily until it was obvious a forced landing would be necessary. The wounded pilot gave the "stand by to dunk" order. Then, trying to give life, if not to himself, to his fellow crewmen, he executed a very difficult full-stall landing about twenty miles from the submarine. The plane was set down with such skill that the bomber's bow window did not break and neither pilot was thrown forward in his seat. Both pilots and the radioman climbed through the escape hatch. The two enlisted men in the after cabin were not seen during the landing because of the smoke inside the plane. Possibly they were suffocated or temporarily blinded by the smoke and fumes. Another possibility is that each tried to escape by means of parachutes which failed to open because of insufficient distance between the plane and the water. Subsequently, one of the survivors reported he sighted two closed parachutes bobbing up and down in the water not too far from the plane.

After about twenty minutes, a PBM from Elizabeth City spotted the survivors and landed to pick them up. Regrettably, the courageous pilot had succumbed to his wounds, and before either of the survivors could reach him, he had slipped out of his life jacket and disappeared.

The survivors reported that the sub was a large one, apparently of the 750-1000-ton class, with three separate gun stations, all manned by personnel. One large gun mount, possibly a four-inch anti-aircraft, was on the after deck. The submarine made no attempt to maneuver or to crash dive during the time it was under observation, and its forward speed appeared slow.

Owing to a slip-up in communications, which were sometimes bad in Eastern Sea Frontier, Headquarters knew nothing of this action until later. Two more Venturas from Floyd Bennett Field took off at 1024 hours that morning and the second plane, while still on the runway, was belatedly notified of the crash and told to proceed to that position to make a search for three men not rescued. At 1206 hours the second Ventura acknowledged a routine message sent her. At that time it is estimated she would have been in the immediate area of the submarine. She was never heard from again. Hornkohl's diary, captured after the war, discloses that the plane dropped bombs accurately, but all were duds, and the plane was shot down in flames with the loss of all hands.

Other attacks were made on U-566 by other planes. Twice she dove, and twice was blown to the surface, where her gunners, undisturbed by two other planes and two blimps circling nearby, kept them at a harmless distance.

All efforts of shore authorities to intercept the submarine failed until after dark on August 7, when another PBM from Elizabeth City picked up a contact at 2217 hours. The destroyer Laub had been diverted from a homebound Mediterranean convoy to join the hunt (it was a good choice—she had joined with destroyer MacKenzie on

May 16 in sinking the *U-182* off Funchal). The PBM attempted to make voice contact with her, but the TBS failed to function. Then the PBM dropped flares but they refused to flare. For the next two hours the plane shuttled back and forth between *Laub* and the target, trying to home her in, but finally had to leave because of a severe fuel shortage just as *Laub* appeared to be making contact. Another PBM from Elizabeth City arrived and passed over the convoy, not knowing that *Laub* had been diverted. At 0135 hours the PBM picked up a good radar target about fifty miles from the convoy and dropped flares which functioned beautifully, only to illuminate *Laub* in their eerie brilliance.

U-566 was sighted in the small hours of August 8, 255 miles southeast of Nantucket Shoals; three new destroyer escorts out of Norfolk made contact and forced Hornkohl to dive. He used the German radar decoy called "Aphrodite" to mislead them and made good his escape once more. On August 10 Commander, Eastern Sea Frontier directed the ships and planes still so engaged to give up the hunt.

There was a scorching letter from Captain W. G. Tomlinson, Commander, Fleet Air Wing Five, to the squadron commanders, in which he excoriated the "unbelievable number of inefficient anti-submarine attacks wherein a material failure has been reported as the cause—failure to insure the proper state of readiness for action, failure to exercise forethought and the failure to use common sense."

He presented the evidence from one investigation which revealed that the ordinanceman had set the flares for 3,000 feet instead of 300 feet, thus causing the mission to fail. Result: the patrol plane commander was suspended from duty and from duty involving flying for a period of ten days. The ordinanceman was disrated. He recommended more such actions.

There was also a candid analysis of the hunt by Captain Stephen B. Robinson of Eastern Sea Frontier staff, pointing out that so many mistakes were made by so many people—blunders in procedures and communications, "failures of bomb release gear, of bombs to explode, of guns to operate, and of radios to function"— that one could not blame any particular unit or command. Almost everyone who took part was a novice, and inexperience is costly.

Perhaps it was just as well that we on *Haste* did not know until long afterward that our ineptness during that search for *U-566* had been shared by so many—some of whom paid so tragically.]

"Gowd sive the flippin' king!"

8

> "And believing that this land was an island, they named it La Florida, because it has a beautiful view of many cool woodlands, and it was level and uniform; and because, moreover, they discovered it in the time of the Feast of Flowers."
>
> Antonio de Herrara
> *Royal historiographer*
> *of Spain. Written of that day in*
> *March, 1513, when Ponce de Leon first*
> *sighted the shores of Florida.*

August 13, 1943

(New York)

EVERYTHING IS ADDING UP TO the *"Waste and Insanity"* reputation around here this evening. Part of it is in connection with leaving for Key West. By eight o'clock tomorrow morning we will have gotten under way.

I have seldom heard so much noise, nor seen so many people stumbling, sweating, shoving, and falling over one another in one place. We're loading provisions on one side of the ship, and ammunition on the other. The chief cook is standing by the big, walk-in icebox trying to direct a bunch of unenthusiastic seamen, and at the same time give directions to the two young stewards, who are supposed to be serving our farewell meal down in the wardroom.

That function is to be attended tonight by two enlisted Waves, especially invited by Mr. Ramsay for the occasion. Mr. Ramsay, we have learned, is separated from his wife, so perhaps he feels a bit at loose ends. However, at present all the provisions are piled across the spotlessly prepared main deck, so there isn't even space for the Waves to come through. It'll be a helluva sight to greet them.

The business about the Waves is a little inopportune for the rest of us. Everybody has a lot of last-minute work to do, or last-minute letters to write, but we are now pressured into dressing up and looking pretty for two women Mr. Ramsay invited aboard when he was not in condition to do any inviting. Fortunately they won't be here long; we're closing off the gangway at nine.

August 15, 1943

Good weather. We are off Norfolk. Have had a blimp over us the past two days and this afternoon's escort signaled she had taken a picture of us at low level which would be made available upon our return to New York. Hope to get a copy of it.

I have gotten acquainted with my Colt .45—I now load, unload, and clean it like an old hand.

On the bridge yesterday we were firing at clumps of seaweed and sea nettles. Then the cook volunteered to position himself up forward and pitch overboard some tin cans, cartons, and paper plates, a few at a time. I actually plunked a shot into a big baked beans can just before it sank. Someone else hit it at the same time, but that didn't lessen my satisfaction.

We didn't do much of this in Bermuda; we were too busy with our drills and usually at close quarters with other ships. Captain Boyce had made the suggestion at lunch that we sharpen up our marksmanship, realizing full well, I am sure, that in the case of some of us there was little, if any, marksmanship to be sharpened.

While I was firing away with my accustomed pumping up and down of my forearm—very much as we used to "Pow! Pow! Pow!" when we were kids in Southwest Washington playing cowboys and Indians—Cooney, shooting beside me, remarked matter-of-factly, "On the small arms range they tell you to keep your arm level and not bend your elbow. And squeeze off the trigger instead of pulling it."

A little later, when I had partially incorporated that information into my efforts, he added to it, "Some of the best shots keep their bodies at right angles to the target."

Down in my room afterward where I was cleaning the smooth, heavy, and still-warm gun barrel, I was aware of a new confidence in the potent little weapon that possessed what Turner described as a "jackass kick."

August 16, 1943

We have two more ships that made a rendezvous with us during the night. Seas were moderate and visibility fairly good, so the operations proceeded without difficulty.

On the bridge Captain Boyce reminisced about something that occurred off here one night a year ago with a big convoy headed south in very bad visibility. "Then the improbable happened," he said. "We ran into a convoy coming north!

"At first we couldn't believe it," he recalled wryly, "but when we heard a couple of whistles the commodore ordered, 'Illuminate.' When both convoys got their lights on we found we were almost in each other's lap. It was a damned hectic forty-five minutes—but fortunately nobody was run down!"

The *Haste* is tossing out a slight spray as she hits the swells. Cooney told us at lunch he had talked with some "Limey" officers at Staten Island and they had identified us as members of the "Admiralty 'S'" class, slightly modified from the older corvettes by a "raked stem" and a little more flare to our bows.

"This flare keeps our foredeck from getting as wet as the older ships," he said. In this weather it was certainly true and tonight we were turning and twisting on our zigzag course with only the shimmering of little ephemeral spray clouds against the low-hanging stars.

Following up our talk at lunch, Cooney, who seems to have gathered a store of information about our type of ship, tonight was comparing us with a destroyer. "There's an impression around that corvettes are faster and shallower than destroyers and therefore can better evade torpedo attack.

"But that's not so," he said flatly. "We have deep holds like the old English trawlers; and our sound dome, which can be somewhat retracted in shallow water and in port, is down there at twenty-two feet, a very deep draft for a ship our size.

"Yet that's our reason for being," he stated, "to listen with that damn thing. Our big plus," he added reassuringly, "is maneuverability. We have a huge rudder which, when put hard over, makes us practically turn a corner. For our purposes these are good ships, and we are ideal for convoying some of these old tubs that can barely turn up eight knots."

We are running with three other escorts in a half circle in front of and out on the sides of the convoy. And each of us zigzags continually. We don't worry too much about the flanks because it is doubtful if a sub, far enough out to escape detection would be fast enough to come around and attack us from the stern.

Our escorts consist of two 165-foot Coast Guard cutters, the *Galatea* and *Triton*, plus the converted yacht *Mizpah* (formerly *Allegro*). Somebody said, "This is an all Coast Guard show!"

The *Haste* is running out front on the starboard side. Commander Boyce is the escort commander and our ship derives the same title from him.

August 18, 1943

We are still at sea, but we are approaching Florida, and the water is becoming increasingly blue.

Weather continues good. The flying fish are more numerous than I have seen them, and dart away from under the bow like swarms of insects. At times there will be several hundred of them. Yesterday I also saw the biggest school of porpoises I have ever seen. There must have been thirty or forty of them in the school, and they outdid themselves cavorting for our amusement. Long after we passed, they were visible jumping across our bow waves.

We are by no means in port yet and, as a matter of fact won't be for several days. We do a lot of sailing, but much of it, as already described, is from side to side, and our forward movement is slow.

August 19, 1943

Our Engineering Officer, Lieutenant Pangle, has finally brought our British engines and other gear under control, and we have been steaming along very smoothly throughout this trip. This is a tribute both to Commander Boyce's patience and to Mr. Pangle's persistence. He is an oldtimer, originally from the Lighthouse Service, a bit senior in age to all of us, but forceful and competent in his particular line.

I have already discovered that his shyness in the chartroom when we first fired our guns was very similar to mine—he had simply never had any war experience. He is devoted to his job and to his engine crew, and when things get rough he goes below with them and is strong and calm amid their labors and troubles.

I was up in the chartroom this morning studying the charts, and it was like meeting old friends. The names of towers, stations, inlets, capes, bays, and rivers, were like a roster of our payrolls at Miami, where we were responsible for paying most of the Coast Guard installations in the southern part of the state. Cape Canaveral and Gasparilla light stations, Sanibel Island, New Smyrna Beach, Fort Pierce, Riviera, and all those others, bringing back memories as I traced them on the charts.

August 22, 1943
(Key West)

The tropical rain is splashing in my port, so had to close it. I can hear the water sloshing off the gun decks back aft. It's a welcome rain, too, because until now the weather has been hot and sultry. But the most marked feature of this place is the stillness. When you walk down the street, a ring of silence goes with you. The palm trees are absolutely still.

We are here in this little city, which is the farthest south of any in the United States, and one hundred miles off the Florida mainland. It is said our old friend Ponce de Leon sighted Key West in 1513 when sailing south along the islands after landing in the vicinity of St. Augustine. The island was later occupied by pirate crews that infested the neighboring seas and who found the place ideal for their purposes. Early Spanish adventurers named it Cayo Hueso (Bone Key) because of the numerous bones found here, but the English corrupted it to Key West.

When I first went ashore I thought we had hit a mid-morning calm, but apparently the weather is as lifeless as this for days. One of the Coast Guard pay officers told me that sometimes there will be no sign of a breeze for several weeks. The town is quite as quaint as legend has it. I understand Ernest Hemingway has a home here.

We tied up on the western side of the island, which is bisected by Duval Street, running from the Gulf of Mexico to the Atlantic Ocean.

Walking along the street, we saw a few Conchs, natives who inhabit the Florida Keys. They are of mixed extraction, from widely diversified groups of early settlers, who for some reason or other migrated to the Keys, and they are supposedly named Conchs from the variety of shellfish they eat. Their costumes are colorful and remind me somewhat of the Seminole Indians we used to see in Miami.

While there is not much to be bought here, the prices are high and the stuff all looks ordinary and cheap, it's still a nice town to come ashore in, with its bleak, unpainted houses and ghosts of the past contrasting with the present.

August 23, 1943

Last night—our first night ashore—we had a sample of the entertainment, and we were frankly amazed at the quality, looks, and talent of the performers. The difference between them and the surroundings in which they work is very marked.

Most of the cabarets are little more than stores which have been converted by minor alterations and decorations. Especially in a place called Duffy's, we were impressed by the girl who sang and by a dancer who dazzled the boys with an Hawaiian number.

There were a number of bearded submariners in the place. They were wild and noisy, but clannishly kept to themselves. There is a deep-seated respect among surface sailors for their undersea brethren, and everyone seemed tremendously pleased to see them enjoying themselves by letting off steam in their own way.

A bunch of our men from the *Haste* had found the place, too. They began sending drinks over to us—which at first we accepted, since to have refused would have been unwarrantedly rank conscious and ungracious. Finally, however, we diplomatically had to get the word to them to stop, because before we could empty one glass, another would be sitting there.

We came aboard about one o'clock (all the bars close at twelve on Sautrday night), after having stopped in a little sandwich shop for a "western" and coffee. Didn't sleep well because it was awfully hot below decks. Up for breakfast at eight. Turner had the duty last night and consequently couldn't go ashore with us. This morning he decided he wanted to look the town over, and asked me to go along.

Our departure was delayed a bit, so we compromised and decided to go to the church service in an interesting-looking old church we had seen near the docks. The structure resembled a Spanish mission and was surrounded by a rich assortment of tropical plants. Dressed in our best "whites," and amid much kidding and a few friendly catcalls, we went down the gangway bound for church.

Mostly we wanted to see the church, but it also gave promise of being one of the coolest places nearby. The walls were high and thick and the floor was of stone, and a furtive breeze managed to get in and wander about among the pews. We sat in the twelfth row, in order not to be conspicuous, and nearly everyone else (not more than fifty people showed up in a church that could accommodate several hundred) sat behind us, so that we turned out to be some of the "down fronters" after all.

While some of the singsong droning of the ritual was going on, my friend Turner started to nod sleepily. He had been up all night and the repetitious cadences and drowsy atmosphere were too much for him. His head just kept drooping until I was afraid he was going to bang it on the pew in front. Every time he sagged, I'd nudge him. That went on for three-quarters of an hour. When it was time for the sermon, the clergyman mounted one of the pulpits closer to the congregation and addressed the listeners on the subject of the war being related to the sins of man, which perhaps it was, but in any case we are stuck with it. He then said a very nice prayer for those in the service, and those everywhere who had suffered because of the war, and we stood with bowed heads down there in the front, feeling a little self-righteous at having gotten there to partipate in it.

Turner seemed to have benefited both physically and spiritually from our churchgoing. "That was a nice nap I had," he whispered to me on the way out as some of the townspeople nodded to us pleasantly.

We came back aboard just in time for dinner and, of course, took a lot more kidding at the table. "Somebody has to pray for you birds," Turner told them good-naturedly, "after all that howling you did last night."

August 30, 1943

Our trip back from below was fairly uneventful but the day after we arrived we were put on "stand by" and all leaves were temporarily canceled. This caused much cursing and grumbling, but I suppose the situation is connected with some emergency. We are tied up at Pier 8 in Staten Island at the Section Base, headquarters for the convoy escorts.

Turner, with his ability to find something humorous under all circumstances, had a great story at lunchtime about a happening on Pier 9 next to us the day before we arrived.

It seems a minesweeper with the pleasant name of *Pheasant* was tied up there and a group of students from Fort Schuyler had been taken aboard and were being escorted around the vessel by a coxswain. The students became fascinated with the hedgehog on the bow deck and asked a lot of questions about the curious contraption and its forward-throwing depth charges. Completing his remarks, the coxswain said, "To fire them, all you do is press this button, like this —"

"And he was right," chortled Turner. "Somebody goofed and forgot to turn the thing off and with a big 'whamo' sixteen projectiles took off for Staten Island."

"Fortunately," he hastily reassured us, "they were set on 'safe,' and they didn't explode. But they went through a roof somewhere and scared the hell out of a lot of people who thought the war had taken a new turn. Just where they landed is a military secret."

We found the whole incident hilariously funny and when we stopped laughing Turner, the forester, concluded, "They'll be talking a long time about how that *Pheasant* laid its eggs on Staten Island!"

September 4, 1943

We are sub-hunting.

They actually call this "killer duty." Subs, they say, are bad enough when they're stalking a convoy, but they prefer the big ships and usually don't waste ammunition on the escorts unless detected or threatened. But when you go out to hunt subs without big ships, then the enemy has nothing else to shoot at. At the moment, all we know is that there is supposed to be a sub out here somewhere and we're looking for it.

Today was significant on two accounts; first, we sighted a whale, and second, later in the day we *thought* we had sighted a submarine. Each occasion brought me hurriedly to the bridge where I grabbed a pair of glasses.

Mr. Levendoski (an old-time Coast Guard Officer, who had joined us when we started out for Key West) had sent for me on the first occasion because he knew I had never seen a whale. There it was, "blowing" fifty yards off the starboard bow when I arrived. With the glasses, I saw it quite clearly and it reminded me of the back of a hippo standing almost submerged in a pool at the zoo. Showing absolutely no concern, it passed lazily off our side, spouting intermittently. I followed it with the glasses for a long time.

During dinner a messenger came down and told the Captain,

"Mr. Cooney wants you on the bridge. He's sighted something." The way he said it was enough to make all five of us grab our life belts and start for the door. The statement had coincided with a sudden change in course we had felt just a few moments before but hadn't mentioned.

The Captain and the Exec were already out of sight when I reached the upper deck, so I went forward to the wheelhouse. I arrived just in time to hear Mr. Levendoski yell through the tube, "Man gun one!" so I knew we were preparing for action. I couldn't see anything ahead of us, so I went around to the ladder going up to the bridge and through an aperture I saw the Captain and several of the officers in an excited huddle near the window of the sound room. The action looked real enough, so I went up myself.

At that time we were in the middle of our "run" and bearing down on some underwater target. Suddenly the Captain gave the command to turn away. "It's a wreck," he said, peering through his glasses. Then I saw what had first attracted Cooney's attention. An object looking deceptively like a periscope was bobbing up and down in the water. It may have been a broken stub of a mast or a stump, but at a little distance it was dangerously suggestive. Besides, the sound machine showed a considerable bulk of it underwater.

Sensing that something was wrong (although we had not been ordered to General Quarters), the crew had crowded out on deck and, when we fired a couple of depth charges from our K-guns, we had quite a large audience. The starboard charge exploded near the object but it stayed afloat; we came back and fired with the port K-gun, with the same result. That was all the firing we did, but it created tremendous geysers on the evening surface of the ocean. Landward, the sun was slipping down through a cloudbank.

We stayed on deck for a long time after that, restless, excited. At eleven tonight we are scheduled to reach the position of the sub we are hunting.

September 5, 1943

We've been searching all day without results. At times the *Nourmahal*, the former Vincent Astor yacht, now converted to war purposes, has been visible on the horizon. She's our partner in the search.

A large crescent moon is hanging in the sky tonight, its reflection dancing across the undulating epidermis of the sea.

[NOTE. At the time I wrote the above entry, I hesitated in using the term "epidermis of the sea," since one doesn't usually connect epidermis with water. When I was making the entry in my diary I was trying to describe how the sea at certain times, and in certain moods and lights, resembles the skin of a great mammal. I experienced this strange imagery several times during my service aboard the *Haste*.

On a trip to Hawaii in 1970 I had this impression confirmed when I visited the spanking new Ilikai Hotel, which was convention headquarters for our group. I asked the cab driver what the name "Ilikai" meant and he said, "The best translation I can give you is 'skin of the sea.'"

Evidently the Hawaiians, some of the greatest and most imaginative sea people on earth, have incorporated my same visual experience into their language.]

September 6, 1943

Word came tonight that we are giving up the search and going home. Almost simultaneously we ran into a strong contact on our sound device and fired "the works."

The occurrence was just before dark with the faintest of peach coloring still lingering in the sky. The moon, almost at the half now, was throwing a brilliant track across the sea. We heard the command, "Man the ready guns," and by the time I had reached the bridge the command to fire the depth charges and K-guns was being given.

The explosion of the charges was the most violent I have ever experienced and seemed to shake every plate in the ship. One of our port throwers emitted a shower of sparks to add to the fireworks. Afterward we circled over the spot, guns ready in case anything should bob up, but nothing happened. We passed half an hour making slow circles in the dusk, and finally the Captain said, "Secure from General Quarters." In the wardroom an hour later, he looked up from his coffee and remarked, "That was fun, wasn't it?"

[NOTE. The Skipper, an extremely well-balanced person, and an excellent seaman, did not intend the quip to be as vacuous as it sounded. It had been a tense, watchful, exciting time for all of us. We had been keyed up for several days, and had put on a performance that was little short of the real thing. We were all experiencing various reactions, and I suppose the Captain, who wanted the glory of bagging a submarine very much indeed, and who had thoroughly enjoyed the action of the hunt, was trying to relieve some of the let-down feeling that follows in the wake of high pressure.

Not until much later, when I was researching some of our activities of that period in an endeavor to find out what was really going on (we were only aware of what we were doing from moment to moment, and were not even too sure of that) did I learn what our search was all about. And it wasn't just for fun!

According to the records, the 740-ton *U-107*, charged with the mission of mining Charleston Harbor, had gotten across, and on the night of August 26-27, 1943, cautiously moved toward the Carolina coast, and—so its Skipper claimed—jettisoned twelve mines southwest of the harbor entrance. Then it promptly hauled off in hope of bagging some heavy traffic outside.

The Eastern Sea Frontier War Diary discloses that on August 28, 1943, the SS *Albert Gallatin,* a U.S. cargo freighter of 7,000 tons, proceeding on a northeasterly course at a speed of 9.5 knots, about one hundred miles southeast of Charleston, was shaken by a "tremor" which was felt throughout the ship. The propeller had been hit by "something"; but an investigation, carried out while the engines were briefly stopped, revealed no damage. At the time of the incident a blimp was escorting the *Albert Gallatin* and had sighted no torpedo or wake. The area was calm, the weather clear, the visibility good. Nevertheless, there was the possibility that a submerged submarine had fired an acoustic torpedo which proved to be a dud. (*U-107's* diary indicates she fired three torpedos which hit but failed to detonate.)

That afternoon, exactly three-and-a-half hours after the *Albert Gallatin* incident, an Army B-25 was on patrol in the general area and sighted a wake about ten miles off. The position was about twenty miles north of the position where *Gallatin* had felt the tremor. When the bomber approached within half a mile, the pilot sighted a U-boat of the 750-ton class, painted white, with a grey conning tower. The sub was proceeding, fully surfaced, at about fifteen knots on a northerly course, as though it intended to shadow the freighter until after dark. With bomb bays open, the B-25 made a run on the U-boat, which had twelve men on her deck. The submarine opened fire with machine guns and heavy anti-aircraft fire; the approaching bomber countered with fire from two 50-calibre machine guns and bullets were seen to ricochet from the conning tower. Unfortunately, the bombardier manned one of the machine guns and because it was jammed he was delayed from making the bomb-release. On the first run, the bomber dropped only one depth charge, from an altitude of 150 feet, and it overshot the target. Before the plane could return for a second run, the U-boat started to submerge, making a seventy degree turn to the right as it did so. The plane dropped three more depth charges and the first landed in the swirl of the conning tower. Although the B-25 remained in the area for three hours, there was no further sighting. Within an hour of receiving the B-25's sighting report, Eastern Sea Frontier ordered eleven ships to make an intensive search, and K-34 stayed out to home them in. The surface craft were the patrol yacht *Marnel*, the DE's *Flaherty* and *J. Richard Ward*, the PG-1262, four SC's and two Coast Guard patrol craft. Destroyer *Biddle*, homebound with a Guantanamo convoy, was ordered to join the search at 0600 hours. Five B-25's were in the search area in addition to K-34.

After about twenty-four hours nothing was sighted and the search was discontinued. We had not been included in that group, having just arrived in New York with Key West convoy KN260 on the morning of August 28.

At 0634 hours on the morning of September 4, another PBM on routine patrol sighted an object on the surface from 2,000 feet. Before the pilot had time to point out the sighting, the co-pilot sighted it through his binoculars, and immediately afterwards, the bow station reported the same thing. This action by three separate individuals did not cover more than three or four seconds. Battle stations were called over the interphone, and the pilot made a turning dive. The plane dropped depth charges as the sub submerged, and the first landed in the swirl. The plane stayed in the area for three hours but observed no results. The sub was identified as German, of the 750-ton class, painted white, with a grey conning tower.

The final description, tallying with the previous one, brought the immediate organization of another considerable "killer group," which included, in addition to *Haste* (PG), which was the way Eastern Sea Frontier seemed to tag us, the destroyer *C. K. Bronson*, CG Cutter *Jackson*, frigate *Asheville*, converted yacht *Nourmahal*, minesweeper *Sway* and five SC's. Numerous planes were also in the groups including five PBM's, two PV-1's, and the blimp K-82. The search continued for several days. Again nothing definite developed and the hunt was abandoned.

And so, although we did not know it at the time, we were searching for that elusive *U-107.* Whether we made a momentary contact with her or a sister sub lurking in the same waters, we will never know. The *U-107* outsmarted all of its hunters and returned safely home.

Eastern Sea Frontier's diary says of the action, "It may be pointed out that although the results of the killer group searches were disappointing, the results from the enemy viewpoint were equally unsatisfactory. For more than two weeks, at least two U-boats were active in frontier waters, but during that time no merchant vessel was sunk, no man-of-war was sunk, no plane was shot down by U-boat anti-aircraft fire. Enemy caution in firing from a safe distance indicates the former daring of some U-boat commanders had been tamed by constant vigilance and attack on the part of patrol and escort craft in the Frontier."

A further satisfaction for ourselves and Eastern Sea Frontier can be that the mines *U-107* had laid eventually turned out to be as ineffectual as our search for her. Although she had apparently been guided by lighted gas buoys up Charleston Harbor, *U-107* had laid the mines so far outside the main channel that ships entered and departed without damage until September 20, 1943, when a British motor minesweeper exploded one with no damage to itself. Sixth Naval District then put on a sweep which disposed of the remainder.]

September 7, 1943

Slept in Turner's cot on deck last night from twelve until four, when he came off watch. He had placed it under the forward gun deck where it was protected from showers and spray.

The sea was fairly calm and I was tired, so I fell asleep rather quickly and slept soundly. Sometime later I was awakened by a shining in my eyes that appeared to be a bright star on the horizon. I was too sleepy to investigate, but merely turned over and went to sleep again. But again, I awoke for some reason and, by that time, the star had come closer and proved to be a large ship lighted up from stern to bow. In the darkness it stood out like a Christmas tree.

At dinner today, the Captain said she was probably one of the neutral ships exchanging prisoners—more than likely Swedish. They must feel like people running around naked on a ship lighted up like that, with most of the rest of the world blacked out.

A tired pigeon came aboard this morning and allowed itself to be caught without a struggle. When we examined him we found a message in a little tube in his leg, with a tag reading, "U.S. Navy." The message was apparently a routine one from a blimp and dated the day before. Her position was given as 155 miles offshore, and evidently Mr. Pigeon had missed his directions. We logged him aboard very formally, put down his number, and replaced his message. When we released him, he merely strutted around in front of the windguard and preened himself a bit.

This afternoon we have run into a heavy fog near the entrance to New York Harbor and have had to reduce speed. Our whistle has been going for some time now, and with the first blast, the pigeon flew away. We thought no more about him until someone spied him again on the forward deck, evidently waiting, as we are, for the fog to lift.

> "The battle of the Atlantic was the dominating factor all through the war. Never for one moment could we forget that everything happening elsewhere—depended ultimately on its outcome."
>
> Winston Churchill
> *Closing the Ring*
> (1874-1965)

September 8, 1943

A HELLUVA TRAIN WRECK HAPPENED yesterday at the same time we were coming in through the fog. And it occurred, of all places, on the Washington-to-New York run.

I speculated on such a possibility on my last trip home when I saw some of the ancient equipment that has been pressed into service. This tragedy involved the Congressional Limited, the fastest train from Washington to New York, and I have been reading the accounts with a great deal of personal interest, since this is the train I usually use when I am home on leave. The two cars that were derailed and carried most of the casualties were those ahead of the two diners, always popular with service people, and where I am in the habit of riding if I can find a seat there. Seventy-eight were killed and one-hundred-fifteen injured, the worst train wreck, said the *Times* in twenty-five years. That was almost like a bomb catastrophe.

Commented one member of our crew, "If we're going to get our asses broke going home, as well as going to sea, we're in one helluva bind!"

Turner added his bit with a wry grin, "Aren't you glad, Carr, you were out hunting subs instead of riding that train back from Labor Day leave?"

Later in the day we took the Staten Island Ferry over to New York and caught the subway up to Times Square. Roamed around a couple of hours, visited a couple of bars, including the crowded one at the Hotel Astor, glad to be ashore and feeling like a veteran, just wandering, looking, and smiling at the crowds.

Wallace Beery is starring in something called "Salute to the Marines," but we passed up the movies. For us the streets, the lights, and the people are a show in themselves.

When we came out of the subway station near Battery Park, we went over to a restaurant nearby for the luxury of a "bought sandwich" and a couple of beers before catching the ferry back. The place is evidently the hangout of a nondescript crowd of merchant seamen and bums, and most of them were pretty far along with their drinking. Through the din we could hear a group talking about the train catastrophe, which was still making the headlines in the evening papers.

One gravel-voiced individual behind us was sounding off about how much worse it was "to get it out there," meaning, of course, to be torpedoed at sea. "In that train wreck," he rumbled on, "if you are still alive they get you to that little white cot with people trying to do something for you—giving you painkiller and that kind of stuff. And if you are 'finished' they'll bury you in a nice cemetery with people around.

"Out there if you're knocked off or hurt bad, you're gonna go down to the fish—and nobody knows when or where in hell you went.

"I'll take that train wreck any time," he finished emphatically, thumping the table with his fist.

Sitting there at the bar we were a captive audience to one guy's opinion on a subject we talked about as little as possible. We couldn't help wondering if this bird was actually attached to any vessel.

When we got out of the place it was Turner who put things back in perspective. "Well, it must be nice to think you've got a choice," he observed mildly.

September 10, 1943

"Italy has surrendered!" blazes the headline of the *Times*.

Forty days after the fall of Benito Mussolini—a welcome development which took place while we were in Bermuda—a secret armistice was signed in Sicily by General Eisenhower's representative and Premier Pietro Badoglio. It was ". . . Three years and three months ago today," says the dispatch, "When the dictator, playing jackal to Hitler, led his country to war on France." that is, June 10, 1940.

One of the pleasures in being in New York Harbor is to read the *Times* and follow its accurate coverage of the news from the various theaters of the war.

September 11, 1943

The Nazis, ignoring the surrender, have occupied Rome and Milan. The British, in turn, have taken Taranto. Roosevelt and Churchill have asked Italy to fight against her former Axis partner.

Over the air waves Hitler has minimized what he calls "the betrayal." Using the "big lie" technique, Hitler extols Mussolini as "the greatest son of Italian soil since the collapse of the ancient empire." He also called the surrender of Italy "unimportant from a military point of view," inasmuch as "most of the fighting on Italian soil during the past three months had been done by German troops."

"Therefore," he continued, "Germany . . . is now free to carry on the war without being encumbered by inhibitions." The Reichsfuehrer accused both the Badoglio government and the Italian king of "having consciously deceived and betrayed an ally." What was that phrase about "honor among thieves"?

Perhaps the Italian surrender will shorten the war, but I doubt it. I never felt they belonged in the war in the first place, or had much zest for fighting their former allies. Nor we them.

Caught the Staten Island ferry and walked from the Battery up to Bowling Green. Picked up some much-needed supplies and new finance bulletins at Coast Guard Headquarters nearby at 42 Broadway.

We will be in port until the latter part of this month. Sat for a few moments in that little park almost disbelieving this first real intermission in our hectic schedule since I reported for duty aboard the *Haste*. Was it really only three months ago—and is it possible I have learned so much about a warship and the sea in such a short time?

Finally sauntered down to Whitehall Street, which slants from the bottom of Broadway down to Battery Park. Was fascinated by the narrow, crooked streets coming in at right angles and bearing the descriptive names, Stone, Bridge, Pearl, Water, Front, and South.

Discovered the Seaman's Book Store at 12 South Street and browsed around a bit among the shelves and tables of musty volumes. Located a worn history of New York City which I bought for fifty cents.

In its first chapter as I thumbed through it I came across a sentence reading, "I can remember when South Street was a forest of masts. . . ."

Outside the store I could picture the multitude of sleek bowsprits, the carved figureheads and fabulous names that formerly overhung the street.

I am beginning to like this big city with its proud and colorful past, even though I don't like the circumstances under which I am here.

September 12, 1943

The *Times* reported today that most of the Italian fleet has escaped and surrendered to the British at Malta. Twenty-two ships are said to be in the group, including four battleships, seven cruisers and six destroyers.

The Allies have captured the port of Salerno, below Naples, and are fighting their way inland in the face of continuous counterattacks.

September 13, 1943

Details were published today on the sinking of the Italian battleship *Roma*, a vessel of 37,000 tons and believed to be the finest in the Italian fleet. The report came, ironically enough, from an English reconnaissance plane that had never before been able to locate the big ship in her hiding place, wherever it was. In bright blue weather, steaming under forced draft through the Strait of Bonifacio, between Corsica and Sardinia, enroute to surrender, she was caught by a Nazi bomber who bracketed her with a stick of bombs. One of the explosives must have entered her stack or an open hatchway, because she was almost broken in two by the enormous blast. At the last minute, the pilot reported, the bow and forward control tower almost made a symbolic "V" before she disappeared beneath the waves.

What an inglorious end for a great ship!

September 21, 1943

A week has gone by and much has happened. Have been very busy.

The Skipper and his wife gave a party for the officers and their wives on Saturday afternoon at their apartment, 14 Washington Place, on the east side of Washington Square.

Dee came up for the occasion and I met her on the crowded platform under Pennsylvania Station. I am becoming very adept at getting about town and I wanted to show off my newly acquired proficiency to her. She seemed to brighten up the whole drab section of the platform with her big smiling cat-eyes and matching green and white suit and small hat. Proudly and quickly I guided her via subway to the Henry Hudson Hotel where I had made reservations.

At the Skipper's apartment, his wife, obviously a skilled hostess, soon had all of us at ease. She is small, attractive, and wears her black hair sleekly pulled back in a bun. Only two other wives were present, Mrs. Pangle and Mrs. Stolzer. The wine helped to get the party going, and we talked about everything but the war.

When I studied Captain Boyce and his wife, I wondered how they could be so outwardly calm and detached from all of the misgivings that were haunting me and must be bothering them in some degree. I decided that perhaps that quality of equilibrium under all circumstances—at least on the surface—was one of the real distinguishing marks of professional service people.

Sunday, the day following the party, I brought Dee over here to see the ship. She enjoyed the trip across the harbor on the big, roomy Staten Island ferry, with the skyscrapers in the background, but perhaps that was an unfortunate prelude to the letdown of going aboard the *Haste*. As usual, even on Sunday, workmen were welding something topside and electric wires and tools were strewn in all directions. The workmen paused to stare through their visors at Dee's legs as she came up the steep gangplank in her high-heeled alligator pumps.

She tried to suppress her shock at viewing the *Haste*, and of course, she had genuine difficulty negotiating the ladders. Fortunately we encountered only a few crewmen enroute. Dunbar, who had the duty, was busy with an emergency leave situation in the office.

In our room Dee observed, "I might have known you'd have a Petty Girl tacked over your bunk."

"It looks like you," I told her.

In the wardroom she remarked, "This is the only decent place I've seen on the ship," and we had a cup of coffee there. I showed her the "heavy weather rack," the wooden rack about the height of a billiard table triangle with its cut-outs of assorted sizes for plates, cups, utensils, etc., that we clamp on the table in a bad sea.

When we had once again negotiated the ladders and regained the main deck, peeking into the office enroute, Dee was straightening her hat and checking her image in the mirror of her compact when she commented, "I feel like I've been climbing around in a circus." Then, with a little laugh, she added, "I certainly gave those sailors a leg-show."

From the dock she cast a final puzzled look at the *Haste* and said, woman-like, "I don't see how you find anything at all on there."

On Monday we checked out of the Henry Hudson and took the subway down to Pennsylvania Station. Our stay at the hotel had been nice, although a little bit hectic. The place is noisy, crowded with service people and slightly run-down. They probably don't have the time to clean the rooms properly between occupants, and there were lapses evident that caused Dee to fume a little. In the crowded cocktail lounge off the lobby, if I turned my back for a moment we had unwanted company.

But so it goes. We were together and that, in war time, is important enough to take the place of many other things.

Put Dee on the 3:30 train. We had a cocktail at the Hotel Pennsylvania across the street, and in so doing recalled a little sadly the Glen Miller hit tune, "Pennsylvania Six-Five Thousand," a title taken from the phone number of the hotel.

There is never enough time and the crowds and the circumstances take over and finally you have settled your wife in a nice seat beside the window and already you observe the glances of fellow officers, and you go out on the platform with her and kiss her goodbye and wish to heaven that you were going to make the trip with her instead of those other bastards.

From behind the window Dee waved and threw a kiss. Her eyes were glistening, and I got the hell out of there. Why wait until the train started? We were going to say good-bye anyway—and I was going back to sea.

September 26, 1943

Just returned from another two-day hunter-killer mission. We were running with the PC-565 and conducting an expanding square search of the area where a sub had been reported at dawn on Friday.

The new ship *Natchez* joined us during the night, and at dawn Saturday we were cheered to see a blimp coming out.

The *Natchez* is said to be one of the first of the new frigate class to come down the ways. We looked her over with a feeling of both curiosity and comfort in the early morning light. She is a little over 300 feet long and carries two five-inch guns, compared to our three-inchers, and both 20-millimeter machine guns like ours, plus the heavier 40-millimeter which gives her a much greater all-around capability. "She looks beautiful to me," Captain Boyce said approvingly as he put his glasses back in the rack.

We were ordered to abandon the search later in the day. Turner remarked with a pleased chuckle that this ended our "Red Dogging of that one," and when I asked him what he meant he explained that our radio voice call as commander of the task unit had been "Red Dog One."

[NOTE. Although we on the *Haste* had been cheered and heartened that night when the new and larger *Natchez* joined us, post-World War II research reveals that the real hero of our group was the *PC-565*.

On a beautiful afternoon back in June 1943, while patroling ahead of a New York-to-Guantanamo convoy, 120 miles southeast of Cape May, New Jersey, the redoubtable little vessel, 173 feet long, had slipped up undetected on the submarine, *U-521*, and sunk her with an attack of five depth charges. The only survivor was the skipper of the sub, who was later identified as an "ace," holder of the Knight's Cross for allegedly having sunk twelve ships, plus a British destroyer and two corvettes.

The Commander of the Eastern Sea Frontier, Rear Admiral Adolphus "Dolly" Andrews, expressed special gratification that one of his PC's, which had gallantly borne the brunt of convoy duty for so long and under such difficult conditions, should singlehandedly have dispatched one of the enemy. Many had argued that corvettes and PC's were too small for combat with submarines, but *PC-565* had proved that, with proper indoctrination and by following standard procedures (with a little luck thrown in), these escorts could triumph over the most illustrious of subs.

PC-565 is pictured in one of the World War II histories with a large swastika emblazoned on a plaque on her bridge, crisscrossed with two broad white stripes of paint.

"It does seem strange," wrote Commander Boyce in reply to my inquiry, "that we were not aware of her triumph, for news like that traveled pretty fast among the escorts." Then he added, reflectively, "I don't believe we were ever close enough during daylight to see her scalp."]

September 27, 1943

Back to catching up on the news reports. The Italians are finally doing some fighting for our side. They have driven the Germans from Sardinia. The Allies have widened their beachhead at Salerno.

The Navy says that we now have "the largest surface fleet in world history, and the most powerful air force in the world. In the midst of the war," the report states, "the United States has built the Navy into the greatest sea-air power on earth." The surface fleet "now has 14,072 vessels—three years ago there were 1,076."

I presume that we are catalogued somewhere among the 14,072. I hope that as a result of the terrific losses we took when we had only the 1,076, we will never again neglect our Navy and merchant marine as we did between the wars.

> "Overloaded, undermanned, meant to
>   founder, we
> Euchred God Almighty's storm, bluffed
>   the Eternal Seas!"
> > *The Ballad of the Bolivar*
> > Rudyard Kipling (1865-1936)

[NOTE. ON SEPTEMBER 29, 1943, we started out with our first convoy for Guantanamo Bay, Cuba. As soon as we got outside the "gate," as the submarine nets are designated, we ran into a violent storm. The convoy was scattered, and for three days we led a precarious and thoroughly miserable existence. It seemed a somewhat portentous beginning for our barely shaken-down outfit.

Mariners are accustomed to classifying weather conditions on a scale from one to twelve. A "one" is hardly more than a light breeze, and a "twelve" is among the more unpleasant things that can happen to a ship. Most seamen exhibit extreme reluctance to employ any of the higher numbers. For example, when a newcomer might say, "Wow! Isn't this a pretty bad sea?" the average salt will more than likely reply, "This isn't even a good 'three.'" The storm in question was logged "eight" by our Skipper, who was a very conservative seagoer. We learned later that it was a near-hurricane in force, which would shift its number quite a bit higher on the scale.]

October 5, 1943

Weather has been good for the past several days, and Doc and I and the rest of the crew have been slowly recuperating from our experience in the storm. Lt. Carroll, the Navy observer, is wearing a bandage like a turban. I found it impossible to write during those turbulent days, and am just getting around to jotting down my own notes and impressions of the cataclysm.

To begin with, we apparently ran smack into the storm when we came out of New York. At first it was just a sort of haze against the land, and a breeze over the water. Later it became a rain squall.

Then it was a full-blown northeaster. After that it became a gale, and a bad one.

By mid-afternoon it seemed to me we had already lost our convoy and were running due south, with the northeast wind and a driving rain at our backs. Things on the ship began to "go." Crashes were coming from all directions, an ominous indication of broken equipment. By nightfall the ship was filled with a repetitious, nerve-racking symphony of smashing, crashing, banging objects.

We came out on this trip with fifteen new men, most of whom had never been to sea before. Cooney described their plight with more accuracy than sympathy, when he reported, "All the new men are in the crew's head, lying face down in a sea of vomit." And there wasn't anything we could do but leave them there.

We slept only fitfully, and early the next morning Levendoski came off watch and said our small boat had broken loose and had to be cut adrift. He added that the seas were even worse than they had been—which wasn't any secret to any of us who were trying to stand up.

Our roll at this time was nothing short of alarming. Everything not bolted down was sliding across our room; suitcases, chairs, books, clothing. Things that had been bolted down had, in many cases, broken loose. The drawers under our bunks had sprung open.

When I stood up to put on my heavy coat, I had to brace myself upright several times against Cooney's bunk. A nauseating stench had seeped down into our quarters from the mess deck, where—as an accompaniment to the crew's misery, and in the midst of it—the toilets began malfunctioning.

Fighting the motion of the ship, I struggled up the ladder to the mess deck, continuing upward to the door leading to the catwalk behind the wheelhouse. When I opened the door the wind almost tore it out of my grasp. The scene outside was appallingly spectacular. Seas as high as the mast rolled up on our stern with a furious hiss. As they picked us up on their crests, we rolled so far over that the wings of the bridge almost touched the water.

I discovered it was easier to stand on something upright, like a railing, than to try to keep my feet on a deck that kept dropping away from under them. The railing seemed to be under me anyway, and standing on it I stared down into a green and boiling sea.

The wind brought me the sound of voices, and nearby I discovered a group of seamen huddled in the shelter of the leeward catwalk. The chief gunner's mate was there, a veteran of twenty years at sea. "This would be a real storm in any man's ocean," he commented. One of the mess boys, his eyes round with excitement, exclaimed, "Them waves look just like mountains with snow on 'em!" It was a good description. The big combers crested with flying spray and white foam did, indeed, have the appearance of snow-covered peaks. In the distance other peaks were visible, lifting high against the sky.

About this time the Captain discovered that some members of our convoy were somewhere around five miles distant, and changed course accordingly. At the same time our shelter along the catwalk was becoming untenable, and I moved around to an enclosed spot under the radar shack. Standing there, I was partially sheltered from the onslaught that came over the bow. The big waves would hit the bow with a terrific thud, followed by a jar as the weight of the water struck the bridge. Then the residue would come slithering down amidships. At times the atmosphere seemed to hold more water than air. However, it seemed better than going below again. I was convinced that a descent into the interior would make me actively and unpleasantly ill.

At noon, Ensign Dunbar came down off the bridge and joined me. He had the same idea I did concerning the inadvisability of going below. Smith, one of the mess boys, gallantly fought his way to the bridge with sandwiches and a pot of coffee, and promised to do the same for us. When he came back with the sandwiches wrapped in soggy paper in his pockets, and two half-filled cups of coffee, we wished we could have promoted him on the spot.

Trying to hold the coffee in one hand and the sandwich in the other was an impossible maneuver, and several times we broke loose and went teetering through space to the outside railing. In the end we were forced to gulp the coffee down to free one hand for holding on. Afterward we settled down to pass the miserable hours the best way we could. Once, for no particular reason, I broke into a rousing rendition of "Sailing, sailing, over the bounding main," that brought Turner back to peer, grinning moistly, down the bridge ladder.

At four in the afternoon, a patch of blue sky appeared and simultaneously six lumbering ships of the convoy were sighted over the wave tops, appearing and disappearing in the watery chasms. We discovered one of the little PC's of our escort group doggedly hanging onto their flank. The sight of the little craft made everybody feel better. Here was a ship smaller than we, taking a worse beating out there in the waves. Word passed somehow and a number of curious faces began to appear on the *Haste* decks to take encouragement from a brave little sister ship whose misery must equal or surpass our own.

I was temporarily routed out of our shelter when Adams, who felt as bad as the rest of us, and possibly a little worse, asked me on two occasions if I would help him decode and encode a message. Last trip I was drafted as a member of the Coding Board, when the Captain discovered I was both a touch typist and had operated other keyboard machines like adding machines and calculators, which he figured made me a logical candidate. So he said pleasantly, "Mr. Carr, I think you could give these gentlemen a lot of help."

At this moment, I cursed the idea of anyone sending messages in such weather, but holding my breath as much as possible to close out the odors, I followed Adams below to the wardroom, where we began to struggle with the machine—or, more correctly, struggled to stay in front of the machine, much less to operate it. We always put an irrelevant phrase in front of the actual message to confuse enemy cryptographers who might be intercepting the communications, and one of these I used was "Shiver my timbers."

The patch of blue sky and the temporary lull were deceiving, for with the coming of dusk the wind veered around to the southwest quarter and the barometer dropped again. Wet, cold, and thoroughly tired out from fighting it, it was obvious there was nothing left to do but go below for the night. Dunbar had crawled into the chartroom to try for a few hours of sleep.

On the way below, a sudden curiosity caused me to struggle aft on the mess deck to the pay office, where I snapped on the light. The scene that greeted me was fantastic. Water was sloshing around depositing papers and pieces of garbage wherever it touched. Chairs were overturned. The typewriter and adding machine we had thought so securely wedged in place were sliding about in confusion among papers, file boxes, ledger sheets, books—all the orderly accumulation of three months of patient, systematic collection

118

and arrangement. Fortunately my most important records were in the safe, which still stood securely on its foundation—an island in a sea of devastation.

Sleep that night was out of the question, mainly because we couldn't lie in our bunks without holding on. Our roll had gone past forty-five degrees and was almost continuous. When Cooney came down from the bridge at eight o'clock, he said we had slowed down to six knots and were practically "hove to."

Suddenly there was a tremendous commotion and yelling outside our room, and it turned out that Smith and Williams, the stewards, who were hauling some garbage on the mess deck, had let the big galvanized can get away from them and it had landed on the head of our Navy observer, Lt. Carroll, who had just come down from the bridge.

Doc was in his bunk in the sick bay on the mess deck, feeling none too well himself, but we led the bleeding lieutenant up there, holding his head, and Doc valiantly got up and tended the wound. Carroll decided to sleep in the wardroom, since he probably couldn't get back aft to the stern house anyway.

Cooney, Turner, and I talked for awhile, disconnectedly and somewhat giddily, rehashing the day's events. At ten o'clock Turner went up on watch, and Cooney and I finally lapsed into silence, listening to the pandemonium raging above and around us. We left the light on because it made no difference whether it was on or off—the background was equally chaotic.

Cooney made an inclinometer by fastening his identification chain to the bottom of Turner's bunk, and we watched it with almost hypnotic fascination as it traveled back and forth to a position almost level with the cross-pieces.

Adams appeared, wraithlike, at our door with another message, and we went in to fight it into the machine. Lt. Carroll was trying desperately to keep himself on the wardroom bench, but despite his obvious misery he was doing his best to laugh it off.

Back in our room, I went through an intolerable period of waking and dozing until my wristwatch said twelve-thirty, and I knew I'd had it. I couldn't lie there any longer. I had to take my misery somewhere else to at least a change in intolerableness.

Slipping over the side of the bunk, I went through the torturous process of putting on my shoes and my heavy coat, then I headed for the bridge. Adams and Turner were there. For ten minutes I held on at the top of the ladder, until their hooded figures became distinguishable. Seizing an opportunity between rolls, I reached the bridge platform, hung onto the binnacle a moment, then gained the windguard. They acknowledged my presence, and that was all. It wasn't an occasion for idle chit-chat. It was all we could do to hang on.

Through the wet glass of the windguard I watched the big ones come at the bow diagonally. There was no end to them. But suddenly a clear space showed in the sky, and a few stars came out. Then more stars. We all saw them and pointed upward. Adams called down the tube for the barometer reading. It had risen a fraction. We looked with desperate hope at that rent in the clouds and the glimmering stars that peered through it.

At one-thirty it was time to call Turner's relief and he dispatched the messenger for Levendoski. He was a long time in coming. The sky cleared and more stars appeared. Almost afraid to mention it, we commented that the rollers seemed to be dying down a bit.

At last Levendoski appeared and Turner went below. The veteran Coast Guardsman leaned against the windguard and groaned. "How're you feeling, Clem?" we asked him, unnecessarily. "I can stand anything but this rollin'," he said. "This rollin' gets me. I never seen such a ship for rollin'."

He hung onto the windguard limply. The old sea-dog of bragging and jesting days was sick. Adams and I didn't say anything, but it was a kindred moment for all of us. At this juncture the Reserves were standing up with the regulars—brothers in misery.

At two-thirty the patch of sky was bright with stars, although the wind continued strong. "How's the barometer?" we yelled down to the quartermaster. "She's up to 30.2 inches, sir, and still going up!"

It was the news we had been waiting for. The low pressure area was behind us. We had taken the worst of the storm, and now it would subside. The wind would continue for awhile, but eventually it would lessen.

Wearily I leaned against the bridge rail and looked upward. For the first time my thoughts turned away from the exigencies and discomforts of the moment and went out toward home and wife and baby son.

"Messenger," said Mr. Adams, "go below and tell the Captain the sky is clearing."

Then, turning to me, he said, "The 'old man' had been on the bridge for sixteen hours straight when he went below, but I don't think he'll object to hearing the news."

Duffy's Tavern at Key West

11

> "Geography without historye seemeth a carkasse without motion, so historye without geography wandreth as a vagrant without certain habitation."
>
> *Fifth Book of the General Historie of Virginia, —New England and the Summer Islands.*
> Captain John Smith (1580-1631)

October 6, 1943

THE MILE-HIGH MOUNTAINS OF CUBA rose out of the sea this morning. Or, to be more exact, they were there imposing their solid and indestructible bulk against the sea when I went on deck after breakfast. They were a new presence and the whole aspect of the sea was changed because of them. It was as though hundreds of pairs of eyes must be watching from their heights, but through the glasses we could make out absolutely no sign of life, or of human habitation. They say this is the barren end of Cuba.

Later in the day we rounded Cape Maysi, which is the easternmost point of the island. On the other side of us was the purple shadow of Haiti, the aboriginal name meaning "mountain country." I thought it described the island perfectly, as I turned the glasses in that direction and tried vainly to bring out the details of the tremendous peaks. The sea through here, a channel fifty-five miles wide between Cuba and Haiti, is called the Windward Passage.

While I was looking through the glasses, one of the mess attendants, who was standing near me asked, quite seriously and diffidently, "Sir, is that where them voodoos live?" Jokingly I answered, "Yes. I can see them through my glasses."

I handed the binoculars over to him. Holding them trained on the island for a few minutes, Williams lowered them, looked at me, and grinned. "Sir," he said, "I think you're kidding me."

"That's right, Williams," I admitted. "I was kidding you. But one day we may not be able to kid any more—so perhaps we'd better do it now."

"You're right about that, sir," Williams said. "Thanks for letting me take a look."

Haiti faded out as we continued along the southern shore of Cuba, and ahead of us the mountains stretched away into the blue distance. The summits of some of them brushed the clouds and I gathered from a chart that this range bears the Spanish name of Sierra de Purial.

We moored at about six o'clock. The trip into this harbor was very beautiful, and the sun went down some time ago behind the mountains. The sky was clear this morning, the water blue, and the mountains, misty purple on the horizon, have been with us all day. Everyone aboard has been in a jovial mood.

I haven't been over the side to take a look around, and am not sure when I'll get a chance to do so. We are gradually cleaning up the mess left by the storm. My typewriter is now bolted to the desk and we are rigging up clamps that can be used to secure the drawers of the file cabinet.

The new Doc (his name is Raymond Hofstra) and I have worked out quite a companionship. We don't stand watches and we have a little more time to lounge on deck together. He is an interesting character, and when I have time I must write down the things he has told me about how he came to be on the *Haste*. The tale of his transformation from wife-and-baby idyll ashore to sea duty, and his experience in that connection, are even more rugged than my own. That's another bond between us.

October 7, 1943

This has been a long, hot, hard day. I haven't yet been off the ship. We've been working all day preparing our payrolls for the General Accounting Office. Every three months we have to submit a summary of our disbursements, and this period right about now is our busiest time, so I have banged around all day in shorts and T-shirt, in and out of the pay office, cursing and grumbling at little insistent delays. But we have accomplished quite a bit.

After dinner Turner, the Doc and I are going to look at the canteens ashore.

Last night, after we moored, we moved to a fueling pier and passed the time until almost midnight taking on oil. Then we shifted back to our previous berth and tied up for the night. It was past midnight then, and I turned in on my cot which was outside, under the forward gun deck. At first I had trouble trying to sleep up there, with the noises and strangeness, but pretty soon I fell into a sound sleep and didn't wake up until the "piping" started at seven, except to pull the blanket over me against the most wonderful cool breeze imaginable, which had accommodatingly come up during the night.

I'm going in now to take a shower before the line forms. With thirteen officers aboard (including Lt. Carroll), things are a bit crowded, but we make out.

October 8, 1943

The canteens here—there are three of them—are the best I've seen. They have some elegant things at bargain prices. After we visited the first one last night, we went up to the Officers' Club, which is also one of the finest I've seen. Located right on the shore of the bay, it has an open terrace with comfortable red leather chairs to lounge in while sipping some very reasonable and very good mixtures. They take good care of naval officers in this war. About a hundred officers were lounging around. The place could accommodate a thousand easily.

Afterward, Cooney, Turner, the Doc and I went up and played a couple of games of pool and some table tennis. We came back about ten-thirty. Talked until twelve, with everybody spreading out his individual purchases from the PX on the wardroom table for inspection.

Slept on the after gun deck in the open. Heat lightning and dark clouds in the distance kept waking me up, expecting a downpour. Didn't happen. Stars later, right up over my head. "Orion in his panoply of gold," as the *Odyssey* described it. Used to see it when I took walks along the Potomac.

October 9, 1943

I have been intensely interested in my first contact with Cuba, even though it has been extremely circumscribed.

Guantanamo Bay is an indentation in the southern shore of Cuba, approximately eighty miles south and west of Cape Maysi. The base, which occupies in turn the southern shore of the bay, is

124

roughly crescent-shaped, with the horns pointing toward the north, and is divided into three parts.

On the western tip as we come in is the air station; in the center, the naval base; and, on the opposite tip, the Marine base. All three operate under the Commander, Caribbean Sea Frontier, who has his headquarters here.

The shore line being rough and characterized by innumerable points of land, the entire establishment covers a considerable area, and a bus system is maintained to afford transportation from one section to another. The triumvirate character of the base was emphasized for us by the fact that each of the services has its own movie and canteen, and we have spent a great deal of time riding from one to another of the canteens, looking, comparing, purchasing. At night we have had three shows to choose from, though we have since found out that the same three shows make the rounds of the three theaters—and our only real choice was when we would elect to see a particular one.

The one Officers' Club on the base is open to officers of all the services. It is certainly spacious and elegant enough for anyone.

The bay is about four miles wide by ten miles long, well sheltered and deep, capable of accommodating large vessels. The place is wild and solitary, and except for the U.S. Naval Base, originally granted by a pact signed in 1902, it had little importance. However, the naval base has now become of even greater importance to us and our Allies than even the most far-seeing could have dreamed.

We went over to the Officers' Club for dinner tonight. There were about ten of us, including the Captain. Before dinner we sat out on the terrace, sipping a drink, and admiring the sunset over the mountains.

After dinner we went over to the outdoor movie to see "My Sister Eileen," starring Ginger Rogers, and then returned to the Club, but I left almost immediately. I was tired and wanted to do some writing. The stars have been waking me up the past two nights, plus the fact that this morning we shoved off at seven for some firing practice outside, and didn't moor again until two.

We are almost ready to shove off on the trip back. It has been a good change from some of our others ports, and the club and canteen features have been a treat. Also I have been finding Doc Hofstra as companionable ashore as on shipboard. His principles, and his desire to do the best job he can, fit into my own scheme of things.

In the spring, before reporting to the *Haste*, Doc and his wife and baby daughter were comfortably located at Pine Lake, Michigan, where Doc was on duty as medical officer of the nearby Coast Guard Training Station. Doc was happy to be there, but couldn't quite understand it, since just before this pleasant assignment he had written a letter to Headquarters from the Public Health Hospital near Chicago, where he was then assigned, requesting transfer to a "more meaningful assignment in the prosecution of the war."

Pine Lake didn't seem to quite fit that category but orders were orders. Then suddenly, at the end of August, new orders had arrived to "Report to Coast Guard Headquarters, Third Naval District, 42 Broadway, New York City, for further assignment."

Doc, a native Chicagoan, had never been east, nor seen the ocean, when he headed for New York. At Headquarters he had been informed by his fellow officers that periodically one of the group drew an assignment for a one-trip tour of duty at sea as medical officer. They indicated they had the situation pretty well under control, even drew lots occasionally to determine who would go out, and that such assignments were few and far between. They also indicated they knew precisely what to do to avoid lengthy sea duty. In the interim, they were busily engaged in forming financial pools, gambling on the stock market and the races, and cordially invited Doc to join in their activities.

This didn't sit too well with Doc, who had a strong sense of duty and was lonely and worried. So being a very direct sort of person he took his problems to the Medical Officer in Command, an oldtimer in the Public Health Service, who played down Doc's chances for sea duty and told him it would be perfectly all right for him to find an apartment and send for his wife and baby.

Doc immediately got in touch with his wife. Train reservations were made and all was set—until a couple of nights later when Doc arrived at his Bachelor Officers Quarters in lower Manhattan to find an urgent message from Headquarters.

They had given him the bad news quicker than they had given it to me. "Report at once," they said, "to PG-92, Staten Island, for assignment to duty as Convoy Medical Officer." They also indicated the convoy might be sailing early the following morning. Doc was aghast.

He phoned his wife; they had a tearful farewell and cancelled their plans. Afterwards he took the ferry over to Staten Island to meet his fate—which at that moment seemed a little like walking the plank.

Turner was the O.D. and he reassured Doc somewhat, both by his friendliness and by telling him that sailing time would be delayed another twenty-four hours. Doc also met his pharmacist mate and saw the sick bay where, according to him, he found "a rusty scalpel wrapped in brown paper and a bottle of aspirin in a medicine cabinet." He was horrified, but thankful for the twenty-four hours in which he might outfit the place. He immediately made arrangements with the pharmacist mate to accompany him early the next morning to the Marine Hospital at Stapleton, Staten Island, to stock up on supplies. Then he went to a restaurant on Bay Street, had a couple of quick drinks and a plate of spaghetti. Glancing down in the middle of the meal, he discovered that the spaghetti was mostly down the front of his uniform, and he said to himself, "Hofstra, you've got to pull yourself together."

I'm trying to write this the way Doc has been telling it to me, but I doubt if I have caught the full flavor of it. His initiation to convoy duty was, of course, a nightmare, since we sailed right out into that near-hurricane.

In the midst of the violence of the weather and the clatter and confusion, Doc was summoned to the bridge by Commander Boyce, who requested him to take the "customary" inspection tour of the ship with him and Ramsay. Doc told me that he staggered miserably through most of the inspection until they started down the engine room ladder where he had to ask to be excused. Thereafter he remained mostly in his bunk feeling the end was near, until late the next day when Carroll was brought in with his bleeding head.

The need for action had miraculously revived him when he set about with the pharmacist mate to tend the wound. "I could see the scalp," he told me, "and I prayed it wasn't a fracture or concussion. We bridged the wound with a pressure bandage and fortunately it held, even though he lost some of the dressing we put on top of it."

Now that things have settled down, Doc has grown to like the ship and has decided to ask the MOC to leave him aboard until further notice.

And thus Doc, along with the rest of, has become part of the *Haste*.

October 10, 1943

This morning, quite early (nine o'clock), I went out in search of a barber shop, and while I didn't find one that was open, I had a delightful ride in the early morning through the hillsides studded with shrubs and flowers of all varieties. Excellent station wagon service furnished officers down here, and the little vehicles have a regular route to follow, hence a miniature sightseeing trip is afforded for each ordinary mission a person sets out to perform.

This afternoon Doc and I went to the barber shop (which opened at one o'clock) and got a very good twenty-five cent haircut. I like barber shops, and this one had much of that good smell and sound that half puts you to sleep. The flies and an overhead fan buzzed, the barber was a stupendous clicker of scissors, and altogether it was a pleasant, three-quarters-of-an-hour doze. Meanwhile, music attended by rapid-fire announcements in Spanish went on in the background.

Left Guantanamo under a brilliant sunset tonight. It was a fitting climax to our four-day stay; not all of it a vacation, by any means, but filled with interest—for me, at least.

Just before we left this evening, a native boat came down from up the bay somewhere, and pulled in behind us. It was loaded to the gunwales with bananas, coconuts, limes, avocados, and so forth. One man in the crew saw it first, a dozen followed him, and soon half the ship was doing business back there. Bananas came aboard in stalks, coconuts by the dozens; even the officers loaded themselves down with them, tempted by the low prices. A whole stalk of bananas was fifty cents. For ten cents you could get several dozen broken or cut from the stalks. Avocados were a nickel, as were coconuts. The little huckster boat was also selling a native delicacy of some sort which resembled an ice cream cone, and was filled with a mixture of coconut meat and sugar cane, and the crew bought them out of that, too.

As we came through the nets tonight, I looked over the railing of the after gun, and there on the fantail the off-watch members of the crew were lounging about, drinking the milk from the drilled coconuts, munching on the bananas, and probing the mystery of the cone confections.

October 14, 1943

Received radio orders from Eastern Sea Frontier today to detach one escort to proceed to the assistance of the tanker *Balls Bluff* which lost its rudder.

We sent the *PC-1225*. Location about ninety miles away from us. Seas fairly moderate, so she is apparently in no great distress unless there is a sub in the vicinity.

October 16, 1943

The *PC-1225* rejoined us today. She said a tug from Charleston had come out to tow the tanker, and a DE was standing by.

October 25, 1943

Have been very busy.

Had three days' leave and returned briefly into that wonderful world of "back home." Dee looked beautiful and was delighted with the presents I brought her from the canteen, particularly the Peruvian silver bracelets.

Bragged a little about my first convoy and the storm. Felt very salty, but kept telling myself, "Remember, you've got to go back there."

Sailed for Cuba again with our second NAN-George convoy. Total of thirty-three ships. Last one was out of the gate at 0715 hours and by ten o'clock they were pretty well formed up into columns.

Seas are bumpy. Almost impossible to write. But what an improvement over our last trip!

> "Columbus found a world, and had
> no chart,
> Save one that faith
> deciphered in the skies;
> To trust the soul's
> invincible surmise
> Was all his science and
> his only art."
>
> O World, Thou Choosest Not
> George Santayana (1863-1952)

November 2, 1943

GUANTANAMO AGAIN! THERE WERE TWO palm trees and a mountain peak through the porthole while I shaved.

We tied up alongside a little Dutch gunboat, the *Jan Van Brackel*, camouflaged in black-and-white and flying the horizontal red, white, and blue of the Netherlands.

We arrived in good order this morning after a fairly uneventful trip—except for the weather, which was atrocious. For four days living was quite a problem, and during that period I believe my waist grew thinner again.

The bay at present is reflecting in spots the warm colors of the sunset. A light soft wind comes across the water, and while it can't find its way through the thick sides below deck, it feels delightful above deck. Have decided to sleep outside tonight.

The boat came alongside to take us to shore, and it felt wonderfully good to know we were going to put our feet on land again.

As usual, we first went to the Officers' Club. Played the slot machines for awhile, and then went on to the movies which I enjoyed immensely. There is a reserved section in the first couple of rows for the top brass, and a less exclusive section behind reserved for other officers. Before each performance, when the sky colors have faded sufficiently, and darkness is descending on this beautiful tropic land, there is the playing of the National Anthem, with our spotlighted emblem, either stirring gently in the breeze, or billowing out on its staff.

As long as I live I will probably hear those stirring strains many times in many places, but I doubt that anything will match the proud, almost tearful, welling-up of patriotism to be felt on hearing it in a foreign land, standing in the uniform of our country, with the perils of a war unwon still hanging like a giant shadow between me and my home.

November 3, 1943

It's a big war in a small world. After the movies last night, when I returned to the Officers' Club, the tall affable Navy lieutenant who manages the Club came over and said, "Lieutenant, haven't I seen you in Washington, D.C.?" It turns out that he had been assistant manager of the Mayflower Hotel. His name is Aubrey Brown, and it was like home, standing there shaking hands and grinning at each other.

Moving over to the bar we reminisced about the famous hotel which had played a small part in my life and a large part in his. I recalled the dates and banquets the name "Mayflower" brought to mind. The last annual dinner of our Washington Chapter, American Institute of Banking, was held there in February, 1942, just before Admiral Gorman signed me up for the Pay Clerk class at Curtis Bay.

In the course of our conversation "Brownie," as he seems to be known to practically everybody, told me, "We have a good package store here, and our prices are right. Why don't you take home a few bottles?" And later, he introduced me to Oswaldo, who presided over a room full of racks, shelves, and famous labels. "Take care of Mr. Carr," he said. "He's from Washington, D.C."

You could really go overboard in there; everything is a tremendous bargain. Old Granddad and Old Taylor are two dollars a fifth, as is Johnny Walker Red Label. Bacardi Rum is one dollar and forty cents for either the dark or the light variety, and that firm's famous product "Anejo," which I learned meant "very old" and is pronounced "an-yea-ho" sells for two dollars and twenty cents.

Oswaldo wrapped an assortment of four bottles while I thought with pleasure of the members of the family and friends who will share the loot, especially brother Frank, who always says of a highball of good whiskey, "Don't stir it too much; you might bruise it."

This was my introduction to canteen goodies and I loved it. Somebody back home must think pretty well of us to treat us in this fashion, and for this I am very grateful. There's a sort of "wealth of the Indies" aspect about being able to take treasures home that temporarily erases the trials and tribulations of our voyages, perks up our spirits and takes our minds off the danger and tedium of our days at sea. This canteen and PX privilege can be a profound thing in a sailor's life.

November 4, 1943

Have been busy aboard, but played tennis again this afternoon with the Captain, the chief engineer, and Doc. After an interval aboard ship it's a genuine luxury to stretch our muscles in any kind of athletic activity.

The Captain and I are the only two tennis players, so he teamed up with Pangle and I got Doc as a partner. It was a sort of "command performance" anyhow; Doc and I had a lot of paper work we should have been doing.

Doc and I diplomatically managed to lose the first two sets, although we dissipated a big lead in the second, but got some consolation by taking the third. Pangle, our engineer officer, is a well groomed, muscular man who keeps his small moustache and black hair neatly trimmed. He is also one of those rare individuals whose skin has a natural retentive property for the rich cologne he uses regularly. But, like the rest of us, after two hours of tennis in that tropical climate, he looked like a big seal dripping moisture.

After a dip in the pool, the Captain's suggestion that we have a "tall, cool one" and sit out on the veranda, sounded like an excellent idea.   /

We lounged there for about an hour and a half, while the usual display of sky colors went on; and we forgot about the bridge of oceans, bad weather, seasickness, and possible lurking submarines between us and our home port.

Then we went inside for a steak dinner, complete with sparkling burgundy. It was all very satisfying, and beautifully served by a dining room staff who always seem pleased to see us enjoying ourselves. That, along with the much appreciated canteen and PX privileges, appears to be among the few fringe benefits connected with being on a fighting ship: when you come ashore you have at-

tained somewhat of a hero status, with the accompanying per-
quisites, just for going out, surviving, and coming back in.

"Luxury ashore, misery at sea," whispered Doc as he clicked
glasses with me.

November 5, 1943

We were out practicing firing again, which brings to mind the
little fellow we have on board who is called Old Dog by the whole
crew. An under-sized, runny-eyed Cajun from Louisiana, he picked
up the name when he first came aboard because he called everyone
"Old Dog." He is an orphan, I understand, and has led what he
claims is eighteen years of pretty tough existence, although we
suspect he is nearer fourteen.

Anyway, he was made the hot shellman on the Number Two
three-inch gun. His duty was to catch the empty case as it was
ejected after firing and throw it out of the way. The first blast from
the gun folded Old Dog against the splinter shield and practically
scared him to death. He got a razzing from the others, who were
shaking so much themselves they could hardly talk, and the bos'n
indicated he would feed Old Dog to the sharks if he missed another
empty. So on the next blast Old Dog really waded in to get the case.
He cradled it up in his arms like a baby, and, as a result, lost two
six-inch square patches of skin in a first degree burn above his
elbow-length asbestos gloves. Doc took care of it—and Old Dog has
never missed another shell case.

November 7, 1943

Surprisingly enough, Brownie paid a visit to the ship before we
sailed. Most of the officers were having a last fling at the Club, but I
had some paper work and other matters to clean up before we entered the uncertainty of the weather going north.

I was hard at work when the messenger came down from the
gangway to tell me, "There's a Lieutenant Brown and another officer come to see you, sir," and there was Brownie, in a gay and ex-
pansive mood, yelling "Hello" from the dock. His friend was a lieutenant in the Supply Corps, and the possessor of a jeep.

I welcomed them aboard and they came down the first ladder
okay, then Brownie exclaimed, "My God, we go down again?" I
showed him how to steady himself with the bar above, but he

seemed to grow bigger as he came down, and I thought for a minute he wasn't going to make it.

When we got to the bottom of the ladder, he looked around and asked with a slight stammer, "You live down here?" I led the way to the wardroom, and then showed them our bunks. "Is this below the water line?" Brownie wanted to know, and I told him, "It sure as hell is." He looked at his friend and both gave an exaggerated shrug. Then Brownie grinned, patted me on the back, and said, "Carr, old boy, any time you get down here and you want some whiskey, you come and see us."

After that I took them topside, and up to the bridge. I offered them some coffee, but they were on their way to a party at the house of another officer, they said, and felt they shoudd hurry on. They both thanked me profusely for the tour and wished me luck. As I watched them climb into the jeep I heard Brownie say, "Sidney, I think we need another little drink." Then they waved a hearty good-by and were gone.

I surmised that some of their reactions might have been a bit of an act, put on for my benefit—but I also remembered my own sinking feeling when I first looked at a corvette. Now I was used to it, but looking at it through their eyes I could well imagine their shocked consternation at the thought of actually being on duty aboard this thing.

November 10, 1943

We have had a pretty good trip back thus far. Weather bouncy, but not bad.

Evidently our crew, like some of the rest of us, was bitten with the "shopping bug" while we were ashore. When we formed up and headed north we discovered, the first day out, that one of our seamen had brought a parrot aboard, complete with cage. He said proudly that he had paid eight dollars for it.

The bird was occupying a prominent spot on the mess deck and proved very popular. It was a pretty parrot, its plumage predominantly blue and yellow, with just a touch of green. It had a light chain around one foot which permitted it to climb around a bit and sit outside its cage. The seaman who owned it said it was a young bird—and it turned out that it could manage a couple of expressions in Spanish, but so far all it could utter in English was "Go to hell."

The Captain told us at dinner, "Too bad about the bird, but it has to go. The laws won't permit bringing it in because of parrot fever." He didn't say much more, and no one pursued the subject, although we were all aware that the bird was becoming more and more a favorite of the mess deck. Probably we all hoped that the Old Man might change his mind.

Today, however, the blow fell. The Captain said to Ramsay, "Get rid of that bird. The weather is good and I don't want to take any chances. I like pets as much as any man, but laws are laws. The bird couldn't live out here if we let it go, so it will just have to be destroyed."

A little later I overheard Ramsay telling the seaman's chief petty officer, "If he doesn't want to do it, you do it. Take it aft and shoot it." I saw the kid starting back with his bird, then handing it to the Chief. The Chief put it on the stern rail between the depth charge racks, backed up a few paces, and fired one shot from the rifle. After that, he looked over at our wake to check the feathers floating colorfully and pathetically on the waters; then, chewing tobacco, he turned stoically and strode forward.

That was all, except the kid came back a moment later, the parrot's cage in his hand, and threw it overboard. It was as though he was defiantly echoing his bird's "Go to hell," and directing it toward the law, the Captain, and anyone else who happened to be in the vicinity.

November 7, 1943
(New York)

Rumors are flying thick and fast these days. They have been assailing us ever since we got back from Guantanamo. The *Nourmahal* is sunk. The *Brisk* is sunk. No, they're not sunk, they're transferred. The *Brisk's* Skipper says she's going east, which may mean the Mediterranean. Someone says eight ships are similarly transferred.

Giving the lie to the first rumor, the *Nourmahal* came in on the other side of the slip this morning. I always find her an interesting ship to contemplate—and to muse upon the great change the war has made in her, a change she shares with so many of us.

The *Nourmahal* was probably the most famous private ship of her kind before Astor, proud of his Navy service and commission, turned her over to the Navy. It was rumored she cost $1,250,000 to build and that, during her days as a rich man's recreation, she carried a crew of forty-two and cost Astor in the neighborhood of $125,000 a year to keep up. And there she sits, across the slip, another changeling of the war—taking her chances with the rest of us.

There's an ominous number of Eastern Sea ships in here at present—perhaps there *is* something afoot.

November 24, 1943
(Enroute to Guantanamo)

"I hope you got some strong black rot in here," Levandoski burst out as he barged into the wardroom this afternoon where Dutch Stolzer, our assistant engineer officer, and I were playing gin rummy.

As we glanced around at him there was something in his voice and the strained look on his face that made us ask, "What's up?"

"After what I just heard on the TBS I sure need some strong coffee," he muttered, filling a cup.

He lifted it to his mouth and took a big gulp before he put it down to tell us, "The commodore was talking to one of the merchant ships out on the flank that just spotted a corpse in a life jacket. They asked the PC over there to investigate."

We stopped playing and were giving him our full attention. "They reported it was headless and practically without arms, and they couldn't see any identification," he said.

"What did they do?" Stolzer asked softly.

"He told 'em to leave it and send the position to Norfolk."

"My God!" I blurted out, "Wasn't there anything else they could do?"

"What d'ya want them to do, put it in the ice box and haul it all the way to Gitmo?"

"Skip it, Clem," I said, unable to repress a slight shudder. "Sorry I asked."

"There's a lot of them poor bastards out here, I guess," Levandoski mused, staring straight ahead, "but I ain't never heard of one like this."

"Mr. Carr," said Stolzer, quietly, "We better get back to our game. I think I go down with six points."

November 25, 1943

Today after lunch Turner stopped by my office and said with

his characteristic grin, "Better come watch the fun, Carr, we're going to open the wooden horse."

I knew he was referring to a tremendous wooden packing case that had been deposited on our after deck, with much cursing and sweating, the day before we left port. The instructions on the monster, which had "SECRET" stamped all over it, prohibited the opening of the crate until we were well out at sea and away from prying eyes.

This had caused much comment and speculation throughout the ship. It was a "secret weapon"; it was a "counter-torpedo device" we could turn loose on a sub; it was a new "radar-sighting attachment" for our guns. One thing all agreed upon—it must be important or the Navy would not have cloaked it in so much secrecy and drama. The Captain himself was inscrutable about it, giving no indication that he had any knowledge of its contents, but we felt certain he had received a briefing on the subject.

I worked on in my office until I had reached a convenient stopping point. The weather is good for November and I have a little catching up to accomplish, but as I worked I could hear some dismayed yells from back aft where the "secret contents" were being bared.

I knew Mr. Ramsay was back there as overseer of operations—and also because of his immense curiosity about anything mechanical and because, moreover, we suspected from his attitude that he had some inkling of the nature of the surprise. By the time I arrived there was quite a turnout. Pangle was there as engineering officer, and Levendoski was there as a veteran bos'n and deck officer. Several of the other officers were there as onlookers, as were a goodly number of crew members. It seemed an altogether auspicious and promising moment.

Instead, what developed was mystifying and somewhat unsettling. From the cavernous interior came a series of steel rods attached to manila lines set more or less horizontally to two side pieces, so that when the thing was stretched out on deck it reached back for twenty or thirty yards and resembled a mobile ladder.

The instructions, which called it "FXR gear," directed that it be streamed astern as a defense against acoustic torpedoes. The vibration of water around its parts was said to create a disturbance louder than that of our propellers.

We have heard, of course, that some ships near the European theatre have been hit in the tail and badly damaged or sunk by the Germans' newest infernal device which, when released by a sub, takes off toward the sound created by the ship's propellers. This then is presumably the Navy's reply to that threatening development. But before the contraption was even in the water it had been cursed and challenged by those in our crew directly involved with it at the moment.

The men exercised great care to try to feed it over one side away from the props, but the weight of the crosspieces quickly created a heavy pull which upset a couple of sailors entangled in the lines. Our chief bos'n mate roared and swore; Pangle kept warning the handlers to keep the contrivance away from the propellers, his special preserve and worry and a source of deep concern for all of us. He not only swore appropriately, but he tried to assist the men physically who were struggling with the lines.

At long last it was dragging behind us, and causing a commotion like a school of heavy fish. The strain on the lines was immense and quickly apparent. "That's a pull on the engines," Pangle moaned. Cooney, who had been skeptical throughout the proceedings said, "I'm going to check the sound room. I'll bet you can't hear anything but that crazy gadget."

Cooney had just started away when a tremendous yelling broke out—caused by the fact that one of the lines had parted, and the answer to the acoustic torpedo was thrashing about with a sidewise motion, and swinging dangerously close to our propellers. "Release that line!" Ramsay roared, and in a moment the FXR gear was disappearing astern.

The curses, grumbling and chuckles that followed represented emotions from rage to relief, to disappointment and disbelief. Was this really the official Navy answer to the problem? Already our crew had learned that FXR was the official abbreviation for "Foxer gear," and one of them commented sarcastically, "That'll fox 'em all right. Like hell it will!"

As it turned out there was a second device in the "wooden horse" exactly like its ill-fated predecessor and, goaded by officers who felt it must be proved workable, the crew again began the difficult task of feeding it over the side. Very little had been learned, and two crew members were dragged violently up against the depth charge rack. But the thing was finally overboard and seemed to be streaming faultlessly. We moved about and breathed a sigh of relief. Maybe it would work, we thought. It was better than nothing. We have always known that if we are hit by a torpedo with our extra fuel and ammunition aboard, it will be serious. We could haul it in, treat it gently, and only use it on contact or in a danger area.

There were even instructions about how to manipulate a set of lines that would cause it to collapse into one long bundle for hauling aboard. "Let it stream for awhile," came word from the bridge. We left it out for almost an hour, despite Pangle's grumbling about pulling on his engines, and Cooney's insistent lament that it was jamming the reception on our sound gear. "Does it make sense to protect your rear and go blind up front?" he demanded.

All seemed well until the order came to retrieve the device. Our chief bos'n's mate was attempting to follow the instructions about releasing one of the lines to convert the ladder-like framework to a narrower shape for hauling aboard. Suddenly, incredibly, the entire device disintegrated into a momentary mass of swirling lines and crosspieces that disappeared astern, leaving a small section of one line dancing and dangling in our wake.

We were shocked and astounded, but momentarily silent. Then the exasperated oaths rolled over the ship again in a storm of vituperative incredulity. "Wouldn't Fritz like to see this!" Levendoski erupted bitterly. "Our answer to the acoustic torpedo! If every ship in the fleet got one of these things, this is the most fouled-up Navy in history."

The din gradually died down as the saving grace of humor that the average sailor possesses under most circumstances finally took over. From the bridge came the command—whether from Boyce or Ramsay was not indicated—"Disassemble that packing case and heave it over the side."

The chief bos'n's mate, curling the remaining section of line from the proceedings, suddenly began to sing in a lush falsetto, "We'll climb that stairway to the stars . . ."

Naturally, at dinner we talked over the subject again. "They'll come up with something better," Turner said, soberly, "but who the hell do you suppose is the poor Joe who dreamed this up? This was just about as substantial as Jack's beanstalk!" And there we left the whole upsetting episode.

November 27, 1943

Clear, flat day; sun sparkling on the sea. We are halfway to Guantanamo again.

One blot on our day—our Skipper received radio orders to St Augustine, and he will leave the ship when we return to New York. We'll hate to see him go.

November 28, 1943

Drew alongside the *Victoria Park*, one of the ships in our convoy, to pass over a cylinder of freon (refrigerating gas). Most amusing thing in connection with the transfer was the antics of our dog, Rip. He pattered all the way to the bow point as we closed the dirty little freighter—sniffing, peering, shuffling, and whining. It seemed almost uncanny that he should have known there was a dog aboard her; but sure enough, when her crew spotted Rip, they held up a mangy, brown-and white hound, we held up Rip, and the two canines exchanged "yips" across the intervening space of water.

Rip is a stowaway of sorts. He was just a stray he-mutt around the docks. We saw him and petted him and, I guess, fed him. And, when we got the convoy formed up and headed south on our first trip, he was mysteriously aboard without the knowledge of any of the officers, and he has been with us ever since.

November 29, 1943

Very sleepily, at six-thirty this morning, I trained the glasses off our starboard quarter and there, lying like a purple streak on the horizon, was San Salvador.

I felt that I ought to pinch myself to realize fully what I was seeing. Over and over I told myself, "Four hundred and fifty-one years ago on October twelfth, this was Columbus' first landfall." Last night I had read an account of that landfall and the dramatic moments following. Now I was near the gateway by which Columbus entered the New World.

I kept correcting the glasses ·in an effort to bring out the minutest details; however, I'll admit there wasn't much to see. Just a line of bluish islands with one predominantly high hill. Meanwhile, on the other side of us, the sun climbed further above the horizon, became caught in a cloud bank, and wriggled a few gold rays free that shot down at the morning seas and up at the higher clouds. The ocean was choppy, but generally level. A fresh, cool wind came from the direction of Cuba.

While I was still searching the island, one of our escorts sailed into my line of vision and looked big against the indistinct line of the land. I swept the glasses only a fraction to the right and the first members of the convoy could be seen. Then I put the glasses down and looked at the scene. The thirty-two ships of our convoy were stretched out in a line and extended from the blue shape of San Salvador seaward. Two of the escorts were visible close to them.

Then a thought-provoking thing occurred. From a cream-colored cloud over San Salvador appeared the black shape of a plane—a big Martin Mariner on morning patrol. It was coming directly toward us, out of that cauliflower cloud and looming up fast. In a few moments she was close enough for us to see the pilot behind the fuselage. That, to me, was the crowning scene of the morning— one of our modern warplanes over Columbus's island. The whole picture was symbolic, for me, of the might of the New World that Columbus discovered, engaged in a crusade to liberate the Old World.

November 30, 1943

Eight P.M. and we are almost at Guantanamo. Lovely evening, air warm and soft, sky colors magnificent. Crescent moon floating over a flat-calm sea.

When we made our rendezvous this afternoon with the other escort group who are taking most of our ships on to Trinidad, there, in the midst, was our old friend the *Jan Van Brackel,* with her black and white camouflaging, acting as escort commander. There is a jaunty and pugnacious air to that little Dutch vessel.

[NOTE. So that our activities at that time may be better understood this may be a logical place to explain the Interlocking System of convoys of which we were a part.

At the end of August, 1942, there was a substantial reorganization of coastal convoys, which produced the ingenious Interlocking System, on which convoys were run on routes and schedules very much like trains.

The two main trunk lines, to which all others were geared, were the Key West-New York and return (KN-NK), and the

Guantanamo-New York and return (GN-NG). It was on these two main runs that we of the *Haste* and our sister ships sailed.

These two routes were likened to those of express trains, the others to local trains which fed into the big lines at their southern termini, Key West and Guantanamo. Schedules were carefully worked out and lost shipping days kept to a minimum.

The big north-south convoys ran on five day schedules; the feeders, from Aruba-Trinidad, from Key West to Gauntanamo, and from Canal Zone-Curacao, on ten-day schedules. These southern routes carried the bulk of trade with South America, and the vital tanker traffic originating in the Dutch West Indies.

In order to conserve shipping time, the "through traffic" did not call at the intermediate termini, such as Guantanamo, but changed its name and proceeded on with a new set of escorts, while the old group broke off and put into the terminus to wait for the next big convoy sailing back to their home port.

"Joiners" were local shuttle convoys which had sailed when necessary and formed a link between a main convoy route and a port along that route. For example, the master of a ship outward bound from Norfolk to Guantanamo, had the choice of proceeding up the coast to New York and joining an (NG) convoy, which would take him down to Guantanamo, or hooking up with a New York-Key West coastal convoy (NK) off the Virginia Capes to proceed to Key West, where he could join a (KG) shuttle over to Guantanamo. The convoy which was formed especially to take him out to the Capes to meet the New York-Key West group was a "joiner."

There were two other important convoys feeding the trunk line, the Key-West-Galveston (KH-HK) and the Key West-Pilottown (KP-PK). The first, the Key West-Galveston (KH-HK) brought loaded tankers from Galveston to Key West in time to catch the KN New York convoy. It then took the "empties" which had come down, back to Galveston. The second (KP-PK) handled ships bound to New Orleans and up the Mississippi.

The system involved thousands of ships and scores of routes and continued, with minor changes, until the War ended in Europe.]

13

December 2, 1943

SPECULATION AND EXCITEMENT WERE RAMPANT this morning as *Haste* and *Intensity* passed through the Guantanamo nets and set a course almost due south from Cuba.

Our abrupt departure itself was cause for conjecture. We left several men on shore liberty, since our regular convoy sailing time was presumed to be at least forty-eight hours away.

The southerly course was a new experience. We had never sailed in that direction before, but have gone either westward or eastward to pick up our convoy and then to head for the Windward Passage and one of the alternate routes we follow through the islands. This switch was novel, indeed, and we speculated so liberally on the subject that no matter what the true purpose might be it would have been hard to come up to our conjectures.

Haste, as usual, was running in lead position, and the day was brilliant. A convoy of tropic birds circled our masts, and swarms of flying fish were stirred up by our prows.

Captain Boyce eventually passed the word in his quiet manner that we were to rendezvous with a northbound convoy whose escorts had been diverted. We were to pick them up south of Navassa Island, which lies between Jamaica and Cape Tiburon, Haiti, and some sixty miles south of Cuba. We felt that this could only mean that sub warnings had been issued somewhere in the area.

The rendezvous occurred as planned, and the only unusual aspect was a distant view of Jamaica off our starboard bow, which left us a little frustrated at having to reverse our course and head back to Cuba. The real excitement occurred a short while later in some totally unpredictable and weird happenings aboard our own *Haste*.

Shortly before lunch time a Summary Court-Martial was convened in the wardroom for two crewmen who had been involved in a nasty disturbance ashore.

[NOTE: At this time a "Summary" was the most serious disciplinary action the Commanding Officer of a ship could take. It was also an option that any enlisted man could exercise, if he wished, when he had been put on report and faced "Captain's Mast," the informal administrative action that was the court of first instance in any command.

A man accused of an offense at Captain's Mast had the right not to submit to the CO's informal judgment of guilt or innocence and of what might be suitable punishment. If the accused wanted to avoid this sometimes arbitrary "mercy" he could demand a Summary, where he would have counsel—though not always as enthusiastically partial to his cause as he might like, since counsel was also one of the officers of his unit—and where a formal record would be kept and the whole proceeding reviewed by a higher authority than the CO.

Really grave offenses were handled by a General Court-Martial, which had to be convened by a Flag Officer and was held ashore.

The two crewmen facing the Summary that day south of Guantanamo were accused of an offense too serious for the Captain's Mast, but not serious enough for a General Court—assault and battery against the Shore Patrol at Guantanamo. Two of our own seamen on obligatory SP duty with the base professionals had been witnesses and could testify at the trial as to what had happened. It also turned out that the two accused were going to plead guilty anyway.

The shore command at Guantanamo, an Admiral's domain, was very interested in making sure that the ship punished its own offenders rather than protecting them, so in a sense our reputation was at stake.]

It was a solemn occassion in the wardroom when the trial began. The three officers in the court wore ties and carried their caps. The Captain's yeoman was taking notes as he sat with his back to the bulkhead, facing the door.

144

Suddenly there was a jolt and an astounding kerboom from a tremendous explosion in the pantry next door. This was followed by a shrill cry, and as the yeoman jerked his head up he saw a yelling, white-coated apparition fleeing past the door.

His face turned pale, and he gasped, "My God! Williams (the mess attendant) is full of blood!"

Somebody on the mess deck heard the blast and passed the word to the bridge, where the loud blaring of the electric alarm system was set off. Turner, who had been present, later commented, "That Court-Martial adjourned with very few formalities. Half of those present thought we had been hit, and made a beeline for the ladder!"

A few seconds later, Nelson, our chief bos'n's mate, and head of the fire squad, came down the same ladder with a gas mask ready to put on if he needed it. He was also followed by the panting, wide-eyed members of his group, some of whom had just been routed out of the sack.

Turner, who was right behind Captain Boyce and Ramsay when they entered the smoking pantry, described the scene as fantastic. The sequence of events that led up to the tumult was, when pieced together, equally fantastic.

It seems the galley range was out of commission because of some repairs, which were in progress when we unexpectedly left port; so the cook had told Smith and Williams, our mess attendants, to warm some baked beans in the warming-oven, to go with the cold cuts and salad he was preparing. Thereupon they placed two unopened cans of pork and beans in the warming oven—and turned it on full blast! Five minutes or so later, Smith had just left the pantry to go up for the salad, when the cans blew up.

Said Turner, "They probably had never heard of liquids expanding under heat, and the gases building up to a combustion level. The explosion blew off the steel doors of the oven like they had been shot out of a cannon. The cans, split open and flattened as though they had been run over by a steam roller, catapulted after them across the room, together with a bombardment of gory-looking pork and beans.

"There were piles of beans everywhere," he added. "I think some of them lodged in the steel plates."

Williams did not stop howling until he reached the sick bay

where Doc, after recovering from his initial shock, had tried to conceal his amusement as he examined the frightened mess attendant and finally determined that he had suffered several superficial flesh wounds and minor burns.

Ramsay broke out the two Court-Martial cases and several other bad-conduct characters to help clean up the mess, and by the time I arrived from my standby station on the bridge, most of the excitement and action were over. As I peered into the pantry I heard one of the cleaning-up crew muttering about "those bean-boiling bastards," and I went into the wardroom where everyone had forgotten lunch in the general confusion and hilarity of the occasion.

And thus did we sail with a fair wind almost to Jamaica.

December 5, 1943

Last night before we sailed Turner, our chief censor, dumped a pile of letters on the wardroom table and asked some of us to help with the crew's mail. This involves reading the letters, sealing the envelopes, then hitting them with the "censored" stamp and adding the date and our initials.

I was routinely perusing a letter from a seemingly shy and reticent little petty officer to his wife when I came across the sentence, "I can hardly wait to see you again, honey, in your new baby blue pajamas—without the tops." Since it had nothing to do with the movement of ships and men I let it go through, feeling a little embarrassed at having seen it and knowing the kid would probably check my initials when he got home.

In our room a little later I mentioned the episode to Turner and Cooney. Said Turner with a huge grin, "Why, that little guy acts just like a mouse."

"Yeah," quipped Cooney, "but he writes like a lion."

December 10, 1943

A wild winter sea outside tonight. Northwest wind blowing out of a cloudy and moonlit sky. Spray shining like snow.

I stood for awhile behind the wheelhouse and watched the big ones tear at the ship from the sides. They growl a bit like animals and lick at our gear. The chief boatswain expressed concern for our boat (our second), which is a bit heavy for its rigging. A solid blow may loosen it.

Climbed up on the bridge for awhile where Levendoski and

Janes were hanging on. The bow was spouting geysers that ripped back at the wind guard. Looking upward for a moment, I saw blue sky between the cloud chasms, with one glittering isolated star.

Tomorrow we are due in New York—which makes this much easier to take.

December 11, 1943

We didn't make New York today, although we were only seventy miles away this morning. The storm has gotten worse and threatens to equal in velocity the one we experienced in September. Wind is around seventy miles per hour.

It was a curious sight this morning to watch that vicious, icy wind sweeping over the sea. The wind was much colder than the water, and, as a result, the contact produced a steaming that made the ocean resemble a vast mineral springs. Another impression I got from the steam and the flying spray was of a movie version of a sand storm on a desert. As far as we could see, the white steam and spray clouds were lifting upwards blotting out the horizon.

Once or twice the sun broke through dazzlingly to paint the whole performance with silver. This afternoon, half a dozen stray gulls appeared nonchalantly wheeling and darting over the wave-tops. "Wind gulls," Levendoski called them.

The convoy has slowed down to six knots, but they are only making good about two "over the ground," as the mariners say. We caught several glimpses of the big ships butting their noses into the sea.

December 13, 1943

Clear, cold morning at Pier Number 8, Staten Island. We are tied up on the outboard end of the pier, the *Alacrity* beside us and a PC beside her. The flag on the stern of the PC is snapping in the breeze.

Thousands of gulls are wheeling and screeching out in the harbor. Two well-painted Norwegian tankers are anchored in midstream. A two-stacker (destroyer) lies ahead of them. In the distance the towers of lower Manhattan seem to lean together like a lot of toy blocks. The Statue of Liberty, looking pistachio green is visible in the haze.

We'll be here five days, then "back to the wars."

Had a little ceremony at two this afternoon, when the Captain said goodbye, and Ramsay took over. Whole business was interrupted several times by the roar of motors around the dock, busily engaged in driving repair machinery. The Captain read his orders, then made a short, halting speech in which he praised us for "having taken over an empty hulk and made it into a ship." Ramsay took the command, saluted, and we were dismissed.

December 18, 1943

At twelve-thirty last night, to the accompaniment of a doleful blast of our whistle, we backed away from our berth and headed downstream on our fourth trip to Guantanamo. On this occasion we had a new Escort Commander aboard—a Lt. Pilling of the Navy, who in that capacity takes the place of our former Skipper.

We heard voices on the dock as we pulled away and made out in the shadows several of the base officers and their wives, who had come down to see us off. We yelled a couple of "Merry Christmases" across the widening gap of water. At the same time we threw back a half dozen pairs of leg irons we had used on our prisoners.

Since Levendoski is sick, I had command of the group who handle the stern lines. The yeoman from the ship's office wears earphones and relays to me orders from the bridge, and I yell the commands with what I hope is a tone of authority, and the lines come aboard briskly. We stay at our posts until dismissed.

The moon was hanging low over the Brooklyn shore, but the wind was icy last night, and we huddled for shelter behind the big gun and its platform until word was passed to set sea watches.

Sometime later I was awakened in my bunk by a messenger telling the Escort Commander that the *PC-1084* had struck a buoy and damaged her port propeller. (Since Ramsay has graduated to the Skipper's cabin on the main deck, Cooney has moved forward to the room on the other side of the ladder, and Lt. Pilling is occupying Cooney's old bunk in our room.)

The same messenger who awakened us returned a few minutes later with the information that the PC's port engine was entirely useless, so there remained no alternative but to order her to return to port. Thus we are beginning our Christmas trip with escorts cut down from five to four.

We have twenty-five ships, too. I counted them from the bridge this afternoon. Four escorts is hardly enough to form a proper

148

screen. The convoy is spread out so far we can only see half of them at a time. Only one of our escorts, the *Alacrity* is visible in the haze.

This trip has certainly started out wrong. Ramsay, as the new Captain, and Pilling, the new Escort Commander, have already had a couple of verbal clashes. Cooney, who has become our new Exec, has such a sore throat he can't talk, Pangle, Stolzer, and Levendoski are in their bunks with the flu, and Hofstra has been violently ill since we left port. I have been doing all the decoding today. If things get worse, I'll be standing an OD watch.

December 19, 1943

We ran through an immense school of porpoise today. Their fins and splashes must have covered half a mile of the sea's surface. I was on the bridge at that time, and Turner steered for them so we could have a better look.

When they saw us and started for the ship, they came with the rush and swish of an express train. There seemed to be a number of young ones in the group swimming side-by-side with their mothers. The mothers were always the first to break off and turn away, evidently as a protective gesture. But the young ones made a good showing, swimming in such unison beside their parents they seemed welded together. As we leaned over the side and watched them below the surface, the big fish resembled iridescent patches of oil.

December 20, 1943

At eleven o'clock last night, with a considerable blinking of red and white signal lights, the PC-619 joined us as an extra escort. For awhile she ran around like a dog looking for its master, first into the middle of the convoy, then up to the *Alacrity*, and finally over to us, blinking all the while, "I am reporting for duty." We assigned her to a station back on the flank.

The fact that she was able to penetrate our screen, and go all the way into the convoy, is a sad commentary on the efficiency of our radar protection.

December 22, 1943

We fired four shots this evening at a stray lifeboat. The shots went whistling out over the surface, throwing up geysers as they struck the water. Two of them sent back curious metallic echoes as they ricocheted and splashed again a mile away.

We failed to hit the target but the shooting was good. Two went over it by inches. One was a couple of feet short. The fourth skidded by the stern. A creditable performance and one that might well have spelled the doom of anything as large as a submarine.

The convoy came on inexorably behind us, and a little PC charged up from the flank, having failed somehow to receive our explanatory message.

"Why the hell didn't we go up alongside that boat first?" I wanted to know, having visions of emaciated forms lying in the bottom. Several of us had the same question, but it was explained that we had gone close enough for the man in the crow's nest to make sure that there was no one in it.

"That's one of the tricks the Germans use in setting their acoustic mines," the Escort Commander said. "You go up to take a look and —bingo!"

That was enough of an explanation for me.

December 23, 1943

Passed San Salvador this afternoon and, at the same time, we were passed by a faster convoy. The escorts consisted of two "cans" (destroyers) and a DE, so its importance is obvious. All that strength was even more significant in view of the fact that there were only three ships in the convoy, a liner of about five hundred feet and two fast, modern freighters (they call them AKA's).

Those ships were out of sight in a couple of hours. It looked like a complete outfit in one bundle—men, supplies, and equipment. We hung around the bridge for awhile speculating on what they were and where they were going. Estimates placed the number of troops the liner could carry at about five thousand.

Columbus's island was in the background, closer than we had seen it before, yet somehow of secondary importance.

The Secretary of the Navy's Christmas greetings came over the radio today. We posted it on the bulletin boards. It was a bit wordy and sprinkled with generalities and guarded optimism. I suppose somebody worked over it a long time, but it really didn't ring very much.

Specifically, it was difficult to reconcile the words. "These one hundred and thirty million Americans whose thoughts are with you, and whose words back you in battle," with the news of the impending railroad strike. The characteristic comment going around was, "Yeah, they back us all right—way back!"

After listening to the discussion, Levendoski came through with one of his brilliantly ribald remarks. "Awright," he observed, "just let them union guys wait. The sun doesn't always shine up one dog's ass. Either the sun moves or the dog does!"

This afternoon I was working in my pay office when a stream of curses erupted from the galley. The ruckus was such that I closed the office to investigate. When I stuck my head into the galley and inquired the cause of this commotion, Tuden, our first-class cook, who is an ex-wrestler, looked up from the pan he was scraping and replied sheepishly, "Aw, sir, I just burned my goddamned Brown Betty."

December 25, 1943

Christmas dawned today with a lovely pale sky dotted with isolated fragile clouds. In the east was the pink of morning, and at its edge the jewel-like stars forming the Southern Cross. That was why I happened to be on the bridge. They called me to see the famous constellation.

The pink was rapidly washing over the stars when I came up, and try as I would I couldn't see more than one or two of them. Repeatedly they pointed out the shape of four bright stars, situated at what might be the extremities of a Latin cross; but the light was quickening so fast I was never quite sure that I had seen it. I made a resolution at that moment to have another look at the Cross before we leave this latitude.

We spent the morning shepherding our convoy into a rendezvous with its new masters. Then, seeing them safely enroute to Trinidad, our job well done, we ran up a beautiful ten-flag hoist reading, "MERRY CHRISTMAS," and ploughed back through the middle of the group. The Coast Guard hero-ship *Campbell*, which had rammed and sunk a German sub in the North Atlantic and was the new Escort Commander, was the first to read our hoist and came back with "SAME TO YOU." Two PC's followed suit and then half a dozen merchantmen belatedly caught on.

We kept our resplendent hoist snapping in the breeze right up to the gates of Guantanamo. It was our intention to go in with it. But, as we were about to pass through the nets, a baleful signal light blinked from a shore tower, "Please lay to for outgoing traffic." In amazement we made out, almost a mile inside the nets, a bulky, slow tanker coming out. We could have made it through there twice without interfering with her. "Break your hoist," the Captain yelled angrily, and down fluttered our flags like so many wounded bright-plumaged birds. "The hell with 'em. We won't wish 'em Merry Christmas."

We sat there for half an hour growling, cursing, and spluttering, until the shore light told us, "You may enter as soon as the ship clears."

December 26, 1943

We had our shipboard Christmas today. Yesterday we were at sea and the prospect of getting in looked too uncertain, so we held off until today.

Our Christmas tree is unique. We carted it all the way down here from New York. Throughout the voyage it reposed on top of one of the machine-gun magazines under the radar shack, where, although partially sheltered, it became as salty as any of us from generous applications of spray.

Now it's set up on the mess deck, properly decked out with glass balls, tinsel, and electric lights. These lights are actually the little red emergency lights we carry on our life belts, each one complete with its own battery. They are tied to the tree limbs in various places, and whenever a display is desired someone has to reach in and twist them on individually. There is also a beautiful pinup girl squarely in the center of the tree, which the guys couldn't resist throwing in to provide the feminine element.

They're singing *Dear Mom* now, standing in the chow-line.

December 27, 1943

I slept out under the stars last night, back on the number two gun platform. I remember turning over just before I fell asleep and thinking what a helluva sleeping partner that three-incher was.

Sometime later I woke up. Orion was directly overhead with about a million neighbors. Also up there were the red trucklights on our mast and those of the ships around us. The *Haste* was sighing and quivering in her sleep as she always does in port.

I remembered about the Southern Cross and wondered if it was visible yet. With a great effort I crawled from under the blanket, put on my shoes, and walked forward to the deck house. Then I climbed up to the bridge. But the phosphorescent hands of the bridge clock showed it to be only three-thirty and there was no sign of the constellation. At least I couldn't find any sign of it.

Back down I went and curled up again beside the big gun. I tried, before going back to sleep, to remember all that I had read on the southern constellations. Orion, of course, is easily the most wonderful, with all the fine stars in its belt. Half surrounding the Southern Cross, and lying north of it, is Centaurus, the Centaur, rich in bright stars and globular clusters, with its two splendid stars Alpha and Beta Centauri, known as the Southern Pointers, since they point to the Southern Cross. It all sounded fine on paper, I thought sleepily, but actually picking them out individually in that stellar myriad was not as simple as the star charts made it seem.

At five-thirty I was on the bridge again. Orion had moved away over to the right when I opened my eyes, and I felt that the time must be about right. Sure enough—there was the Cross, directly south, in a dead line at 180 degrees down the azdic repeater.

I felt very elated at having gotten up there to see it. The constellation was actually much larger than I had expected and seemed at least a third the size of Orion. The Cross sits low in the sky at a slight angle with the top inclined toward the east.

I realize that to many it might prove disappointing, because of the unequal brightness of its four principal stars and the lack of one at the center, but I was willing to join those others down through the centuries who have traced its configuration with fascinated eyes. The brightest star in the Cross is Alpha Crucis, a double star, but to me it was the brilliance and the perfect placement of the four stars that made the whole array a wonderful thing to see.

At seven o'clock I turned out for the third time and went below to finish my nap. It was delightfully cool even down in our room, and the air had a washed and fragrant quality.

I rolled in under the Christmas cards I had tacked over my bunk from wife, family, and baby—and although the "night before Christmas" had passed, and we were well toward the year's end, visions of sugar plums certainly danced in my head—the only sugar plums that mean anything to a man in the service this year; those of wife, family, civilian clothes, a regular job, days off. With all those things in my mind, I think I smiled a little going to sleep way down here in this hemisphere under the Southern Cross.

December 28, 1943

At the Officers' Club last night I met a fellow I had gone to night school with at George Washington University.

Going into the Club, I saw this big, dark-haired lieutenant sitting at a table with another officer and mentally I put them both in the category of Skippers. They had that tough, jaunty air of command most of them wear as easily as the jodphur-type boots they sport.

When the dark fellow looked at me a couple of times, as though trying to place me, I said, "Weren't you a Sigma Nu at G.W.?" The big guy smiled all over the place and acknowledged, "Sure was!" Then he added, "If I remember rightly, you were a Kappa Alpha." That did it! After a lot of back-thumping he introduced me to his friend by saying, "Back in our college days this was one of my old 'Knights of Alcohol' buddies." It had been a long time since I had heard that popular varsity corruption of our fraternity initials. The war almost faded away—but not quite.

As I surmised, these were both Skippers on the Panama run, and I made the mistake of asking how things were "down below." Immediately they sobered up. "We've been catching hell," one of them said bitterly, "The Germans are knocking off ships right and left. I mean, they're right outside the Canal, and off Trinidad and Aruba."

I started to ask how this could happen with all the air cover I was sure they have, but they brushed my question aside. "This is almost like '42," my friend persisted. "We've lost a helluva lot of ships but most of them are independents. Every time we get to port they're running our asses right out again. This is the first break we've had for two months."

Flabbergasted, I moved on after a few minutes and left them to their drinking. I wondered if they were exaggerating. My God, it's hard to see how the Germans can still be knocking off ships near the Canal at this stage of the war. I'm glad we're on the New York run. The weather may be lousy at times but if that's how it is on the southern run, we're luckier than we realize.

154

December 29, 1943

Left the green hills of Guantanamo today at four o'clock. The *Alacrity*, which was outboard of us, backed away first with a snort of her whistle. We followed a few minutes later, slipping away so imperceptibly I had to look at the pier to make sure we were moving.

A big convoy was coming in as we approached the gates, and we had to wait until they broke them off. Then the signal tower blinked, "You may proceed out," and we led our little flotilla through the double nets, then across the demarcation line between the green water and the blue.

The incoming convoy was steaming around out there, probably cursing as we had a few days before. Our sister-corvette, the *Action*, escort commander of the incoming group, ran over to signal "HAPPY NEW YEAR" No one can say we do not observe the amenities!

At sundown we ran alongside the merchantman in our group which is carrying the temporary Commodore, and talked to them through our loud-hailer. (That's what we call it, although it is nothing more than a loudspeaker on the bridge.) We asked them their "night intentions," a curious phrase meaning their course and speed during the night. We wanted to check our figures.

Our broadcast boomed over the ocean, and their megaphone replies came back faint and muffled, but somehow intelligible. We thanked them and pulled away.

We are meeting the rest of our convoy in the morning.

December 30, 1943

The star-filled beauty of last night was deceiving. We saw a flare at ten-thirty, so faint and far away it looked like a yellow star on the horizon. Then the radio message came back from the planes telling us, "Sub sighted," and giving a position twelve miles ahead of us and slightly to the east. We saw other flares after that and doubled our watches. But the planes had evidently done their work well and kept the sub submerged. Nothing further occurred, although we spent a tense couple of hours.

This morning we figure the sub has had time to radio, "There's one on the way," and we are looking for trouble up the line.

That would certainly be an eventful climax to a year of events—coming face to face with a sub!

December 31, 1943

We had extensive firing practice this afternoon. Among other things, we fired a three-inch shell which bears the unpleasant title of antipersonnel shrapnel.

Even if we do not sight a sub, our year seems to be going out with a bang.

[NOTE. After-the-war reports indicate that Grossadmiral Doenitz had decided early in November to try a three-boat attack on Caribbean shipping. When my Greek-letter friend told me during our Guantanamo meeting that they were catching hell on the Panama run, he wasn't kidding. Kapitanleutnant Hans Tillessen and his *U-516* was doing most of the damage, moving so rapidly and continuously that authorities in the area were sometimes unsure how many subs they were contending with.

Tillessen's own diary, captured after the war, reveals that he entered the Caribbean by the Dominica Passage in the Leeward Islands on November 5, a feat which the Navy Department deemed totally impractical, if not impossible, because of heavy sea and air cover and a ring of sonobuoys moored around the Caribbean approaches to the Canal area.

Three days later, on November 8, the first entry concerning him appears in the War Diary of the U.S. Naval Operating Base at Trinidad, reporting that at 1039 hours a Ventura flying at 4,600 feet developed a contact and eventually sighted a submarine three miles distant, traveling at a speed estimated at eight knots. The plane attacked the sub with six depth charges. All the charges overshot, but the first two entered the water very close to the vessel. The sub fired on the plane as it attacked and damaged it so seriously with twenty millimeter shells that it was forced to depart for its base after only twelve minutes. None of the plane's crew was injured, and when it departed, the submarine was still underway on the surface, apparently undamaged and steering the same course.

This unruffled attitude set the tone of the arrogant, contemptuous raid that Tillessen carried out for fifty days against the Isthmus and its adjacent sea areas.

U-516 headed for the Spanish Main, and on the night of November 12, off the north coast of Colombia, sank the small Panamanian freighter, *Pompoon*, which had departed Cristobal for Barranquilla on November 10, giving her estimated time of arrival as November 12, 1943. This little vessel was well known in the area. When her ETA expired without any word from her, an extensive air-sea hunt was organized, but no trace of the ship was found.

It later turned out that the only survivors of *Pompoon*, three armed guard bluejackets and a sailor, drifted for twenty-two days on a raft without being picked up, despite sighting numerous ships and planes. They reported that no SOS had gotten off because the ship went down in less than one minute.

An entry in the San Juan War Diary of November 21, records the arrival of the Honduran freighter *SS Oratona* at Cristobal on November 20 with seven injured survivors of the small Colombian Coaster *Ruby*, which Tillessen had shelled and sunk at 0500 hours on November 18. The master, mate and two sailors were killed in the action.

Entries in the War Diaries of both the Panama Sea Frontier and the Caribbean Sea Frontier cover Tillessen's next two victims, which were sunk, respectively, on November 22 and November 24. San Juan reported that a large enemy submarine on the surface fired two torpedoes into the American freighter *Melville E. Stone* in a position seventy miles off the Canal entrance. Seventy-three members of the crew of ninety-five were landed at Cristobal.

Panama's slightly conflicting version states the ship received one torpedo in her deep tanks and one in the forward hold and sank in ten minutes. Their report said seventy-three survivors out of a total complement of eighty-nine were rescued by patrol craft.

The next victim, the tanker *Elizabeth Kellogg*, reported San Juan, was attacked by an enemy submarine firing one torpedo into her amidships section abaft the superstructure. Guards and crew departed the ship at once, believing the vessel would not stay afloat, but the *Kellogg* burned for twelve hours and ran in a circle for two hours. Thirty-two crew members survived.

The Panama entry on the *Kellogg* stated that thirty-eight survived, out of a complement of forty-eight.

The slight contradiction in the accounts typifies some of the confusion and consternation accompanying Tillessen's attacks. After each sinking, search and destroy orders went out in greater urgency and numbers.

In none of these sea frontier accounts is there any mention of a "fix" from a direction finder as a result of a radio message sent by Tillessen. He must have craftily given up the satisfaction of reporting his successes to Berlin.

At dawn on November 24, a few hours after sinking the *Stone* Tillessen aimed for the tanker *Point Breeze*, escorted by a lone Kingfisher, but he missed. Not having seen a plane in a remarkably long time—considering the swarm of them hunting him—his aim was evidently spoiled by its presence.

The Diary of Headquarters, Gulf Sea Frontier, Miami, carried an entry at about this time noting the suspension of all independent sailings of merchant ships under 14.5 knots in the Caribbean, south of and east of a line joining Cape Gracias a Dios to the south coast of Cuba at Long, 80-00 W. All vessels bound for ports in the area were sailed via convoy system.

Tillessen apparently sank his fifth victim on December 8. She was the small coffee freighter *Columbia*, steaming through the Gulf of San Blas, just below the Canal. He missed two tankers on December 14, one of which, *Balls Bluff*, was the same ship that lost its rudder not far from our convoy coming out of Guantanamo on October 14, and for which we were instructed by Eastern Sea Frontier to detach one secort to screen her pending the arrival of a tug.

On December 16, in two separate attacks, Tillessen didn't miss. He sank the unescorted and loaded American tanker *McDowell* about thirty miles off Aruba.

San Juan's report on the *McDowell* states that an Army pilot reported sighting four life rafts and five lifeboats with fifteen to twenty persons in each. Sixty-three survivors were later picked up by the SS *Fairfax*.

Two nights later, on December 18, the Trinidad diary reports, Tillessen got into his most serious scrape with a PBM equipped with the new L-7 searchlight. (This searchlight had been urgently requested in one of the reports filed after the investigation into the Hornkohl-*U-566* debacle, following the sinking of the *Plymouth* in August in Eastern Sea Frontier.)

The PBM, while flying at 900 feet at a speed of 110 knots, made a radar contact with a target at 2113 hours. As it turned to a homing course, the plane descended to 200 feet and switched on its searchlight at a range of three quarters of a mile and caught the submarine in the beam of the light.

Sweeping the beam along the length of the ship revealed that it was fully surfaced, with the bow well up and cleaving the water at fifteen knots, causing considerable white water. The brilliantly illuminated conning tower was revealed in detail. About five seconds later the U-boat opened fire on the plane. Despite the amazing strength and volume of fire, the pilot held to his course and, as the plane passed 150 feet over the submarine, released four torpex depth charges spaced at eighty feet apart. The pilot firmly believed that the stick straddled the U-boat, and the tail gunner observed the white plumes from the explosions.

The submarine was about 250 feet long, was light in color and camouflaged, and had a streamlined conning tower which resembled French and United States designs more closely than typical German U-boats. (We would have had to stretch out the bow of the *Haste* by forty-three feet to match the length of this vessel.)

The rate of fire from the sub was described by the crew as unbelievably rapid, but apparently the gun crew of the U-boat, partially blinded by the searchlight, believed the plane to be at a higher altitude since most of the bursts passed ahead of and above it. The PBM had returned the fire with its own bow twin 50's and bullets were seen to ricochet from the conning tower. No accurate assessment of the plane's gunfire or depth charge attacks could be made, as the submarine submerged immediately following the encounter.

The diary of *U-516* discloses that it suffered no crippling damage, effected emergency repairs, and made good its escape.

Patrols and sweeps continued until Christmas Day, but to no avail. *U-516* celebrated Christmas Day submerged near Saint Eustatius, southeast of the Virgin Islands, her record of destruction and enemy frustration hundreds of miles behind. She reached blue water and the open sea by a seldom used passage the sea-frontier commanders had ignored and returned home safely.

The monthly summary in the War Diary of Gulf Sea Frontier for December, recounts the torpedoing of SS *Touchet* in the Central Gulf. This was a 10,000-ton tanker on her maiden voyage, with a speed obviously better than 14.5 knots, since she was running independently. Seventy-one out of an estimated seventy-nine were picked up. According to their testimony and that of the vessel's master, three torpedoes struck the ship, though one failed to explode.

This attack was not Tillessen's work, but that of one of his more cautious sisterships, *U-193*, which had worked through the Florida Strait into the Gulf of Mexico, where on December 3 she sighted *Touchet* 185 miles west of Dry Tortugas. *U-193* then returned home via the Yucatan Channel and the Windward Passage (the latter being an area we traversed each trip).

The third sub, *U-530,* came in north of Martinique on November 21, warily patrolled the Gulf of Darien, missed a tanker off San Blas Point, and torpedoed but failed to sink the tanker *Chapultepec* east of Colon on December 26.

The Panama War Diary carries an entry on that date stating that a plane from Fairwing squadron three, circling the scene, received a blinker message, "We were hit. Not know what hit us." The plane reported the tanker was zigzagging and leaving an extensive oil slick, but showed no damage above the water line. The ship proceeded to port at eight knots.

The skipper of *U-530*, evidently believing he had made a kill, and having no stomach for the extraordinarily heavy sea and air cover Tillessen's forays had brought forth, also headed home.

And so it now becomes clear, some thirty-two years later, that there was reason enough for our sudden orders to pick up the ships off Jamaica on December 2 and the heavily guarded ships that passed us on December 23.

The submarine activity in that vicinity went on into January—and since, at that time, no one could be sure just where *U-516, U-193,* or *U-530* might pop up—it accounts for the fouling up of our New Year's celebration (next chapter) and the silence of our convoy on that night. Obviously the commodore had some knowledge of what was going on, and our change of course might have been connected with it.

At any rate, it was a much busier ocean than we realized at that time; and when the Guantanamo recorder made his entries in the War Diary for Christmas Day, 1943, we could be thankful (although we were not aware of it) that he wrote simply:

"Escorts *Haste* and PC-619, etc., in from NG-405 at 1145 Q."]

14

> "The old, old sea, as one in tears,
> Comes murmuring with its foamy lips,
> And, knocking at the vacant piers,
> Calls for its long lost multitude of ships."
>
> *Come Gentle Trembler*
> Thomas Buchanan Read (1822-1872)

January 1, 1944

AND SO A NEW YEAR BEGINS. What it will hold is impossible even to speculate upon.

We had planned a little celebration for last night but something went wrong. During the afternoon the Commodore had signaled that a course change which was to have been made at 0200 hours would be moved up to midnight and would be indicated by whistles instead of lights. This sounded exactly as though the old boy wanted to give the group a chance to whoop it up on New Year's Eve.

Since the turn was to port, this meant that the Commodore and each of the lead ships in the columns would blow two whistles—a goodly amount of noise. Our Captain gave orders that we could join in with a long whistle and three short blasts of our siren.

At five minutes to twelve a little crowd of us was collected on the bridge. Dunbar was standing by the siren and I was standing by the whistle. The night had cleared and was tremendously starlit. The wind was only moderate and it was a good night for whistles. We watched the clock and waited.

As the hour approached, a voice suddenly came through one of the tubes saying, "Radar to bridge."

Turner, who had the watch, answered, "Bridge, aye."

"Happy New Year," came back the chuckling reply.

Turner was so taken aback by this divergence from the usual bridge communications he could only mumble, "Same to you, but you're a half-minute early."

Then we heard a door open somewhere below, and members of the watch extending good wishes to one another. We could also hear the faint sounds of merriment and whistles from over the radio which filtered out somewhere. But not a sound came from the convoy.

Patiently we stood by and listened. The radio sounds died out. Men began to move around restlessly. At five after twelve Turner picked up the TBS to call the *Alacrity*. "Goldbrick, this is Gangster. Over." (These are our code names for talking between ships.)

In half a minute the answer, "Gallant, this is Gambit." He has caught us asleep and has changed to our new call names for the New Year.

Turner, grinning sheepishly, "I correct. Gambit, this is Gallant. Did you see or hear a course change. Over."

"Negative. We were just going to ask you. Over and out."

"Gallant out."

The same inquiry was made to the PCs *Gander* and *Gadfly*. No answer. They must have been so blue they didn't want to hear. And that was just about the story of the evening. We learned later that the turn had been executed promptly on schedule, but for some inexplicable reason not a whistle was sounded.

At twelve-thirty we went below to the wardroom where the Captain had charitably agreed to expend sixteen ounces of medicinal brandy for the "grippe." We poured it into Coca-Colas and clicked the glasses at each other in a belated welcoming to the New Year. But the commodore had fouled us up. We would have enjoyed that little tootling greeting to the New Year.

January 2, 1944

At 1230 hours today a lookout called, "Signals from the commodore," probably after the commodore had been signaling for fifteen minutes. The message read, "Doctor urgently needed on ship number 84."

We passed word to other escorts, "Form four-escort screen. We are dropping out to transfer doctor to merchantman."

"Roger. Roger," from escorts.

Doc is about to get his first taste of transfer at sea in a small boat. He is scared, but doesn't show it. The transfer is hastily completed and we take position number five in escort screen, awaiting word from Doc.

Soon a big puff of smoke arises from the other side of the convoy and a PC comes heaving over to our side. The skipper grabs the TBS. "Gander, this is Gallant over." No answer. We bet the PC conveniently did not answer, already suspecting something was wrong.

"Signalman, ask them what the hell they are doing here!"

"Aye, aye, sir." Signaling, "Why over here?"

From PC: "*Alacrity* ordered us."

"Now who the hell told them to give that order!" fumed the Skipper. By blinker light the order goes out, "Return to station two."

"Roger." Another puff of smoke and PC is going back to station.

On TBS: "Gallant, this is Gambit. Over." "Gambit, this is Gallant. Send your message. Over."

"We told the PC *not* to cross over. Gambit out."

"Roger. Gallant over and out."

And once again the poor buck is passed, is unclaimed and left hanging in midair.

Levendoski, his obsidian eyes crinkled at the corners, was chuckling on the bridge this afternoon. When I asked him what was up, he shoved his cap back, wiped his hands across his broad forehead, and explained with amused incredulity how a seaman, who was relieving the lookout in the crow's nest for the first time, and was apparently uncertain of his terminology, had stepped up to the bridge platform and said, "Permission to relieve the crow, sir?"

"We have some characters out here," Levendoski concluded. "No wonder they call this the 'Hooligan Navy'!"

Dunbar, who was lounging against the windguard said, "Remember, Mr. Levendoski, the rejoinder is, 'Call us hooligan if you must, but don't call us Navy!'"

January 3, 1944

When the general alarm sounded at twelve-thirty last night I was propped up in my bunk glancing through a *Collier's*. I lunged for my lifebelt, missed, lunged again, then rounded the corner heading for the ladder. Going past the mess deck I heard the tense, sleepy noises of the crew fighting their way upward in the dim light to the accompaniment of the loud, urgent *urk, urk, urk* of the bell.

Outside I bumped against several unseen figures, kept getting stepped on, and finally decided to go up on the bridge where I could see something.

A neutral ship of some sort was glowing brightly up ahead. I heard the Escort Commander explaining over the TBS that we had picked up on our radar a target between us and the lighted ship. Mr. Ramsay was calling through the tube for another bearing. Machine guns were being turned on, magazines were being clamped down with a businesslike "click," steel helmets were being distributed. The helmet I received was too small, and I nearly choked myself trying to hook the strap. At that moment I became aware that I was barefoot, had on only a thin pajama top over my khaki shorts, and was cold. The deck, the wind, and the excitement had started me shivering.

Word passed over the phone for all hands to keep a sharp lookout for a submarine target on the surface. The radar shack again reported a target "bobbing up and down" at four thousand yards (two miles). The neutral ship was four miles away.

Then a message over the TBS: "Gallant, this is Gambit. Over."

"Gallant, this is Gambit. Say, is that you coming up on my stern? Over."

"Gambit, this is Gallant. Roger. You may return to station. Over and out."

And once again the sub contact turns out to be the good ship *Alacrity*, out ahead investigating the lights, too. Immediately the command came to secure from general quarters.

A little later, completely awake and restless, I threw on a jacket and joined Turner on the bridge.

The clouds were coming in heavier and heavier. Visibility was reduced at times to one thousand yards. The PC on our port kept coming in too close as their radar was out. About 0200 hours the silence was broken by, "Gambit this is Gaucho. Message for you. Over."

"Gaucho, this is Gambit. Send your message. Over."

"Gambit, this is Gaucho. Would you mind playing in your own backyard for awhile. You have me crowded out of mine. Over."

"Gaucho, this is Gambit. Roger. Over and out."

"Gaucho out," from the PC. And once again the USS *Alacrity* has wandered off station and tried to pluck off a PC.

We had been saying earlier in the evening that nothing had happened for awhile, which always seems to be some kind of psychic signal for something to happen, even if it is a false alarm.

But at three o'clock events took another turn when the *Alacrity* intercepted a radio message from a merchantman saying, "Torpedoed by sub. Abandoning ship. Position Lat. — —, Long. — —. Levi Woodbury." And another member of our merchant service has joined the long list of those below the waves, and people are fighting for their lives a short distance northeast of us.

We are plowing through the darkened seas and will be in their latitude tomorrow night.

January 6, 1944

No subs. But three days of pounding, deadening seas. Slam bang, up and down, over and back again. All the way from Hatteras to the sea-buoy we fought it out with these waves. We won, but we took a terrific amount of punishment and general misery.

Yesterday the galley range finally succumbed and we had only sandwiches handed out between lurches. For three nights, sleep was a highly diluted product.

Some day I must write a treatise on seasickness. That malady hits a person long before the upchucking stage. It starts when these fragile craft begin their complicated maneuvers, and continues in a variety of forms right up until it's reasonably smooth sailing again. Some people heave over the side. Most of us simply suffer in a determined, tortured, nonheaving state. The malaise attacks brain, body, and spirit. A better term would be "sea misery."

We made the swept channel at two last night and were immediately enveloped in a blinding rain. Progress up the channel was slow, halting, and tedious. We docked at about ten this morning with a sharp, splintering crash as the tide caught us and slammed us against a corner of the pier—reminding us with that last, lashing gesture that the battle is to be resumed.

January 11, 1944

(New York)

The news about our prospective leave is the best I've heard. So good, in fact, I'm a bit skeptical of it. At dinner last night Mr. Ramsay explained that we were getting a complete overhaul and a lot of new equipment next time we come back in. "So be prepared with work lists for whatever you need for your department; also figure out when you want your leave," he said.

That's the first time I have ever been invited to ask for leave. Mr. Ramsay seems to think we'll be in port for at least two weeks, probably longer, so I think I'll ask for a solid week. Never hurts to ask.

It's nice to think that after this trip we probably won't go out again until late in February. That will be the start of the ninth month. The pay officer at Headquarters here in New York told me today he was sure I would get shore duty after a year.

January 17, 1944
(Enroute for Guantanamo)

This morning was the first time the sun made a decent appearance on this trip. We have had five days of high seas, rain, mist, gloom and uneasy stomachs. Of all our trips this, I believe, was the most colorless; or perhaps I'm becoming so accustomed to it all that the routine, including bad weather and "sea misery," approaches boredom.

I didn't even bother to jot down daily entries. The usual things happened this trip, but they just seemed to duplicate everything that has happened before, so I just let them go by. Besides, I felt too miserable most of the time to do more than dream of the "someday" when life would be normal again.

I did get some reading done. Despite boredom and discomfort I find that reading is stimulating and helpful. I have been doing very well with a five-hundred page volume by Pierre van Passen entitled *Days of Our Years*, which I bought at Brentano's near Headquarters. It's one of the best books I've ever read, and I'm going through it carefully, dictionary by my side, annotating the pages.

January 18, 1944

Turner sent the bridge messenger down to call me early this morning. He wanted me to see what he called the "blue Bahamas morning." Everyone is in good spirits because we are only one day out of Cuba.

Our Commander Task Unit, perhaps feeling good himself or merely wishing to exercise some authority, sends over to the *PC-568* for their morning position.

Answer: "320 degrees true; 500 yards from the commodore."

"Trying to be funny with me, are they?" murmurs CTU 02.9.7., his regal feathers ruffled, "I'll fix them. Messenger, have the signalman send this over to them. 'Upon arrival at Gitmo Bay submit log and navigation notes for inspection.'"

Back quickly comes an answer. "Are all vessels submitting these, or are we picked out for this signal honor? Our morning sights, Vega 0702; Mars 0705; Polaris 0707; Moon 0711, etc."

The CTU is taken aback. This is more than he bargained for. The commander of the little vessel is showing a great deal of spunk. He sends back, "Forget it. We will joke about it over a good dish of your ice cream in Cuba." The *PC-568* is noted for their ample supply of this luxury. They seem to have a couple of extra freeze boxes for the stuff. We think they swap it at a nice figure for rum and cigars, or perhaps deliver some of it directly to the Admiral to get in his good graces.

January 19, 1944

The CTU used to be in the advertising business. If you didn't know that fact, you might possibly guess it from his antics on a day like this.

We are "rendezvousing" with another convoy. Mr. Pilling is very fond of talking on any and all occasions and subjects, and—as indicated in yesterday's entry—he loves to send messages. On a day like today he outdoes himself. The TBS is either worn out, or just plain not working. As a result the signalmen have been running frantically from side to side of the bridge, flapping the lenses.

Earlier in the day we ran alongside the commodore so he could talk through the loudhailer. Later he called a PC over and shouted through a megaphone. And between times he keeps up a running line of chatter, interspersed with oaths, speculations, exclamations, orders and unessential bits of information.

Our former captain, who served also in the dual capacity of Escort Commander, was a singularly quiet, efficient officer. He accomplished much with little show of authority. Perhaps it's the contrast that's getting us. But we can't help feeling that half of this noise and commotion could be avoided.

But, despite the CTU, the day is very pleasant. The sun shines warmly and the surface of the sea is crinkled like seersucker from the touch of little vagrant winds. In the distance, the ochre-colored mountains of Cuba beckon alluringly with the promise of good firm land under our feet.

It is 1030 hours and we just entered the harbor. There is a great collection of colored lights outside. A launch that came suddenly out of the gloom produced a voice that yelled through a megaphone, giving us our berth at the fueling pier. Tired as we are of the sea and everything that pertains to it, our first job is always to refuel and prepare to get under way again. That takes about two hours. Then they tell us where we will berth while here. We hope it will be alongside a dock and not out in the bay, where we have been known to be isolated on other occasions. In any event, it will be long after midnight when we settle down.

January 20, 1944

It's a blue night, in the sense of dreariness and low spirits. I suppose it is partly caused by the weather. All day the grey, beating rain has come down, and it is not unlike Washington in the fall. We were even a little reluctant to leave the ship.

Tonight, at the Club, I sat on the terrace and watched the yellow and red lights of the ships at anchor mix with the fog over the Bay. It was cold. A light, biting cold that slipped under our khaki uniforms and made us think of the joys of being cozily warm before a fire somewhere in the north. The hibiscus were drenched with rain. As always they took me back to Florida—back to the Blue Ocean Apartments, and the long vistas of Sheridan Avenue and Pine Tree Drive, and all the rest of Miami and Miami Beach that had once meant so much in our lives.

The six feeble, struggling royal palms were waving their arms in the wind, seeking for a growth that somehow seems to elude them. They are even more scrawny than when we first came here.

January 24, 1944

With the sky above us like an enormous blue baldaquin glittering with stars, we slipped out of Guantanamo harbor to begin the return voyage of our fifth trip.

The Southern Cross was dead ahead of us as we came out, with the two Southern Pointers, Alpha Centauri and Beta Centauri off to the left. Venus, the morning star, hung over the land to the east, so bright we thought for awhile it was a light on a tower. When we got well out to sea, she was throwing a track like a moon.

Eleven ships were to come out of Guantanamo as the initial body of the convoy, and we dodged around outside waiting for them to appear. At fifteen minutes a ship, we figured they would require almost three hours to get out. We had passed through the nets at five-thirty.

The temperature was cool enough to require a light jacket and we hung about on the bridge, sending for coffee from time to time and chatting about what had happened at the Club and who had hit the jackpots. It was always good to be starting back—but no matter how we felt about it while we were there, we knew there were much worse ports than Guantanamo. There was always that brief interlude of excellent dinners at the Club, with maybe a little tennis and a swim thrown in. It was only when we were out here facing north again that we remembered about the bad weather ahead of us and what it could do to the *Haste*.

At seven the light in the east was strong enough to bring out the shape of several clouds on the horizon. They looked, as usual, confusingly like the mountains that run up and down this rocky, southern coast of the Oriente province of Cuba. Suddenly in the center of the dawn a skeletal moon became visible, looking like a lost or strayed world. Then the light brightened, moon and stars faded, and day began in earnest. At twenty minutes to eight, the rising sun turned the clouds on the horizon into red and gold banners. Shoreward the mountains came out of the blue mist to appear in the more prosaic brown homespun they wear by day.

Eight ships were smoking up the horizon behind us. The members of our escort group were calling back and forth to each other like the braying of a pack of dogs. "There's our blimp," somebody said, pointing to the elongated silver globule over the ships. She would sweep the track ahead of us throughout the day.

[NOTE. The last of the Navy's "bloopy bags" disappeared from the skies in 1962, ending an often unfortunate, frequently glorious, and always controversial career in the nation's military history. During World War II, the blimp had its finest hours. The Navy had only six in service when the war began, and the new enthusiasts who manned them were called "balloonatics." But in a crash program, the Navy commissioned 168 blimps whose duty was to escort convoys and chase submarines.

The blimps patrolled at forty-five to fifty knots and were radar-equipped early in the war. Many thought that their slow rate of flight would help them spot targets, even under water, which might be missed by faster-flying planes.

Rear Admiral J. L. "Reggie" Kauffman, Commandant Seventh Naval District and Commander Gulf Sea Frontier, with headquarters at Miami, was one of the staunchest and most influential supporters of the blimp program. Admiral Kauffman's brilliant record as first commandant of our Naval Operating Base at Iceland, before transferring his talents and energies to Gulf Sea Frontier, made him a forceful advocate in their behalf.

In a letter quoted in the November, 1943, War Diary for Gulf Sea Frontier, he stated in replying to Cominch's (Commander in Chief's) inquiry concerning the blimps' usefulness, that their endurance particularly their ability to maintain patrol for long periods, especially at night, had been of great usefulness. He also sighted their "generally more dependable special equipment" and their "lower fuel consumption as compared to PBM's and PV's," a factor which was "especially desirable at isolated bases."

Whatever the relative merits of the blimps vis-a-vis other aircraft, they unquestionably contributed to seagoing morale, and seamen in some areas where there was limited protection, threatened mutiny unless given blimp cover.*

We on the *Haste* invariably felt better when we had a blimp overhead. And for us, perhaps, they were lucky, since we had them a large part of the time. We actually felt they could "see" with their special visual aids and scientific instruments down in those clear or unclear depths and give us warning of a submarine approach.

Despite looking like gigantic whales moving majestically against the skyline, only one blimp was destroyed by enemy action. At midnight July 18, 1943, thirty miles off the Florida Keys (while we were still at Bermuda), blimp K-74 flying at 500 feet picked up a strong contact. The night was clear and the moon, just past full, brilliantly lighted the calm sea. Very soon, half a mile distant, a surfaced submarine was sighted clearly, proceeding at an estimated fourteen knots. No sign of life was seen aboard as the blimp circled twice; she then made the fateful decision to violate her own lighter-than-air-

*The crews of the bauxite shuttle ships between Trinidad and the Guianas, a route for which no surface escorts could at first be spared, are said to have threatened mutiny unless they were given protection; they were afforded blimp cover all the way and the men were satisfied." *History of Naval Operations in World War II.* Volume I. Samuel Eliot Morison.

doctrine and attack the surfaced sub. Approaching up moon at forty-seven knots, she got within about 200 yards before being detected probably betrayed by the noise of its engines. The U-boat quickly fired at the big target, puncturing the balloon and starting a fire in the fuselage. The airship's forward but sinking momentum carried it over the U-boat where it might, incredibly, have completed its mission, except that its bomb-release gear (perhaps from long disuse) refused to function and it settled in the water as the sub dived. Nine out of ten of its crew were rescued off North Elbow Cay by destroyer *Dahlgren.*

Since the war, blimps have become outmoded, since they were especially vulnerable to the post-World War II proliferation of surface-to-air missiles. Nearly all of their old and invaluable functions are now being performed either by helicopters or by standard aircraft. But those of us who remember the comforting feeling when we saw the huge shape hovering over us will always think fondly of the "bloopy bags."]

January 25, 1944
We ran back through the convoy today to pass some orders to a ship that had just joined us. Running back through the convoy is a thing we like to do. It seems to place us on a new intimacy with the ships that make up our group.

Nothing in the way of a display occurs. As a rule the crews do not even wave back and forth, but there is a certain feeling of strength and comradeship that comes from the mere proximity of the ships. Together they create a sense of solid unity and indestructibility.

The ship that had just pulled up was a tanker named *Spidoleine,* flying the Panamanian flag. At the time, she was the fifth ship in the seventh column, so our mission took us all the way back to the rear. We used a "line-throwing gun" which fires a brass pin carrying a light flaxen cord. When the members of the tanker's crew retrieved the pin, they hauled in on the shot line and we payed out the heavier line which was tied to it. In a few minutes we were ready to start the tin can across which holds the orders.

Everything went off as usual until it came time to haul the line back in. Then, instead of simply heaving it overboard, the tanker's crew tied something to it that immediately pulled the line astern, and we nearly lost it in the propeller. One or two quick jerks brought the object splashing up alongside where somebody grabbed it and yelled out that it was a bottle. When it came up to the bridge, we opened it and sure enough, there was a bottle of "Golden Wedding" and a note from the Skipper, on the stationery of the Gulf Oil Company, saying, "Greetings! We are glad to be with you."

We sent back a hearty "thank you" while the Captain and the Escort Commander engaged in a heated discussion as to who rated final possession of the bottle.

January 27, 1944

We have a second class quartermaster aboard named Watson, who looks just like his name sounds, only more so.

Watson must be about thirty; he's small and baldish and neatly moustached. He speaks in accents as English and clipped as the shadow on his lips, and even in sailor clothes he looks dapper, which is a supreme accomplishment.

Because of his evident good qualities and inclinations, we became interested in the fellow and were anxious to send him to Officer Training School. We found that he used to be a "customers' man" for a Broadway bond house and had made good money before the war. But Watson seemed only mildly interested in our efforts in his behalf. He flunked the exam we gave him, and there were indications that either a lot of things had been left out of his education or he deliberately chose not to make a passing grade. In any case, he didn't seem to be at all disappointed at the result.

We have just found out the answer. Aside from his philosophy that one place is as good as another to serve, and he doesn't want to be bothered with the responsibility of being an officer, Watson is a painter. He brought out a set of water colors he had worked on surreptitiously over the past several months and they are decidedly good. A number of them were done in Guantanamo and he has caught the spirit of that sun-drenched port. Now with our approbation he daubs quite openly and we even watch him.

The weather has been good on the way back and this afternoon Watson was on the stack-deck with his paint box, measuring the convoy with a brush.

We are all hoping to get one of his pictures.

January 31, 1944

Off the Jersey coast today with a surprisingly flat sea and a misty horizon. Nothing to see except an occasional gull circling our wake, and in the distance the dim shape of the convoy.

At five-thirty tonight the ships will "double up," forming a line of two's, preparatory to going up the channel. We are expecting to hit the sea-buoy (called "Point Zebra" in all dispatches and official documents) at six in the morning.

> "This new ship here, is fitted according to the reported increase of knowledge among mankind. Namely, she is cumbered, end to end, with bells and trumpets and clocks and wires which, it has been told to me, can call Voices out of the air, or the waters to con the ship while her crew sleep. But sleep *Thou* lightly, O Nakhoda! (Captain). It has not yet been told to me that the Sea has ceased to be the Sea."
>
> *Foreword to the Publisher*
> Rudyard Kipling (1865-1936)

February 1, 1944

New York did it again! Every time we get there, the weather pulls another trick out of its bag. When I went topside at five this morning a northwest wind was roaring out of a starlit sky.

We were following the thin, scattered line of lights marking the convoy, our position being back on the port quarter. Over our shoulders, our own masthead light glimmered like one of the old-fashioned lamps so often seen on Christmas cards.

At five-thirty, Venus was just appearing around to the right and almost astern of us, looking a bit wan and yellow, as if undecided whether or not to rise on this wintry morning. The contrast in her position with that of the morning we left Guantanamo was very marked. One red light wavered directly behind us. We speculated on whether it was another patrol ship or a member of the convoy. We didn't care much. It was well marked and proceeding in the same direction.

At six-twenty the big moment came. Turner and I remarked simultaneously that a light had gone out up ahead of us and then we saw it again. Immediately it assumed a regular cadence, one long flash, one short, and we knew it was "Zebra." Behind it are eight similar buoys three miles apart making the safety of the swept channel into Ambrose Lightship. This was our landfall, our pinpoint objective since we left the mountain-enclosed bay of southern Cuba. Once you hit the sea-buoy, most of your troubles and fears are behind you.

Buoy Zebra (which is also "Buoy Able," for it has a large "A" on its side) glittered like a phantom before us for an hour and a half, while we "fishtailed" beside the convoy and butted our nose into the rising seas. Meanwhile the temperature was going down, and the wind velocity going steadily up.

At seven-thirty Zebra was a diamond sparkling against the drab background of a grey and foam-crested seascape slowly emerging from its nocturnal obscurity. The string of lights was becoming a string of ships. The red light off our stern attached itself to the purple superstructure of a tanker. Behind us the morning made an almost colorless entry and Venus, having striven above the haze, was assuming a chaste and detached brilliance preparatory to retreating completely from the scene.

We increased speed to move up on the convoy and the waves started breaking over the bridge. My knitted cap under the hood of my coat became soaked through, and salt water started running in a steady stream down my face. It had long since become impossible to chase the cold out of my feet by stamping them. Ducking to escape the spray became an almost fixed posture.

At eight o'clock, the relief came up and Turner and I went below for breakfast. "Buoy Able" had finally been passed off the port side, rolling and caterwauling mournfully in the big waves. Ahead of us another convoy was coming out, led by the little corvette *Fury*, belonging to the "passion class" ships.

February 3, 1944

We got the details of the sinking of the converted yacht, *St. Augustine*, which went down on January 6, the day we docked on our previous trip.

The sinking of the *St. Augustine* was not due to enemy action, but is certainly an example of the "anything can happen, and you never know what to expect" theory.

Some background on the ship, turned up later, deserves mention. She had been acquired by the Navy in 1940, converted at the Boston Navy Yard, and commissioned as *PG-54*. Formerly the pleasure yacht, *Noparo*, and owned by Norman B. Woolworth, this million-dollar yacht had often come before the public eye when Woolworth loaned it to his cousin, Barbara Hutton.

The *St. Augustine's* overall length of 272 feet and her weight of 408 gross tons, made her one of the largest converted yachts in the Frontier Task Force.

On the morning of January 6, 1944, the *St. Augustine*, as escort commander, led the convoy *NK-588* out of the New York harbor gate. Aboard was the convoy commodore and his staff, because the only merchant ship in the convoy was the tanker *Tydol Gas*. Two other escorts, the Coast Guard Cutters *Argo* and *Thetis*, (*Thetis* was also the possessor of a scalp, having destroyed the submarine *U-157* in a depth charge attack off the Florida Keys on the night of June 13, 1942) completed the convoy. It was known that two other ships were due to join the convoy off the Virginia Capes. Throughout the day the three escorts and one tanker proceeded south from Ambrose without incident. Heavy NNW winds, force seven, built up high seas and conditions were moderately unpleasant, but visibility remained satisfactory even after darkness set in because a near-full moon and thinly scattered clouds reflected ample light on the uneasy surface of the foam-flecked ocean.

This was the weather we had described in our entry on January 6. "No subs. But three days of pounding, deadening seas. Slam bang, up and down, over and back again. All the way from Hatteras to the sea-buoy we fought it out with these foam-tipped waves. We won—but we took a terrific amount of punishment and general misery."

At about 2200 hours *St. Augustine* established radar contact with a vessel in a sector which was normally *Argo's* and proceeded to investigate. At 6,000 yards, she challenged by blinker light and later flashed her running lights, but received no answer. She turned sharply to port, increasing speed to full ahead, getting into a dangerous position in relation to the other vessel, which was the tanker *Camas Meadows*, proceeding independently out of Delaware Bay. The vessels collided, the bow of *Camas Meadows* striking *St. Augustine* about midships on the starboard side, penetrating her hull ten to fifteen feet and rupturing the boiler or steam lines, allowing live steam to escape.

(We had learned some of the details of the collision and the heavy loss of life from accounts circulating around the Staten Island Base after our arrival, but the real story had to await the declassification and subsequent perusal of the Eastern Sea Frontier War Diary of January, 1944.)

The Secret and Confidential entries disclose that the first word of the disaster received at Headquarters, Eastern Sea Frontier, was an SOS from the *Camas Meadows* at 2325 Queen. The message stated, "Torpedoed. Please get bearings." Within six minutes, bearings from eight stations in the Direction Finder Net had been received in New York, but at 2332 hours another message from the *Camas Meadows* was received: "Please cancel previous. Have collided with another craft sixty miles southeast Cape May." Again from the *Camas Meadows* at 2344 hours: "Please send assistance to pick up survivors. We are not able to do so."

At 0015 hours, about fifty minutes after the collision, *USCGC Thetis* informed Commander, Eastern Sea Frontier that the *St. Augustine* had been sunk at 38-00 North, 74-05 West, that the cause was not believed to be enemy action. At 0102 hours, the *Camas Meadows* sent an amplifying message in compliance with a request made by Commander, Eastern Sea Frontier, stating that two small vessels were picking up survivors, that the tanker was having difficulty in trying to maneuver, that she would stand by until daylight and then would return to Cape May in order to survey her own damage. Within the next two hours, a large search team of ships, planes and blimps was organized, but the brunt of the rescue work was accomplished by the escorts *Argo* and *Thetis*.

Aboard the *Argo*, the tanker had been picked up on the radar screen some minutes before the collision. The OD reported the contact to the Captain, who ordered that the information be given to *St. Augustine* by TBS. The message was passed by voice radio and the *St. Augustine* acknowledged. Lookouts on *Argo* soon reported they had sighted the tanker three points off the starboard bow, and possibly five miles distant. It was also observed that the *St. Augustine* had left her station in the van of the convoy and was turning right toward the tanker. At that time, it appeared from the *Argo* that the tanker would cross the bow of the convoy, which continued on course.

As the range closed, it was decided that the *Argo* should turn right, in order to go around the stern of the tanker, and course was changed until the fast-moving merchant vessel lay about 2,500 yards off the port bow of *Argo*. Although the *St. Augustine* and the tanker were both clearly visible to the naked eye at the time, the radar operator continued to report the relative positions of these two images on his screen. When the *St. Augustine* appeared to be about 3,000 yards from the tanker those on the bridge of the *Argo* observed the blinker challenge aimed at the tanker from the bridge of *St. Augustine*.

By this time the *Argo* was swinging wide around the stern of the tanker, and gradually the outline of the ship cut out the image of the *St. Augustine*. It was presumed that the *St. Augustine* would come around the merchantman's stern from the starboard side and the OD watched through his glasses. In a few moments, the boatswain's mate on watch reported that he could see the *St. Augustine* breaking away from the merchantman, and the *Argo* came right still further to allow room for the *St. Augustine* to pass between him and the stern of the tanker.

Then the OD observed that the bow of the *St. Augustine* appeared to loom up out of the water at a very high angle. As the OD watched, across the 2,000 yards of water, he saw the bow loom even higher out of the water, then seemed to settle completely out of sight, exactly as though she were going down stern first. He couldn't believe his eyes. He called to others on the bridge and asked if they could see *St. Augustine*. They said that they had seen her, but she had disappeared momentarily in a trough of the seas.

At that time *Thetis* began calling *St. Augustine* on voice radio without getting an answer; then called *Argo* to request that since she was nearer, she try to raise *St. Augustine* on the TBS. The OD tried without success. Then the radarman was asked if he had the ship on the screen; he reported that he had had it right after she left the merchantman but he had now lost it. At that point *Argo* noticed that the merchantman on the port quarter had stopped and put on all running lights—a strange circumstance which made the OD fear the worst for *St. Augustine*. He immediately called the Captain of the *Argo*, and sent the coxswain of the watch to rouse all officers and crew. When the Captain arrived, he immediately took the deck and headed for the merchantman, at the same time ordering the signalman to call by blinker and find out what had happened. The signalman began his message.

"Did you have collision?"

No answer.

"What made him sink?"

"Survivors to left of you," came the first blinker message from the tanker.

"What is your name?"

No answer from the tanker.

"What happened to the other ship?"

No answer.

"Did other ship hit you?"

"We rammed her. We are taking on water."

"Do you have any survivors aboard?"

"No."

At approximately 2350 hours, some twenty minutes after the vessel had sunk, the *Argo* reached the scene and sighted survivors in the water or on rafts waving the red lights on their lifejackets. Five searchlights were turned on. Because of the heavy seas, it was difficult to tell which men to rescue first, but it was decided to leave individual men until last in order to get to the largest groups which might be washed off rafts and scattered.

As soon as men had been taken from rafts, heaving lines were thrown across the bodies of individual men in the water. If they failed to respond to the line, it was presumed that they were dead and preference was shown to those who were waving lights or showing other signs of life.

There were many remarkable examples of self-sacrifice and heroism displayed by the crews of these two Coast Guard vessels during the rescue operations, and a number of their officers and men were later recommended for citations.

Within the next two hours all survivors had been picked up, a total of thirty—twenty-three by *Argo* and seven by *Thetis*. The two officers who survived, and who were the last to be picked up, had been sleeping at the time of the collision. They had managed to climb into the damaged starboard lifeboat which had broken loose after the collision. Sixty-seven bodies were found in the area in the next two hours. The final tally showed a loss of 106 men and nine officers.

Survivors later testified that within three to five minutes after the collision, the *St. Augustine* settled by the stern, stood on her beam's end, and sank.

"We were floating there," one of the enlisted men said, afterwards, "and the last time I saw the *Augie* she was pointing skyward against the moonlit sky. She looked like a big, tall building. She was settling down and I turned my head around and clung to the life raft; I was starting to feel cold."

The Master of the tanker later testified before the Board of Investigation that he had been ill and had turned in after leaving port. The OD was his third mate. The only qualified signalman aboard was a member of the Armed Guard Navy gun crew who had also been given permission to turn in because of illness. He had only reached the bridge moments before the crash. The OD should have been qualified to send signals as a licensed officer but evidently was not able to do so.

The Master later testified that his crew had been on board less than ten days, and many of them had never before been to sea. He felt them completely unqualified to put over lifeboats in such heavy weather. He also said if he had released his life rafts, the direction of the wind would have carried them on a course which would have brought them nowhere near the survivors. Finally, he said his radio operator, not knowing what had happened, had sent the SOS because of his fear that before any distress signal could be sent, the radio equipment might have been knocked out.

The conclusion of the Board was that the turn to port made by *St. Augustine* just before the crash was an error in judgment on the part of her officers and was the principal cause of the tragedy. The Board also stated that, if the blinker challenge had been answered promptly, the collision might not have occurred.

Admiral Andrews of Eastern Sea Frontier was livid at the loss of one of his escorts in such a manner. He proposed to COMINCH that all merchant vessels be required to carry two qualified signalmen in addition to their officers, but apparently very little came of the suggestion.

Our Escort Commander, Lieutenant Pilling, came off the *St. Augustine* early last year. His only comment was that if he had been there it wouldn't have happened, because he always left strict orders to be called whenever a contact was being investigated. Despite his somewhat noisy, individualistic approach, which is that of a yachtsman rather than a professional naval officer, I have developed a great deal of confidence in his competence, so perhaps there is a good foundation for his statement.

February 10, 1944

Have been extremely busy getting things into shape here before I head for Washington and some wonderful days of almost-normality with my family.

However, the *Haste* couldn't let me go in peace. She had to stage one of her little scenes to show what she could really do if she was in a temperamental mood.

I heard the general alarm ring once, a long ring like an abbreviated fire alarm, and then I heard the sound of running feet on the upper deck. But it must be a mistake, I told myself, because we're in port and they don't use the general alarm system in port. In my half-awake state, that explanation seemed sufficient.

Suddenly I smelled smoke, and putting two and two together I threw off the covers just as a seaman stuck his head in the doorway.

"What's up?" I demanded.

"There's a fire in the fireroom, sir," he said. "The man on watch just discovered it."

At that point I realized that people were running all over the ship and somebody, somewhere, was yelling orders.

"Turner," I bellowed, switching on the lights, "there's a fire in the fireroom!" In retrospect it sounds a little funny, but at that moment I was thinking of the 80,000 gallons of fuel we had loaded that afternoon, and the forty tons of ammunition we carry at all times.

Turner came down from his bunk with the jerky motions of someone torn from a sound sleep, and the two of us struggled with our clothes while the smoke grew thicker and the excitement overhead increased. Buttoning a button at the moment was a complex operation; tying a shoelace too involved to be considered. And along with the rush and confusion, I could not help thinking of my packed suitcase and the twenty days' leave that had just been granted me, and what this might do to change things. I had purposely stayed over an extra day to straighten out some loose ends and to give the crew a special pay before they left—and here I was caught in a fire and with a good chance that my clothes would be burned up, my office records destroyed, and my leave spoiled.

Turner was through the door first, but I was right behind him. The dazed seaman standing on the mess deck looked as aimless as the lengths of fire hose that rained in all directions. Smoke was pouring from the entrance to the fireroom, and our bearded boatswain's mate was yelling for gas masks. A lot of strange faces were present and I found out in a few minutes that the fire squad from the dock had come aboard.

After about fifteen minutes, it was announced that the blaze was under control, but when I went topside, the PC next to us was backing away feverishly, and a fireboat was coming in with her searchlights playing on us. Quite a crowd had collected on the dock, and a heavy-jacketed figure who was addressed as "Chief" was speculating whether or not we would have to be towed out in the stream.

That was sufficient to send me below for my suitcase, into which I hurriedly tossed the articles necessary to complete my uniform. Over and over I cursed myself for my conscientiousness in staying over that extra day. When I lugged the suitcase topside, however, and past the frightened-looking seaman, I felt like the proverbial rat leaving the stricken ship. The feeling was so strong that I left the bag in the office and returned all the way down to the fireroom ladder to put in an appearance.

There seemed to be absolutely nothing helpful I could do. The fire was being fought by a handful of engineers and firemen, who obviously knew what they were doing and who would only be impeded by well-meaning incompetents. The only officers down below were Dutch, our warrant machinist, and the Captain. The rest of us wandered around helplessly, trying to appear calm.

The fire had broken out at four o'clock. At five-thirty it was definitely extinguished and the fireboat and a waiting tug pulled away. I had been saved the ignominy of fleeing over the side, which I most certainly would have done if they had decided to tow her out into the harbor. I could rationalize that intention on the grounds that I was officially on leave, and the decision to stay over had been my own, but I was glad to have been relieved of the necessity of "leaving under fire." I felt too much a part of the *Haste* now to be guilty of anything resembling a desertion.

At seven-thirty the snow was falling in thick, heavy flakes, and when I left the ship later in the morning she had several inches on her decks. The convoy was scheduled to sail at eleven. It certainly looked like a good trip to miss—and I was going home.

[NOTE. While this book was in the process of shaping up, correspondence with my friend and former shipmate, Turner, turned up the surprising disclosure that he, too, had occasionally kept notes and a spasmodic diary. These records he generously forwarded with his cordial permission to use them as I saw fit.

I thought it might be interesting to compare Turner's account of the fire, exactly as he wrote it back there on February 10, 1944, with my own diary entry of the same date given above, and to follow it with Turner's record of the trip I missed.

There were lapses of several months in parts of Turner's diary, but he made a number of entries throughout that particular trip almost as if to compensate for my own absence. His version follows.]

February 10, 1944—Turner's diary
Home port N.Y., 0410 in the morning. It began with Carr yelling in my ear, "Fire alarm! Fire alarm! Get out of that sack!"

I hit the deck running. Smoke everyplace. Up on deck hoses were already strung out and fire extinguishers setting around like gals on Broadway. It took only a minute to find the fire was in the bilges in the fireroom. Black smoke was pouring out everywhere. However, it was completely locked off and we felt that the vapor from the sprinkler nozzles would quickly smother the fire.

We called the PC moored alongside us to prepare to cast off. No one was stirring. Finally its Skipper came out rubbing his eyes. Janes says, "Get ready to cast off. We are afire and a tug is alongside of you."

He said, "I can't. My men are all asleep."

Janes says, with that little mustache of his bristling, "What the hell do you think all of us were doing until two minutes ago!"

There was some talk of taking us out in the stream. Almost magically Carr came from below all dressed in his blues, with his suitcase. Somebody says, "Carr, where are you going?"

He said, "There is some talk of taking us out in the stream to fight the fire, so I want to be sure to be ashore, and not miss my trip leave."

This morning there was a howling blizzard and snow everyplace. What a day to leave the States. First a fire, then a blizzard. What next? Fortunately sailing time was delayed ten hours.

Just as bad tonight. Cold and ice everywhere going down the channel. As soon as we got outside, she started kicking up. That was a signal for all the new men aboard to start feeding the fishes. The crew's head was jam-packed with men on the deck and laying around, all singing the old sea song, "Harrumph, harrumph, harra."

Four days later. Still stormy and not a single star sight since leaving. Warmer tho. We are down below the land of the ice and snow. If we don't get a sight soon it is going to be embarrassing trying to make Crooked Island Passage.

What a convoy! Ships straggling, breaking down, getting lost. Worse than a bunch of sheep. This trip has been snafu from one end to the other. Oh, well, two more weeks and we will be courting the fair wolvettes of Broadway.

February 17, 1944 — Turner's diary

The routine was interspersed with a little excitement today. At 0900 hours I came out of a sound sleep with the jangle of the general alarm in my ears. Grabbed my lifebelt, woke up, stuck my feet in my shoes and was up the ladder before the late breakfasters made it. Almost beat the captain to the bridge. Turned out to be a false alarm.

The humor came out at the rehashing of events. Tex Phillips, a lieutenant who reported aboard last trip, was well soaped down in the shower. He made one swipe with the towel, jumped into his pants and beat his crew to the number two gun. One man was late. When Tex asked him what was wrong he said, "I couldn't find my lifebelt."

"To hell with the belt! When Fritzy gets after you he won't wait for no belts. After this be goddamn certain you beat me up here," narrated Tex, as only a westerner could do. He had to send a man to look for another of his men. This individual couldn't find his clothes. After Tex had pulled out a couple of handfuls of his already-thin hair he began. "Well, I'll be damned! You're getting damned-awful modest around here. No goddamn U-boat is going to give a damn whether you have any clothes on or not when he fishes you. You'll look a hell of a lot better abandoning ship with no clothes on than hunting them down in 4,000 fathoms of water. It's deep around here you know."

At 1300 hours all hands turned to chipping rust, and painting specialists who hadn't seen the light of day for ages were on deck bitching with the rest of them. And at 1330 hours there went that old alarm again. This time we dropped a full pattern of charges. Apparently no "boners" pulled and very few light bulbs broken.

Today we have picked up the islands and at daylight tomorrow we should see the coast of Cuba. Another trip nearly completed.

February 29, 1944—Turner's diary

Ah, the last night out of N.Y. The off watches are dreaming sweet dreams of the gals, the wine, and song on the beach for tonight. I came on for the 000-0400 [midnight-to-four] watch. It is a cold, quiet, foggy night. Very limited visibility. The first quiet weather we have had at this end for six months. A perfect night for a collision at sea.

The radars are all busy searching out the unseen targets. A ship here, a boat there; and mostly for Buoy Zebra, that point forty miles out of N.Y. that the shipping of the world steers for when entering.

At 0200 hours the *Alacrity* came across the TBS. They have just intercepted an SOS. Tragedy at sea. Two ships have collided. A check of their position shows they are some distance astern of us. One of them we detached only a few hours earlier to proceed independently to Boston and Halifax. Tragedy strikes fast at sea.

The radar picks up a target on the other side of the convoy. The *Alacrity* reports it is a fishing vessel.

We pass on. Suddenly the PC farther astern on the port side calls over the TBS, "We are picking up targets all over the screen. They are from 200 to 400 yards away." Then a short time later, "We have found a mast about ten feet long with two lights burning on it. What is it?''

I say, "It is probably a trap. Lay off."

Quick as a flash, Rollinson, an old salt on the *Alacrity*, comes in, "That mast the PC has out there is a marker for the fishermen's net. If you don't get the hell out of there you will be all messed-up in that net and have a bunch of fishermen on you."

You can see somebody's face get red. We would have something to kid the PC about when we get in.

And at 0347 hours, "Flashing light sighted bearing zero zero five relative." Buoy Zebra. Forty miles from N.Y. and a short relaxation before we head out to sea again.

16

> "It is an old adage that there
> is nothing worse than the
> sea to confound a man, be
> he never so strong."
>
> *Odyssey, Book viii*
> Homer (*c. 850 B.C.*)

March 3, 1944

FOR THREE WEEKS THE *HASTE* has not controlled my life. It was a good three weeks. Too short, but good. I feel refreshed in body and mind, even though the transition from family and home back to ship is not easy.

The trip back was uneventful, except that the train came into New York on time—an event in itself. We pulled into the station at exactly eleven, and I reported back aboard a few minutes after twelve.

When I started up the gangplank, the quartermasters were standing there grinning; and one of them couldn't resist saying, "Boy, are we glad to see you, sir!" And then I found out that the *Haste* had been here since the morning of last Tuesday. As would be the case in my absence, they had a record trip, both in the shortness of the time consumed on the way home (six and half days), and in the flatness of the sea. Turner tells me they hardly had a breeze all the way up here. They've been looking for me every day, hoping I'd show up a day or so early, and they were almost tempted to call up long distance since they were all so broke. It's a good thing I didn't know they were up here. It would probably have spoiled those last days of leave.

March 4, 1944

As nearly as I can make out, we're going to be here for the whole of next week and probably sail around Sunday. It seems that we're to have our annual "military inspection," which reportedly entails an inspecting board coming aboard us. Then we'll go outside somewhere for one, possibly two days, to drop charges, fire the

187

guns, practice quarters, and so forth. It appears to be something that ships have to go through annually, and it's responsible for another longer lay-in for us. As far as I'm concerned it makes an ideal setup for catching up with my paper work, since I'll have very little to do with the inspection.

The run seems to be the same, and there's no talk of any shifting of it. No transfers this time. Charlie Gifford came in to see me this afternoon and said last trip they went down to Key West.

The officers were glad to see me, most of them *very* glad, which is one of the nice things about being pay officer, I guess. People are especially glad to see you come back.

Wrote a long letter home tonight and went outside the yard to mail it; retrieved my laundry from the Chinaman, drank a couple of beers, read the morning paper, and came back on board. Getting back into the routine like this makes me feel I have never been away.

March 7, 1944

The harbor has been foggy and rainy all day, and late this afternoon one of our baby flat-tops, a converted carrier, dropped anchor for awhile just astern of us. She looked business-like with a tremendous load of planes on her deck. She drifted away like a ghost shortly afterward, and so did a lot of other ships nearby so guess they're on their way somewhere.

There's not much foolishness around here. Things are done quietly, efficiently, and without fanfare. Even the ships themselves seem to feel the way we do: "Let's get this thing over with." It makes me proud to be part of it.

March 8, 1944

Dropped in at a service club last night and acquired a pig (inanimate)! It is really a knockout, and will be a fabulous addition to the pig collection I began when I bought my first one as a souvenir in Guatemala back in 1939.

When I walked into the place last night, I spotted the pig in a front room where the hostesses keep their coats. It was an enormous Mexican pottery "piggy-bank" at least a foot high, and fifteen to eighteen inches long, luxuriantly—and somewhat gaudily—decorated with large painted poppies. During the evening, when one of the hostesses struck up a conversation I told her I collected pigs and had been fascinated ever since I saw that big one in the front room; whereupon she said I ought to have it if I collected them, because everything around this house was more or less donated anyway for the men in the service. She told me to stay around for awhile and she would see what she could do about getting it for me.

I thought that perhaps she was making a little pleasant talk, but about an hour later she grabbed me and said it was all set, and the pig was out on the front entrance, behind one of the brownstone pillars. She said she had discussed the matter with the woman who was the manager, and had been told it was all right to give it to me provided no one saw me walking out with it.

I felt a little embarrassed and did not relish the surreptitiousness of the deal. I even offered to pay for it, but she brushed aside my offer and protests, and to have refused to accept the pig now, after all her trouble, would have been extremely awkward. To simply leave it behind the brownstone pillar was unthinkable. So I got my coat and cap, thanked her profusely, and grabbed the pig from behind the pillar as I departed.

I felt awfully silly carrying the thing through the streets and into the subway, since I was wearing my overcoat with the gold-braided shoulder-boards, my grey suede gloves and white scarf, and had every aspect of a well-dressed, dignified officer—except for that damned pig! It is almost as big as the live pigs we had seen running across the roads when Gibbons and Bergmann (those old friends from the bank, and classmates at Curtis Bay) and I were on our way to our new assignments in Miami. At the time the roads of Georgia seemed to be generally without fences, and a favorite scampering place for a vast assortment of pigs.

Finally, when I got to the ferry, I bought a newspaper and wrapped up my porcine curiosity. This morning the rest of the wardroom members got hold of it, and brought it out on exhibition. They ended up by nicknaming me "Piggy," which is a helluva penalty to have to pay even for a tremendous pig with poppies on its sides.

Later I stowed it away in the big drawer under my locker, stuffing newspapers and underwear and socks around it to help prevent it from shattering should we do any heavy depth charging. We make an offering of broken dishes and coffee makers every time one of those big cans goes into the water.

March 9, 1944

We made a good showing in our trials. We've been up at the Officers' Club celebrating. It turned out that I was a hero in a very small way.

When we started out, I remembered that we hadn't decoded anything for the last ten days, and I mentioned to Janes, the communications officer, that perhaps we should set up the coding machine for March ninth, as they change the combinations on the machine every day. He agreed that it might be a good idea and told me to go ahead and do it. So I went down and set up the necessary parts in case we had a surprise message in conjunction with our examination.

Sure enough, right at the moment the party came aboard, a message from Eastern Sea Frontier Headquarters came through and was handed to me as coding officer. Since I already had the machine ready, it only took me about thirty-five seconds to run it off, and then I rushed up to the Captain on the bridge with the message, which read, HAND THIS IMMEDIATELY TO THE COMMANDING OFFICER OF THE EXAMINATION PARTY. Well, all in all, we broke a record for decoding messages, and they're still talking about it.

Without being too cocky about it, I have a feeling I helped our records in other ways, too. When we had abandon-ship drill, the Commander in charge of the drill came up to my raft first and asked what I had under my arm, and when I replied that the waterproof satchel contained pay records, he said, "Good!"

I have charge of one of the life rafts back aft. Our raft is down in the "waist," as we call it, the cut-down part of the ship between the quarterdeck and forecastle; and we were on the windward side. Consequently, for the first half hour we had to stand there, we took a constant drenching from the big ones that kept splashing over the side. We were mighty glad when that drill was over.

I've got some good men on my raft. I've got Dutch Stolzer and Tuden, the cook, the latter being the strongest man on the ship. I told him if we ever need to put the raft over the side in earnest, to grab half the galley.

In the middle of the practice, one of the Examining Officers asked me to come up to the bridge and fire my .45. When I turned in a fairly practiced performance, inasmuch as we have continued to do some firing over the side nearly every trip, he gave me a nod of approval and told me, "I've seen some supply officers who are not very familiar with their sidearms."

Everything went off fine during the drills, firing, depth charges, (the pig survived), K-guns, everything. We hope to get a very good mark on the exam as a whole. So, like a lot of lugs, as soon as we docked, at seven-thirty this evening, we had to pile up to the Officers' Club to have a few beers to celebrate. And we did pretty good by our victory!

But before the drills were over, the old wheeze about pride going before a fall held good in my case. To keep me from feeling too smug about my efficient performance in connection with the coding machine and saving the pay records, I fell all the way down a ladder and smashed up my shin a bit. The Doc said it didn't amount to much and he didn't put anything on it. It sure hurt like hell. We had to wear those kapok life jackets during the drill, which are new to us and make us look very roly-poly. When I was trying to go down a ladder I couldn't see my feet, and consequently missed the ladder completely until I hit the bottom step.

March 11, 1944

Our examination report came back today and we find that they rated us one of the best corvettes in the fleet. I think that's pretty good. Even though I don't like this business, I am still proud to be a part of it, and want us to be one of the best of outfits, and to do our job as well as we can. Our personal identity and inclinations are inevitably converted into identification with our country and our immediate group in times like this. It has to be that way or the great overall effort would surely fail.

The weather has moderated up here today, and we can almost smell spring in the air. Too bad it couldn't have been like this the day of the drill, when we were outside and it was freezing cold and a strong wind blowing.

The *Haste* is champing just slightly at her moorings. She acts as though she were mildly anxious to get on with the war. The moon is hanging over the water behind us, thin and wan, and looks like a light through a blanket.

There's a certain mystery and romance surrounding sailing time, even though it's a sad business—especially after being home on leave. You hate like the devil to leave everything in the world that's precious to you, but the challenge of making a successful trip and the hopeful expectation of coming back again seems to make each of us a little bigger and braver than he really is. And I guess, in spite of all the lonely hours we spend out there, we wouldn't change it much. We have to do something in this battle for civilization; and though very few of us are sentimental about it, in our way we feel that each time we come in we are a little more deserving of the things back home.

March 13, 1944

The first day out of New York was too perfect—sky blue, sea flat calm—which somehow always turns out indicative of contrasting things to come.

They came today. We have hit the tail-end of a storm, and huge ground swells along with a wracking cross-wind are making our lives miserable.

The Escort Commander sailed aboard the *Alacrity* this time. He is already beset with troubles. Two of the PC's couldn't get away from the dock because of engine trouble, so instead of five escorts we have three, to guard the largest southbound convoy we have had for weeks—twenty-nine ships. Now the *Alacrity* reports that her radar, newly installed this trip, has quit completely.

I was seasick this morning. The malady caught me in my bunk and I had to fight back an active nausea while I threw on some outer clothing. I chose the catwalk around the wheelhouse as my balcony of misery. While I was there periodic cascades came from the corners of the bridge above me, and two of the radiomen came out of the wheelhouse to join me on my perch. I do not feel that it is necessarily true that misery likes company, especially in the case of communal seasickness.

I had soup and a sandwich for lunch and kept it down. Same for dinner. Sea legs and sea stomach coming back. Too long ashore.

March 14, 1944

The *Spidoleine* is with us again—the Gulf Oil tanker that two trips ago passed us a bottle of Golden Wedding when they returned our shot-line. We are hoping to do her another favor.

This is the *Haste's* seventh trip to Guantanamo; my sixth. Missed last trip with that long, luxurious holiday home, which is beginning to seem more and more dreamlike.

Just secured from general quarters. We evidently had a sub but lost him. Picked him up on our radar at 7,000 yards. Closed to 4,500 and he, too, started some maneuvers and proved to be faster on the surface than we are. We talked to the Escort Commander on the *Alacrity*, which was closer than we, and tried to conn him in from our radar bearings but without success. The *Alacrity's* TBS is only partly in commission and her engines have broken down twice. The Escort Commander's having a tough time, but the two PC's finally caught up with us and we now have a screen of five escorts, though the equipment of most of them is defective if not downright inoperative.

We stayed at general quarters for nearly an hour, while the target came and went on our radar dial. We wanted to get close enough to fire some star-shells but couldn't. Shortly after midnight the moon came out and put an end to it all.

We are slow because our bottom needs scraping. We are scheduled for drydock after this trip to have it done.

March 15, 1944

During the night one of the PC's made a contact and dropped a pattern of ashcans. Net result: one nice whale. I'll bet the whales have it in for the subs right now, being mistaken for them so many times and being blown out of the water.

The Escort Commander couldn't stand it any longer. I guess the *Alacrity* got the best of him. At eleven o'clock this morning he came over in a small boat from the *Alacrity* and brought his flag with him. He no sooner stepped aboard than the messages and signals started to fly. He appreciates a good ship, even if as rumor has it somebody "deepsixed" (threw overboard) his fancy English bicycle which he used when ashore for his own brand of transportation and exercise. We don't know what happened, but one night the thing mysteriously disappeared.

The small boat that brought the Escort Commander brought us a load of firebrick at the same time. Some of the bricks had dropped out of one of the boilers, which necessitated shutting it down. We've been limping along on the other one while some new bricks are installed. The jinx seems to be hitting us, too.

Good ship this *Haste*. Our breakdown lights shone like two rubies in the almost-dark sky a few minutes ago, warning the rest of the convoy that we were having a steering casualty. We were uncomfortably close in front of the convoy but the big, dark ships, like wraiths, moved silently up to and around us while we sat there wallowing in the big swell and chattering on the bridge like a pack of monkeys. Turner remarked that we were lucky "no Liberty ships came into the wardroom."

After about thirty minutes we were able to take station again— out front, where the *Haste* is at home.

We sent in a message to Eastern Sea Frontier Headquarters today, telling them the Escort Commander had changed ships and claiming a "probable contact" for last night.

March 16, 1944

Took the conn today for about two hours as Officer of the Deck. Turner instigated the situation when he suddenly motioned to me and said, "Mr. Carr, I think it is time you stepped up and took the deck."

To my protest he said, "Hell, you know this routine as well as the rest of us." Then he added, "I want to check something out in the radar shack. You have ten minutes until the zig change. It's yours," and he stepped down from the platform smiling enigmatically.

The ensign at the windguard looked at me curiously, and suddenly I found myself thinking, "Hell, I *do* know the routine! I'll take it."

I moved over by the voice tube and looked around. The day was clear and calm and the convoy seemed in perfect formation. We were headed slightly to port in the lead position, two escorts out on either flank. I studied the horizon quickly and carefully with the glasses, feeling an immediate and magnified sense of responsibility. No matter that other lookouts were studying the same horizon, including the sonar and radar devices.

The ten minutes to zig change was up before Turner reappeared, and I heard myself saying into the voice tube, "Come right to one six five." My voice sounded normal, but the helmsman's (it was Watson) did not as he repeated, "Come right to one six five, sir."

I knew that he had been startled and probably was already whispering to his partner in the wheelhouse, "Mr. Carr has the bridge." When he came in again, I could detect a slight trace of amusement as he reported, "Steering one six five, sir," and in my most casual voice I replied, "Steady as you go."

It was invigorating and I found myself feeling quite salty and at home as we swung to right and left in front of the group. Turner reappeared shortly but insisted that I continue as OD. He is determined to make a line officer of me, despite my lack of training. And he understood instinctively, too, that this was a proud moment in my sea experience to date.

Later in the afternoon the spotlight shifted to Doc, when we had to transfer him to the commodore's ship to take care of a patient. We used our boat for the transfer and I watched the proceedings through a pair of glasses. That ship is a Liberty job and she is evidently running in ballast, because her decks are far out of water making a nice high climb from the small boat to deck. Chubby Doc, wrapped in his life jacket, looked like he was climbing a penitentiary wall when he started up the swinging rope ladder and he had a bad few minutes maneuvering the ascent. He thinks he likes tankers better. They are closer to the water.

Coming down an hour later, the small boat dropped away as he was about to step into it and left him hanging in mid-air. The boat had to row another quick circle and catch a sufficient swell to get them under him again. He looked desperately relieved when he arrived back aboard.

March 17, 1944

At eleven-thirty tonight we had another general quarters. The *PC-1182* fired a star-shell over a target, and it proved to be a fishing boat. We have our little flurry every night.

Today is St. Patrick's Day—may the good saint preserve us! We expect to make Guantanamo Sunday morning. Weather is much warmer. Saw two long-tailed tropic birds today.

March 18, 1944

Off Cape Maysi at sunset tonight. Temperature of air and water have gone up; and down in our quarters the atmosphere is stuffy and uncomfortable.

We have a new observation deck on the *Haste* which was created when they took off our British radar and left bare the upper part of the little tower behind the bridge where it used to perch. Now, with a railing around it, it resembles a crenellated top of a castle tower, and has been designated the "officers' sun deck."

Spent a couple of hours up there this afternoon in a deck chair. Most of the other officers were lounging about the bridge, some shooting with .22's at flying fish or clumps of seaweed, including Cooney, who fires everything. Our small arsenal contains Thompson .45 submachine guns, Springfield .303 rifles (which have five-shot bolt action and were the standard U.S. Infantry rifle in World War I, and are still being used in this war. It has tremendous power and kick, and Cooney refers to it as the "elephant gun") and Colt .45 automatics, which are our own sidearms.

Cooney, who also has a World War I German Luger, which he says his father "liberated" in 1917, does more firing than any of us. Ramsay practices drawing his .22 target automatic from his shoulder holster like an old-time Western cowboy, and the rest of us shoot if and when we must. It was Cooney's dedication extended to his position as battery officer on the number two gun that complemented Turner's work up on number one and brought us that fantastic shooting score in Bermuda.

Cooney is, on the whole, quite a versatile and unusual guy, who refers to himself as a "real freak" and explains, "I got a commission by direct examination in navigation and seamanship which I boned up on from scratch. My only preservice nautical experience was on a small power boat on Long Island Sound. I never went to the Coast Guard Academy or any other Officer Candidate School; in fact, I never did a step of close-order drill. I went direct from home and hearth to sea duty on Greenland patrol, back there on a date engraved forever in my memory—September 20, 1942."

On one of our early trips, Cooney put a lead on a tropic bird with the elephant gun, fired a single shot, and amazingly the thing fluttered for a moment and then dropped down dead in the water. "That was one helluva shot," said Ramsay later. "It was out there about two hundred yards and we were making a turn at the time."

When we were kidding Cooney about it later in the wardroom, he said, "Now I know why the Ancient Mariner shot the albatross." "Why?" several of us asked. "He was just plain bored," Cooney answered, and shook his head sadly.

March 21, 1944

There has been an aftermath to that accident I had on the ladder during our inspection drills out of New York. At first I just cursed it and held onto it and thought, like Doc, that it would take a certain length of time for the hurt to stop and the subsequent swelling to go away. But it didn't act quite right, and the swelling kept increasing on the way down here until I had a sizable knot where the bump was and my ankle was swollen. So Doc suggested that I go with him to the hospital here on the base and let them take a look at it.

The local medics went over it and finally concluded that I had just knocked the blazes out of a couple of blood vessels, and it would be all right in a couple of weeks but must be strapped up. So every morning the Doc does the necessary strapping and I go around with a bandage like a plaster cast over that ankle.

March 23, 1944

Just walked down the dock to mail a last letter home. It's past eleven and we are sailing early in the morning; but instead of being in their bunks, most of our crew are hanging around the dock, leaning against the gang plank, half-dressed, talking and laughing as though they had a holiday coming instead of a week's trip back with its usual uncertainties.

March 24, 1944

Came out of the harbor at six this morning to find an almost flat sea. The convoy got away well, and we have been making eight and a half knots most of the day.

A few events of yesterday seem worth noting. We were out practicing with an American sub, and after a morning of making runs on her it was decided that she would fire a fish at us, or as Levendoski put it, she would "throw one at us."

The sub submerged and we ran out quite a distance to zigzag on a base course that had been agreed upon earlier. We climbed up on every conceivable eminence on the *Haste*, everyone bent on spotting the torpedo first. It seems hardly necessary to mention that the torpedo had been disarmed—had its charge removed. However, that didn't seem to lessen the excitement.

The sequence of events after that was a cause for both apprehension and confidence. They didn't hit us. Turner, who was OD on the bridge at the time, spotted their periscope at about 3,000 yards —a mile and a half—when they stuck it up for only a second. Thus, when the time came to fire, we had already given the sound operator their bearing and our gear picked them up at about 2,200 yards. At 1,700 yards, they put up their 'scope again, and simultaneously we saw the air slug from a discharged torpedo. We immediately ordered "right full rudder," and several other maneuvers, and the torpedo missed us by fifty yards.

But the uneasy part is that we didn't see the torpedo at all. We only knew from a later report from the sub how near it had come.

Torpedoes being expensive gadgets, we went out in company with the sub (now on the surface) to recover it. I was wondering how we would find anything so low in the water as a drifting torpedo, when suddenly we slowed down and then I had another lesson in the infernal devices. Dead ahead of us the object was floating, not lengthwise but perpendicularly, with the red cap of it out of water. Bobbing up and down, it resembled a huge lipstick projecting from the blue surface.

We ran up as close as possible, then put our small boat out to assist the sub in the recovery. When the boat drew alongside the torpedo, we saw our coxswain jabbing at something with the boat hook. We later learned that about half a dozen sharks were swimming around the projectile. Some of them actually bit at our oars. Nelson, the coxswain, had been contemplating going over the side to put the line on the torpedo, thinking that the cool water would be refreshing, when, to use his own terminology, "a big sonuvabitch came floating up from nowhere."

Before we got our boat in, several sharks appeared around us and we started shooting at them with tommy guns. One came up so high after a piece of meat, his fins were out of water. Bullets from two tommy guns hit him at the same time, and he flipflopped violently and turned over, showing blood. Immediately the other sharks forgot about the meat and went after him. Judging by the swirl of brown shapes, blood, and white bellies, they cannibalistically made short shrift of their companion.

March 25, 1944

We transferred Doc again tonight, just at sundown. The *Alacrity* called over to say that they had what appeared to be a case of acute appendicitis aboard, and after some discussion it was decided to transfer the man over to us for Doc to examine.

The *Alacrity* came alongside just as the sun dove under a low-lying bank of clouds. We hauled the patient aboard from their small boat. He was a thin, sandy-haired kid, looking white and sick even under his heavy tan.

With ominous speed, word came up that Doc had diagnosed the case as "a hot appendix," and we were going to transfer him and the patient to a ship in the convoy that had operating facilities and another doctor. The light was fading fast and the Escort Commander instructed us to run over into the convoy to reach the transport without waiting for her to pull out.

The boat was an Englishman, of about 12,000 tons. There was a short delay when we came in on her starboard side, and she asked us to come around to port. Then, with both of us stopped, we placed the patient in our boat, Doc climbed in and we lowered away. The Captain of the ship had said from his bridge that they'd pull the stretcher up with a "power fall."

Our boat had just started away when the Captain yelled. again, "Bring rubber gloves and needle-holders." Doc had neither, so they had to come back in while his pharmacist mate rushed to procure some. Then, in the half-darkness, they made a second start for the side of the big vessel.

The last line of the convoy had passed before our boat reached the side of the *Rimataka*. For what went on after that, I was dependent upon Cooney and the Captain, who were looking through night glasses. "They've got the lines," they reported, and a few minutes later, "There goes the stretcher . . . Nelson's going up the ladder to steady it." Then, "There goes the Doc!"

At last they seemed to have completed the transfer, and the boat was pulling back toward us. The Englishman called through the loud-hailer, "I am rejoining the convoy," and his props started lashing the water.

There appeared to be a number of women aboard the transport, and, while it was impossible to see in the darkness, word passed somehow, and several among our crew started the usual wolf calls. When the boat was coming in, they yelled at Nelson to know if they had seen any girls.

"Hell, yes," was his reply. "Didn't you see 'em throwin' roses and silk pants down at us?"

March 26, 1944

This morning we ran back to the *Rimataka* to pick up Doc. Word must have passed on the big ship, because when we came around her bow we found the port side alive with onlookers. Every vantage point was crowded as though the sight of a corvette was a real curiosity. The ship had come all the way from New Zealand and is bound for England. Her passengers include a number of nurses. The unfortunate group were not allowed to disembark at Guantanamo, but had to sit out in the bay for three days waiting for the remainder of the convoy. I suppose anything out of the ordinary is a welcome break from the monotony.

When we came in close, I was on the forward gun deck with a pair of glasses and I looked over the throng at the railing in considerable detail. There were several girls in sunsuits and they waved at us and we waved back. For the moment, although we were doing nothing remarkable, we felt like heroes.

Doc reported that he had done the operation himself, that it was a nasty one but seemed to have been successful, and that he was assisted by two doctors, one the ship's doctor, the other a passenger. Doc was quite impressed with the accommodations aboard her (it was his first look at a passenger vessel), and, while the *Rimataka* is obviously old, they say she is very commodious and well furnished.

Doc also whisperingly confided that they had given him a bottle of Scotch.

March 27, 1944

Clear, flat weather again today. We are getting very tanned.

Was on the bridge this afternoon practicing with my .45. Our targets were patches of gulfweed, flying fish, and an occasional Portuguese man-of-war. We didn't hit any of the flying fish, I am glad to say, but it was exciting to pump bullets after their skimming forms. My aim is improving.

March 28, 1944

An ominous mist hangs on the horizon today, although the sea is still calm.

Sighted a dead whale this afternoon, an immense floating bulk forty or fifty feet long. A flock of birds hovered around the carcass and it trailed an oil slick like a tanker.

We ran in close and saw the creature's white underbelly as it rocked in the swell. The eye-sockets were there, but not the eyes. The birds have gotten them, no doubt.

We decided that this was probably the whale the *PC-1182* depth-charged on the way down. She picked up a contact closing the convoy at about four knots, made a run on it, and dropped a full pattern of charges, whereupon the whale surfaced, turned over, and died.

It seems too bad to kill off any more of these great sea mammals, but that is another of the casualties of war.

March 29, 1944

Rough sea and rain. We passed Hatteras this morning. Today is Wednesday. We will probably make New York Friday morning. Doc hears that his patient is doing well. It's a good thing he's over there because in this sea, aboard the *Haste,* he'd be bustin' wide open.

At second chow tonight, all hell broke loose in the wardroom. Doc, seated at the end of the table, was being served stew by the mess boy from a huge silver bowl, when a tremendous wave hit us broadside.

Doc is not especially agile even at best, but under the impact of this wave he was lifted from his seat and hurled across the room. Curiously enough, when he was propelled from his seat, he grabbed the tureen of stew and carried it far enough to empty its contents on the head of Stolzer, the machinist, who was sitting on a bench over by the wall reading a magazine.

Doc was wild-eyed and white; Stolzer was roaring in astonishment while dripping onions, potatoes, gravy, and meat; and the rest of us were doubled up with laughter. That scene was right out of an old Mack Sennett comedy.

We heard yelling from topside, and somebody came down to

report that the boat had gone, and the "Charley Noble," which is the little stack from the galley range, had gone with it. Apparently the boat was "rolled under" and the weight of the water tore it loose.

This always happens when we near New York.

March 31, 1944

When I walked into the Supply Section of Headquarters pier this afternoon with a requisition for another small boat the genial Commander there really let me have it.

"What d'ya do, cut 'em loose and use them for target practice or somethin'," he wanted to know, referring to the fact that we have already lost two boats.

"She was too heavy for her rigging anyway," I reminded him.

"I remember. I remember," he said pleasantly, "but she was all we had at the time." Then he added, "Lemme make a couple of phone calls."

I went about my other business of arranging for the repair and replacement for the Charley Noble stack for the galley, and on my return he told me, "I found one over in Jersey. We'll have it here in a couple of days." Then, suddenly changing his tone, he looked at me sharply and said, "Some of your classmates are having troubles."

Mystified, I waited for his explanation.

"One of 'em, who was on a corvette not in your group (he named the ship), accidentally shot himself through the fleshy part of his leg while he was cleaning his .45. They had to fly him ashore in a helicopter."

"Another one," he continued, squinting at me, "on an attack transport, loading here in the harbor, accidentally left two thousand dollars on top of his safe while he went to a tavern ashore. When he came back and found the crew had staged one of the biggest crap games in Coast Guard history, he had a nervous breakdown and they had to send him to the hospital."

I studied the commander, wondering just what other intent was behind his words and he finally concluded, peering over his pipe and the top of his spectacles, "That's a hazardous post you're occupying, Mr. Carr, but you seem pretty well adjusted. And you look okay."

Then, partially changing the subject, he scrutinized me with a little quizzical grin, and said, "How was the trip otherwise?" I gave a routine reply, and he ended the conversation with, "Keep up the good work. We'll take care of your boat for you. And this one is the right size."

On the way back to the *Haste* I was suddenly aware of a new sense of strength and confidence in my own seagoing performance.

"There's our blimp."

17

> "O, that man might know
> The end of this day's business
> ere it comes."
>
> *Julius Caesar*
> William Shakespeare
> (1564-1616)

April 3, 1944

BACK FROM ANOTHER "FORTY-EIGHT." How many more, I wonder before this business is done with. At least I got home for my birthday. I was thirty-six yesterday. The years are piling up, and somehow birthdays are conducive to speculation. What will next year bring . . . and the next . . . and the next.

It was cold in the train and I kept my overcoat on until we were well started. Outside of Washington the landscape was still gray and cheerless, and the smoke rising from the early morning chimneys mingled with the low-hanging mists. There was very little to see, and at the moment I found my thoughts depressing, so opened the *Washington Post* and the *New York Times*, and had finished scanning both papers by the time we arrived in Baltimore.

A contingent of paratroopers boarded the train. The car was filling rapidly, and one of them asked politely and unnecessarily if he might sit beside me. The train started up again, and in a few minutes the camouflaged buildings of the Martin bomber plant came into view, some of them looking like mobile equipment in their bright painted designs. A line of blunt-nosed bombers glinted in the sunlight.

We passed Edgewood Arsenal, then Havre de Grace and the high trestle over the Susquehanna. A white-coated porter came through the car with a metal basket and I treated myself to a cheese sandwich and a carton of milk.

Soon the dirty industrial scene began; smoky factories, starkly bare manufacturing plants with their grimy outbuildings, foundries, mills and dockyards, stretching almost without interruption from Wilmington to Philadelphia. A bomber could hardly miss hitting a factory or a shipyard along here. Thousands of cranes stick up over the skeletons of ships. Many half-finished ships are tied up along the creeks and canals. "E" awards are flying in abundance. One of our great strengths in this war must be that we've never been bombed. How obvious the ultimate defeat would be to Hitler if he could take this trainride.

With much good-natured banter, some of the paratroopers dismount at Philadelphia. One of them, who is smaller and quieter and older than the rest, is met by his wife and baby. He grabs the baby and kisses it and cries frankly, oblivious of onlookers. Then he remembers us on the train, sees some of us watching from the windows, and still crying, holds up the baby for us to admire. By then, nearly all of us feel like crying a little. Two older women, one of whom might have been his mother, seem unable to do anything more than lovingly pat him on the back over and over. The little group moves away just before the train pulls out. How many times, and in how many places, has that scene, in its many guises and with its many implications, been repeated?

I let my thoughts take over for awhile, remembering my own baby and the two words he has learned to say since my last visit. What a nice thing that one of them is "prit-tee"; it's a little sad that the other one is "bye-bye."

The train roars through New Brunswick and over the Raritan. I crane my neck to the left for a glimpse of the campus of Rutgers, where I spent those two pleasant weeks at the Graduate School of Banking back there in the summer of 1941. In one of the classrooms we used to hear the roar of the trains on this main line to New York.

Trenton comes, then Newark, finally the reed-covered flats behind the Palisades. With a final view of a formation of rock we used to know in geology as a "volcanic plug;" the train plunges into the darkness of the tunnel. Why, I wonder, do people always hurry out of a train, even at the end of the line? The escalator going up into the station is mobbed. People force themselves and their luggage onto it and then scatter in all directions at the top. I turn toward the subway, and invariably stop for a Coke in the Station Pharmacy, one of the stores along the subterranean corridor. It is one of the "habit spots" of my new life.

New York offers a miracle of travel for a nickel. The Express pours me down the tracks to Chambers Street, far downtown. There I wait for the pesky local that runs to South Ferry. The station at South Ferry always smells musty. I don't know why. You'd think the salt air would clean it out. Perhaps it is very old. Certainly it's the dirtiest of the lot.

I have to run for the ferry. With a great rumble of its propellers it starts out of the slip and gives a little blast of its whistle. The tugs dodge out of the way. The harbor is sunlit but misty. Many large ships are riding at anchor. New York harbor is always crowded with big, fine-looking ships. One of them has a PT boat on its decks. Several carry planes.

A sadness settles down upon me as we pass Governor's Island. This is our bridge of sighs, this coming back on the ferry. The ride in the other direction is a ride on the clouds. Returning this way, the cold, hard facts of the future take over. What a difference direction makes in our lives.

I hurry through the ferry station to catch the untidy-looking bus that is marked "Via Bay Street." The bus is crowded with sailors, all looking as dejected as I. All coming back from leave, no doubt. In a few blocks, the driver calls, "Piers seven, eight and nine." We get off and cross the viaduct over the tracks of the Staten Island Rapid Transit Railroad. As we come down the other side, there are the blue-gray piers and the blue-gray ships, dozens of them, and men walking in all directions. The man at the gate hardly looks at my card.

I pass Pier Seven. Pier Eight is the next one. There's the *Haste* on the outboard corner, a thin-steam smoke rising from her stack. Another corvette seems to be berthed in front of her. From this distance, it looks like the *Action*. I turn into the covered pier and walk rapidly toward its outer end.

When I pass the *Action* I wonder if my pay officer friend, Charley Gifford, is aboard. Probably not. Strange how little we see of each other, although we are on the same run. In port our time is exclusively our own. Seagoing men have an unspoken agreement to that effect. A sailor off the *Haste* passes me and says with a smile, "They're waiting for you, Mr. Carr." It's good to have somebody wait for you, even if only to be paid.

The quartermaster on the *Haste* snaps up to a smart salute. I make a little circle around the mast, then come back to the door leading below. I stop into the office for my mail, and the yeoman asks if I had a nice time. My grin must tell even more than my answer in the affirmative. With difficulty I squeeze my two bags down the ladder to the mess deck. Another ladder leads below. I go down awkwardly, leaning backwards to balance the weight of the luggage. A turn to the right and there is my room, empty, the beds made up neatly, the electric fan running.

I leave my bags and walk over to the wardroom, but find it empty. Everyone is ashore somewhere, either on leave or on business. The place gets a rest in port. Back in my room, I take off my overcoat and hang it in the closet. This may be the last time I'll need it; it'll be spring when we get back. I open my suitcase and stow my clean clothes away.

I lay out my khakis and start to change back to the war again.

April 4, 1944

The talk here is very encouraging. Turner said he had been in conversation with several of the ordnance men, both here and elsewhere, and they all seem to think that the corvettes will be on this coast for the duration. The reason seems to be that we're both too large and too small for the more active combat areas. We're too big for the work in the Mediterranean and too small for the long hauls in the Atlantic and Pacific. We don't have enough armament to fight ships, and not enough anti-aircraft to combat planes in a "hot" area like the waters around Italy, so the consensus is that they'll keep us at convoying on this coast for a long time—maybe even after the war with Germany is brought to a close.

April 5, 1944

It has been snowing here all day, and a thick gray sky seems to hang just over our masts. This afternoon we went across on the ferry in a station wagon—an extra armed guard with an automatic rifle in the front seat and the driver and I wearing our .45s—to get some money from the Federal Reserve Bank, and the old tub was blowing and whistling throughout the whole trip. But then, she hasn't got a radar to reach "seeing fingers" through the fog for her.

April 6, 1944

Left New York last night for our eighth trip to Guantanamo. Throughout the day, snow had fallen and appearances indicated that we would have a bad time forming up, but just before midnight the sky blew clear and the moon came out.

When we backed away from our pier at three-thirty, the moon was hanging over the hills of Staten Island and the harbor was glittering with light.

We had a pilot aboard who had been called in anticipation of bad weather, and he made a great arc around a number of loaded tankers lying at anchor and took us down the main channel. The big tankers waiting for their convoys cast heavy black shadows over the surface. Solitary lights shone on them, giving out the only signs of life. They seemed to be sleeping the good harbor sleep that is a boon to both ships and men.

The sky was still clear this morning and the ocean has been comparatively calm. We have thirty-three ships in the group, one of them a large French passenger ship named the *Cuba*.

April 7, 1944

Our dog, Rip, went over the hill in New York a couple of months ago, and we haven't heard from him since. The boys looked around for something to replace him, and the next thing we knew we had two puppies aboard. They both lived, somehow, through their stepped-on stage and have now officially taken their places as the ship's mascots.

Their names are "Skipper" and "Suggee," and they are both of some breed that is smallish in size. I should probably make that plural, since their breeds are definitely mixed and uncertain. Skipper's only distinction is that he looks more like a cinnamon-colored mop than anything with legs. Suggee, who must have some black Scottie in his ancestry, is much more individualistic. Among his idiosyncrasies is his liking for coffee, which he drinks in great quantities. But only with cream and sugar. Leave out those two ingredients and he will turn up his nose at the brew. He also has a voracious appetite for raw onions. Added to these two quirks, he is taken with fits of barking at intervals and will yap for an hour.

Suggee was taken sick last trip, and for awhile it appeared that he would have to be shot for distemper. There was an atmosphere of gloom on the mess deck as thick as fog, until he recovered.

April 9, 1944

Today was a gray, drab, colorless Easter. It is quite a contrast to last year, when we were still in Florida.

There was a thin sunlight this morning, but it faded out gradually as the day wore on, and tonight it's raining and the seas are rising. We must be in about the same latitude as Savannah, but we're far out.

This morning in the daily sub reports, we received word that there are two subs ahead of us. One of them, by our reckoning, should be almost in our path by morning. This was confirmed by a later report from a shore station that had charted that sub as moving across our track. The shore station picks up a radio broadcast from the sub and is able to tell by the use of the direction finder where it originated.

We are keeping an exceptionally sharp lookout tonight, and at five-thirty in the morning we are going to general quarters. The Skipper is playing this one safe.

This Easter, I guess, is in tone with general world conditions. There must be hundreds of thousands of men in the world having a worse Easter than we—and it is good to remind ourselves of it.

April 10, 1944

With the moon still high and the first faint glimmerings of daylight in the east, we went to general quarters at five-thirty this morning. I had hardly taken my position on the bridge, when a radio message came in and it became my job to go down and decode it.

At the decoding machine in the wardroom, at the bottom of the ship, and with everyone else topside, is a lonely place to be at such an hour. The message was from the Commander, Gulf Sea Frontier, telling us that another "df" had fixed the sub as directly in our path, and cautioning us to keep a strict lookout. Copy of the message, it said, had been sent to the RAF at Nassau where, undoubtedly, planes would be sent out.

When I took the message topside to the Captain, the spot of daylight had broadened and the first dim shapes of the convoy were appearing in the distance. Our men stood tensely at general quarters, guns turned on, depth charges set on "ready." Slowly, as the minutes passed, the surface of the sea emerged from the darkness. And nothing happened.

At six-twenty, word was passed to secure and everyone breathed easier. Another little crisis had passed. Back aft one of the firemen was lifting the night covers from the engine room skylight.

Later in the morning, several planes appeared. One of them came in almost at mast level and signaled, "How is everything?" We were glad to be able to signal back, "All's well."

April 11, 1944

Had a long talk with Tex Phillips on the bridge tonight. He is standing our eight-to-twelve OD watch.

Tex is a former All-American football player from Southern Methodist. In 1936 he participated in the Rose Bowl game against Stanford. He loves to tell about it, and tonight he gave me almost a play-by-play description.

I became so enthralled with the idea that I had met and talked with a genuine "Rose Bowler" that Phillips, evidently suspecting that my interest was more than casual, looked at me sheepishly and said, "Hell, Carr, don't get too excited about that game—I was only in there for the last five minutes."

Phillips is a big, amiable guy with a wide grin and a slow drawl. In keeping with Texas tradition, he can twirl a rope and has often diverted us with some of his tricks. One day Levendoski was standing on deck a good twenty feet away, with several stanchions between the two. Tex let go with his rope and threw it clear of the stanchions and over Levendoski.

Tex is also an excellent shot with a pistol, and has some strong southwestern characteristics beneath his good-natured exterior. Not long ago, our newest mess boy refused to do any work. Simply said we could put him in the brig or do whatever we wished, but he was on a work strike. Tex asked permission to handle the case. He picked up a belaying pin, found the recalcitrant and took him into the head for a "chat." We never knew exactly what happened, but the mess boy came out without a scar on him, but willing and eager to work.

April 12, 1944

"It's the same on every ship," Turner was saying this afternoon, "after awhile, the main thing you're fighting is boredom."

210

We were complaining because our lookouts had been so lackadaisical about reporting a plane that had come in overhead. Every time we near land, there is a dangerous tendency to "let down" in efficiency.

"Someday," said Cooney, "a periscope will pop up right out there and they'll all be so goddamned tongue-tied they won't be able to report it." The point was partially illustrated in what happened tonight.

We were coasting along easily at nine-thirty, waiting momentarily to hear that Cuba had been picked up on the radar. (Our new radar has a range of 42,000 yards—twenty-one miles—and has been working beautifully.) The alarm went off and Turner just missed me as he vaulted down from his bunk.

We got topside in time to see two plane flares dying over the horizon. The radar reported two targets, one quite close less than 1,000 yards, and one at 18,000 yards, nine miles away. We ran in on the nearer target and the Captain gave orders to illuminate with star-shells.

At the command, "Commence firing," we heard the shell rammed home and the breech closed and the voice of the gun captain singing out, "Ready One." The white shell roared out like a shooting star, but the parachute flare failed to appear.

"Ready Two," the deep voice rang out, and the second explosive burned its trajectory through the night. But still no flare.

"Goddamn it, they're duds," Turner said.

We were closing the target fast and the Captain gave "Cease firing" as we turned away and started searching the area with night glasses. Then the radar reported that the second and larger target was closing in fast and was now 16,000 yards away. We turned our attention to it.

Cooney, in the chartroom, was plotting the bearings and very soon he said, "The target's 7,000 yards away. We're runing a reciprocal course and going like hell," which meant that we and the target were headed at top speed directly for each other. At 4,500 yards we made out the object, and it was obviously a tanker. We challenged her with a light, and immediately got an identifying number. The Captain sent over a course for her to steer to keep away from the convoy, and that phase of the night's proceedings was closed.

As nearly as we could reconstruct events, what happened was in the following sequence. A plane picked up a lone tanker on its radar and dropped flares thinking it might be a sub. Phillips, on the bridge, saw the flares and thought somebody had started shooting. At the same time the radar got a water echo instead of a real contact ahead of us, which became our first target. Then we picked up the tanker and closed in for the identification.

But as to the duds—we discovered that our overanxious gun crew had gotten into the wrong "ready box" in the dark and had fired antipersonnel shrapnel by mistake. We had never even gotten off a star shell. Reminded me of the night in Bermuda when we were firing star shells level at the target instead of high for illumination.

The Captain intends to have a night practice down here to iron out the mistake.

April 15, 1944

There is a vicious shark story current here. It concerns a PC on the Panama run that got in the same night we did.

On the way up, they lost two men overboard in a number four sea, and the Captain and another officer went overboard with knives to assist them. They found that one of the men had a horrible back wound where a shark had bitten out a chunk of his flesh.

Just as they seemed assured of getting them both back to the ship, the sharks came back in force and attacked the bleeding man. Testifying to the strength of the creatures, they dragged him out of the grasp of his would-be rescuers and pulled him under the surface. Nothing further was seen of him. The second man and the officers were hauled safely aboard.

Doc got the story from the hospital here, where the second man is recovering from shock and hysteria. Prior to that time, we had heard all sorts of wild tales but the true version itself is tragically pathetic.

April 16, 1944

We took partial vengeance on the shark clan today. We were firing and drilling all morning and part of this afternoon, and in the several hours we had to wait before night firing, the Captain decided we might do some fishing.

We rigged several shark-hooks on a good stout line and threw them off the stern, meanwhile reducing speed to almost nil. Several sharks began to sniff around the lines, but we thought nothing much of it until Levendoski yelled, "I've got one," and started hauling in on his line. Sure enough, he had a six-foot shark hooked solidly in the mouth.

When we pulled him up under the stern, we knocked the daylight out of him with a tommygun, and with the first two shots he showered all of us with water and blood. When he seemed thoroughly subdued, we hauled him around to the side and got a couple of grappling hooks into him and dragged him aboard Some of the crew sliced at him with their knives as he came over the side.

Levendoski cut off his jaw, containing the three sets of razor-sharp teeth (and I do mean razor-sharp; I had an opportunity of examining them), which he is preparing to skin down and dry as a souvenir. Doc came running up to me with the creature's heart in his hand to show me how it was still beating. The organ was definitely pumping spasmodically as he held it. It was just like a confounded doctor to enjoy that sort of thing. Meanwhile the whole ship had turned out to watch the dissection.

Suddenly there was another yell from the stern and they had a second shark on a hook. This one was about a foot smaller than the first, and we went through the same process of shooting him while he flopped around under the fantail. As he came over the side, we threw back the remainder of the first victim and the knife-wielders went to work anew.

Tonight we had an unpleasant sequel. Tex had cut off a steak of shark meat and asked the steward to fry it for him. The steward got violently sick in the process because the meat was still working and quivering when he threw it into the pan. Tex finished frying it himself and brought it down to the wardroom. One small taste was enough for all of us.

During the day we received a radio report in plain language stating that a ship was torpedoed about three degrees due east of New York (180 miles).

Tonight we had more firing practice and now we're on our way back to our berth. I'll be glad to get in. This has been a long, hot, wearing day. The decks were so hot today they burned right through our shoes. Coming from one climate to another, the sun down here takes a lot out of us.

I did pretty well back on the gun deck on my cot last night, from one o'clock until six, when the engine crew started making such a racket they woke me up. Then I moved down below, although sleeping down in our quarters is next to impossible.

April 17, 1944

This is our last day in Guantanamo. It seems incredible that we had snow on our decks two weeks ago. The temperature here continues to mount.

For awhile we were berthed at a new dock called "Repair Dock Number One." This dock is built part way up a lagoon-like body of water that is formed by the fingers of land that jut out into Guantanamo Bay. The dock is long and low and has a gigantic crane mounted on it which never seems to be used. As a matter of fact, the huge piece of machinery still wears its christening red lead and seems not to have been wholly put together.

On the other side of the pier is a ponderous floating drydock, whose grey-painted sides effectively afford a barrier to whatever breeze might try to approach from that direction. Across the lagoon on the opposite side is a high ridge of land covered with cottages and green vegetation, forming another windbreak. Thus the *Haste* sweltered all day in the flat, windless area below, and at night its decks were almost unbearable.

When we rode back to the ship on the buses, the cool wind from the hills would be sweeping across the upper levels and rustling the palm trees around the officers' quarters. Then, when we dismounted and started down the embankment, the heat would come up and the breeze die away with every step, until by the time we reached the ship our clothes would be soaked with perspiration.

Several times I walked from the ship to the Navy canteen, my walk taking me up to the head of the lagoon, where a crude flight of steps was cut into the coral rock, forming an access to the habitated level.

On one of those trips I stopped in the coppery sunlight to watch a pelican diving for fish in the shallow water. It brought back memories of my lunchtimes in Florida when I used to walk down to Bayfront Park to witness the same spectacle. That was when the pelican became one of my favorite sea birds.

Whenever I saw those ungainly-looking aquatic fish-eaters I would fondly recall a little jingle which had been a favorite with my father who used to repeat it to me when I was a child. While I learned later it did not depict this odd creature very accurately, it was a whimsical little rhyme, and I remeembered my father's recitation of it with affection.

A funny old bird is the pelican
Whose beak will hold more than his bellican,
He holds food in his beak to last him a week,
But I'm damned if I see how the hellican.

Quite by accident, but also with careful, patient, and fascinated observation in Bayfront Park, and along the close-to-the-shore piers of McArthur Causeway, I had discovered that the pelican's beak is not a beak at all in the sense that a kingfisher, or heron, or egret has a beak. It is rather a distensible pouch, a magnificent fishing apparatus, which balloons out like a net as the pelican strikes the surface in its dive, and traps a gallon or two of water and whatever else might be there, including fish.

Then when the bird emerges, the water drains out through a small round opening on either side of what might be described as its chin, at the base of the pouch, leaving only the "goodies" inside, which he then swallows.

My interest in the bird led me to a reference book where I had learned that the pelican is one of the oldest bird species on earth, and has been here for some thirty or forty million years.

"Bravo, brown pelican!" I thought, as I resumed my ascent of the rustic steps. "You have been here a long time and you are a very clever bird, but I'll still always connect you with the jingle!"

When we returned from our drills last night, they put us at the main dock, which is bordered by an open stretch of paved roadway and numerous shops and offices. There is quite a wide reach of open water on the outside of this dock, and the wind has a clear sweep from the first high land at the head of the bay, which is a good distance away. But the temperature has gone up so high today, it seems to have offset all advantage of location. We are thoroughly ready to sail.

April 18, 1944

We drink a beer down here called "Hatuey" (pronounced "AH-tway," with accent on the first syllable). Hatuey is a trade name of the brew, which is manufactured by the Bacardi Company of Santiago. The stuff is stronger than the average American beer and is very popular among the servicemen.

Last night, as we came out of the harbor, we saw the "Hatuey boat" going out—a dirty little schooner that plies up and down the coast between Santiago and Guantanamo Bay, bringing down cargoes of beer. The small craft has a high stern like a Chinese junk, and against the distant conical-shaped mountains, its appearance was decidedly Oriental.

We received a report yesterday that the sub which torpedoed the ship off New York has already been sunk. Three DE's did the job within thirty-six hours and brought back seven survivors to prove it. That's fast work. I think we are all getting better in our jobs.

April 24, 1944

The ocean is alive with phosphorus tonight. None of us has ever seen anything like it before.

The ship's wake is always outlined in white, but tonight the glow is on all sides and extends some distance away from us. A strong wind is blowing, and each wave is a silver streak in the darkness. At times the effect is like a score of searchlights playing across the wave tops. The coruscations and flashes are visible for at least half a mile and create a sort of visibility. On the bridge a man's face takes on a greenish pallor. And this on a dead-black, starless night, with rain coming down in a steady drizzle to add to the overcast. No wonder the ancients thought they saw spectres.

April 25, 1944

We sighted the New York sea buoy at one-thirty today. We pulled it out of a hat, so to speak. A heavy fog had settled down and visibility was limited to about a hundred yards.

Our radar had picked up a small "pip" at about three and a half miles. At about the same time, the commodore had asked us over the TBS to please endeavor to find the buoy and keep him informed. We tracked down the first target and it proved to be a fishing boat. We picked another close by and it, too, turned out to be a little yawl with sails furled, sitting out there in the gloom. The third target was the buoy. We heard its moaning lament even before we could distinguish it.

But that was not the end of our troubles. In a couple of minutes, whistles sounded back in the convoy and the Captain, cocking his ear, said, "Did you hear that—three short blasts? That means, 'I'm going full astern.'"

For corroboration the TBS started buzzing and the commodore came in excitedly with, "We have just had a near miss with an independent—a very near miss! This ship is coming down the starboard side of the convoy and she nearly got us. Please send somebody back to find out who she is and get her out of here. I repeat—please send out somebody to find out who she is and get her out of there."

We tried and failed to get the other escorts on the TBS, and we were too far away to do the job ourselves. Finally we got one escort very faintly and he promised to relay our message, but in that fog its immediate execution was doubtful. It seemed far more probable that the independent would bounce off every ship in the convoy before the escorts managed to head her off.

A big convoy showed up to starboard on the radar dial and we could hear the faint sound of their whistles. They evidently were trying to run up the channel at the same time we were and the result promised to be something novel in the way of confusion.

April 26, 1944

We're going into drydock someplace tomorrow. We don't know just where yet—maybe Brooklyn, maybe Hoboken. We're coming out again on Friday and I am due another forty-eight-hour leave.

Picked up a couple of rather encouraging pieces of information—including the fact that we may be going to Key West next trip. Apparently after eight trips to Guantanamo, they want to give us a change. It gets tiresome going on the same run all the time, and I like Key West very much.

Ramsay says he's coming down to Washington, but he's pretty changeable, so I won't bother about it until it happens.

April 27, 1944

Writing is more difficult than usual tonight despite the fact that the *Haste* is in port. Reason: she is sitting up in drydock with only a few much-too-small-looking blocks wedged along her keel. When we look over the side at the sheer drop of fifty feet or more, we have a sudden and uncomfortable sensation of height.

We have had a busy afternoon. We were brought over here by two tugs which came alongside over at Staten Island at two-thirty

When they had finished installing us, it was five o'clock. And now we are sitting up here like a cardboard toy with a wooden base awaiting the arrival of the workmen.

A grey, slanting rain was falling throughout the afternoon—the last cold rain of winter, and we were all thoroughly drenched enroute. The tugs, whose names were *Swatane* and *Sassacus*, were lashed on each side of our stern and they ran us through a gauntlet of shipping.

When we neared the Brooklyn shore, we peered ahead for an open and likely looking space which might be our drydock, but there didn't seem to be any. It was all up to the tugs anyway; we had no power of our own and our rudder was lashed amidships. We were no better than the barges they haul around. The tug captains kept up a running line of chatter across our stern. Once the starboard captain spotted a tug-and-tow crossing our track and gave two blasts on his whistle. Instead of replying with two blasts, the stranger came back with one, indicating that he intended to continue across in front of us.

The starboard captain yelled to the other to go astern, and they both started backing down to slow us up. Peering through his glasses, he yelled again, "That's that goddamned *George Harris*," and they both joined in the vituperation. Evidently a tug captain's life has certain moments not unlike a taxi driver's.

You would have sworn they couldn't get us into the place they got us into. For a long while we couldn't see the entrance even as we approached it. Then we spotted it running off at a slight angle to the right and looking like a canal. The port tug pushed us around and we squeezed in. Some distance ahead the narrow channel opened into a sort of basin and there must have been a hundred ships in there, parked like cars on a lot.

Big, ponderous ships were sitting on all sides as we came in with propellers showing the height of three men, and rudders the height of four. People were peering down at us from their decks. Corvettes, I always notice, seem to be a curiosity. Perhaps it is our baby size that attracts attention. In this place we were like a two-story building beside a lot of skyscrapers.

We were sidled and shoved and pushed up to the end of the place where there was a smaller drydock, and there we sat and waited until the *Action*, which was ahead of us, was floated off and dragged out by the tail. My friend, Charlie Gifford, was on deck and we yelled a couple of greetings. They're sailing for Guantanamo in the morning.

They maneuvered us in finally and pumped the water out. Then we discovered to our dismay that the only way off the ship was by means of a wooden ladder that reached from the bottom of the dry-dock. The arrangement looked suicidal at first. We were certain that by morning the place below would be littered with our broken bodies. After we tried it once, we found that our fears—like most fears—were exaggerated. The ladder was wide, the rungs stout, and the angle not so steep as it appeared. It was only when we mounted the rail and backed onto it that we experienced a vertiginous moment.

After supper a little party of us climbed down to take a look at the *Haste* out of water. That was an experience! There she sat above us—slimy, green-encrusted, and dripping. The amazing thing was her lines, which are like a yacht's, and the enormous height to her from the floor of the deck. We noted her bilge keels, which are like two enormous flukes running along the sides under water to give her extra stability, and which probably kept us from capsizing during the storm last September. We also observed the salt water intake covered with metal grating.

The porthole of my pay office was way up there like a window in the shoulder of a truncated building. The sailors were already beginning to go on liberty, and each one let out a dismayed yell as he came to the top of the ladder. But they all came down. Just as I'm coming down tomorrow with my two suitcases.

Dunbar, Levendoski, and I just returned from a sortie outside the Yard into Brooklyn. In some respects it was like going ashore in a foreign port. The sights, the sounds, even the language struck us as strange. The place seems to bear no resemblance to New York City.

We just climbed up the ladder to come aboard. A number of steel-helmeted workmen were already milling around below the ship. The ladder looked twice as tall when we peered up through the glare of the arclights. The rungs seemed awfully far apart, and our agility had not been helped in the least by the friendly tavern we had found on Fourth Avenue. When we made the final manoeuver at the top, stepping around the ladder to the ship's rail and then to the deck, assisted by the worried CPO on duty, we breathed a sigh of relief and Dunbar, puffing slightly, peered back over the side and mused, "Erie Basin! They sure named this place right!"

"You ain't just a-bird-turdin," Levendoski assured him as we headed below.

I had already confirmed the fact that the name of our berth is the Erie Basin, and we're all in agreement that it is an eerie place to be sleeping.

April 28, 1944

Traveling home today on another "forty-eight." Spent long, restful minutes staring out of the lounge car windows.

The clouds of good weather were over the hills, and the fruit trees beside the tracks were wearing their pink and white blossoms.

My heart was lighter than it has been for weeks. Maybe it is the inevitable resurgence of spring.

Doc is left (momentarily) hanging from the rope ladder

18

> "What next morn's sun may bring,
> forebear to ask;
> But count each day that comes by
> gift of chance
> So much to the good."
>
> *Odes to Thaliarchus*
> Horace (65-9 B.C.)

May 3, 1944

IT'S DEAD QUIET ON THE ship tonight and there's a certain sadness in that quiet. The original *Haste* crew has been shattered for good. Five of our officers received transfer orders last night. They're all ashore somewhere having a last fling together. I stayed aboard to get their pay accounts ready so they can take them along tomorrow when they leave.

Went down to our quarters just now to get my pipe and the sadness has crept in there, too. I could feel it in the signs of hasty packing, in the disarray of clothing and gear, and in the discarded articles thrown into the trash. It was all symbolic of the disarray of human lives in connection with the war.

It is bothersome having to say goodbye to all these guys. Funny how you get attached to people—even people you wouldn't ordinarily pick out for friends. There is something about shipboard life that does that.

A ship is a strange thing, and as I saw the worst side of it (or surely almost the worst side!) aboard the *Condor*, I have seen another side aboard the *Haste*.

I suppose we hated many things about the *Haste* when we first came aboard; and she certainly has made us miserably uncomfortable many times. But her antics were inflicted upon her by the sea, and she always carried us through. Somehow, without realizing it, a transformation takes place when you're on sea duty and you get to

221

love a ship and the men aboard her. But it's like a lot of other affections; you only become fully aware of it when you're faced with a separation. Those birds ashore tonight are probably drowning a lot of sentiment in their liquor.

Pangle's going to New Orleans for a frigate; Levendoski is catching a transport over at Kearney, New Jersey. Phillips, Janes, and Dunbar are going to the Academy at New London; for just what they don't know yet. That leaves just five of us out of the original gang.

There are no signs that I'm to be transferred any time in the near future. Ramsay apparently didn't discuss me at all with Headquarters; and besides, my case there is handled entirely by the Finance Office. There is a major change coming up in the pay system effective July 1, and with that in sight I don't think there will be much changing of pay officers. It seems to be one more reason why I'll be on here for some time. But you never can tell.

We'll be going out on this trip with only five line officers aboard, including myself. Cooney's on "trip leave" and one of our new ensigns is away at fire-control school. This trip will be a "dilly," as old Tex would say.

May 4, 1944

Last night I sat in a restaurant-bar waiting to call Dee to say goodbye before we sailed. As far as anyone in the place was concerned, I was just a lonely lieutenant who kept ordering beer and sipping it down in slow, deliberate gulps.

Conversation blows around a bar like surf around a beach. Most of it is equally ineffectual. People gurgle and bubble about imaginary ills, swollen troubles, and despairs that are largely a product of inebriation. Nearly all of it is introspective. There were few to note whether I was deep in my beer or just filling up time.

But the clock in back of the bar moved with annoying slowness. The radio program filled up the minutes, stretched them out, and gave them a fullness they actually did not possess. They were measured by the programs as miles by a speedometer. The hands moved with calculated and almost demonical casualness.

I'd had several beers and a few more made no difference. Occasionally I saw people looking at me, but their faces were as empty as the unencumbered areas of the counter. Most of them were civilians. I was experiencing that mixture of misery, self-righteousness, and anger which sometimes settles upon us before sailing time, and I wanted no companionship with strangers.

The fat bartender watched my glass like a hawk, and finally I pushed it out to him again, moving it through a river of suds that sat on the mahogany bar. He slopped another one down and slid a dime back from the change that was also immersed in the liquid. Then the inveterate cloth commenced its semicircular motions and I picked up my glass as if obedient to a spoken signal. The bartender mopped the counter dry and moved along the bar, driving the glasses as he went.

The hands of the clock had finally reached ten-fifteen. In looking at them this time, I noticed two bouquets of snowballs that sat in vases among the pyramids of glasses behind the bar. The dimpled whiteness of the blossoms reminded me of one thing—a certain white evening dress my wife had owned when we were married. I remembered how devastatingly lovely she had looked in that dress, and how I had hated it when the cleaners had finally ruined it.

At ten-thirty I could stand it no longer. The agreed time was ten-forty-five, but she would probably be at home. I left the bar and went to the phone booth. My voice seemed to resound in that small enclosure when I said, "Operator, I want to call Washington, D.C."

In a few minutes I heard her say, "Hello," and then, after I deposited the necessary coins she said, "Hi, darling," and the softness and sweetness of her seemed to come through the phone and envelop me.

The conversation was mixed up and hurried, and I said little that I wished to say. The mundanity of little affairs crept in to dilute everything. But it was always like that. Yet in the end I could only remember how she said, "Of course I'll wait for you," as though my inquiry had been silly and childish. But I always ask it, and she always comes back with her wonderful assurance.

When I left the phone booth, I walked deliberately through the bar and scowled at the circle of drinkers. I pushed open the front door and stepped out into the misty night. A light rain was falling, and I turned up my collar and felt a slight comfort at the desolateness.

May 7, 1944

This is our third day out, enroute to Key West. We have five visiting naval officers aboard. All of them have been thoroughly seasick. Weather has not been too good. Last night Hatteras sent out its milder devils of wind and sea.

Several of these officers have made sea trips before, but never on a corvette. They have already acknowledged the difference.

We had a convoy of nine ships until two of them dropped back last night. This seems like child's play after the big groups we took to Guantanamo.

May 10, 1944

From the bridge of the *Haste* at sunset tonight I looked through the glasses at the familiar sights of Miami Beach. We were only four miles offshore.

Naturally, it was the upper end of the Beach that interested me most because we used to live there. There was the Broadmoor, one of the newest and farthest north of the beach hotels, where we had spent our honeymoon. Beyond it, apart from a few scattered homes, there was little on the beach side but sand dunes and mounds of sea grapes, reaching all the way to the tidal inlet known as Baker's Haulover, the former haven of a swank fleet of tourist fishing boats. Left of the Broadmoor were the two smaller hotels, the open stretch of public park and the drugstore at 71st Street. Left again was the McFadden-Deauville and then the white structure of the Tower. In the background were the radio towers of the upper causeway, and somewhere, out of sight among the Australian pines and coconut palms, the Blue Ocean luxury apartment and villas— first home of our little son.

When I first strolled up the sand from the Broadmoor in 1941, I was certain it would be some years before we returned to Florida. Next year we would find ourselves living there! When, eleven months later, we bundled Roland Junior and started north in the car, that seemed definitely the end of my association with the state. But on the *Haste's* first trip the towers of Miami were sighted, and now I had the glasses turned on them again. The only thing wrong was Dee could not see them with me.

The *Haste* was much closer to shore than last year, and I could even make out a few bathers frisking in the surf. As we turned out

224

again on our "zigzag," the downtown hotels came into view, looking like a cluster of crystalline stalagmites on a cavern floor.

Darkness was accelerated by a rain squall, and then it became obvious that Greater Miami had abandoned the blackout. Lights began to spring on—red, yellow and green—and the great miracle city of the Keys was glowing like a tiara.

Evidently the war is nearly over down here as far as they are concerned. Even the Navy's Dupont Building was brilliantly aglow over in Miami. Somebody suggested we ought to drop a couple of shells over there to let them know there's still a war going on. In the darkness, several officious patrol boats, not much bigger than our dinghy, challenged us, and we answered them grudgingly, not saying some of the things we would have liked.

May 11, 1944

Looking as inconspicuous as a city can look from the sea, Key West came out of the flat calm haze today. A half-dozen water towers, three radio stations, and some flat roofs make up its distant aspect. Closer inspection reveals an old fort, a strip of sand beach and some green trees. But if you were ten miles away you might pass it all by and never see any of it.

It is the popular impression that Key West is the last of the keys to the westward, but that is a prodigious error. Keys crawl like worms across the horizon in all directions. Key West is apparently only the largest of them.

The Navy has quite a base down here, and a number of ships and several submarines were in the harbor. Just as it had been last year, not a palm was rustling as we pulled up to the dock. This place is a burial ground of the winds. Big, soft-looking clouds sit out on the edge of the horizon as if warding off all trace of wind.

We'll be here two days.

May 13, 1944

One of the visiting naval officers and I were roaming around the town in search of a present for him to take home to his family. I knew from my experience the year before that there is very little of value to be purchased in Key West, and finally he, too, became convinced and we just ambled up and down Duvall Street, the main thoroughfare.

At about this time, I remembered "Sloppy Joe's," which is the restaurant where Ernest Hemingway used to hang out when he lived in Key West, and I volunteered to show it to Barron, although we had no intention of lingering and doing any drinking. We heard, incidentally, that "Sloppy Joe's" was one of the few places in town that still operated on an honest basis and gave full value in its drinks. We headed in that direction, slowly, haltingly, peering at all the sights as we went along. The place is located at one end of Duvall Street and was on our route back to the ship.

When we stepped inside we were not immediately aware of what was going on, except that there was a crowd back of a partitioned section in front of the bar, and there was an orchestra of some kind playing back there.

We strolled the length of the bar, looking at the crude murals on the partition; one of Jack Dempsey in his prime, under which appeared the title "The Manassa Mauler," and another of a nude Cuban dancer, with a shawl behind her, labeled "Mama Inez." The noise on the other side of the partition increased and we went around to have a look. It was there we found the jam session.

A cadaverous-looking character with a beard hovered over the piano beating out something hot. A saxophonist in his undershirt was salaaming while he played, and a drummer was slashing at his instrument. In a semicircle around them were a number of people in slacks and fatigue clothes of various kinds, who were apparently some of the nightclub entertainers. A .crowd of onlookers had gathered, occupying the chairs in the place and standing in the doorway leading to the bar.

The pianist sounded so good that Barron and I ordered a beer and sat down at one of the vacant tables. Thus began the strangest two hours either of us had ever spent.

The bearded character at the piano was obviously an artist in his line. He was improvising at random, but he and the other two musicians clearly knew what they were doing—and they were turning out good music. The pianist wore a green sport shirt, yellow slacks, and beige suede shoes. His hair, thin in the center, was long over his ears. He was in a lather of perspiration which had soaked through his shirt. The saxophonist, too, was dripping wet. They never stopped playing. It was all one long number.

Then we recognized the entertainers from "Duffy's" over at

one side—the three girls we had seen perform last night, all wearing dark glasses and slacks. Everyone was clapping and stamping in rhythm to the music. Finally, the bearded one at the piano finished up with a bang and jumped up. Everyone applauded enthusiastically, and then another individual disentangled himself from among the entertainers and ambled over to the piano. He was a slight, bespectacled gentleman, also casually arrayed in sport clothes. He sat down, fumbled a moment, then started playing very slowly at first. The tall, bearded character grabbed a bottle of beer, drank it down in one long gulp, then pushed the drummer out of the way and sat down at the drums. Within two minutes it became evident that he was even more adept at the drums. The pianist turned out to be equally as accomplished as his predecessor, and the threesome started again.

This sort of thing went on for an hour, the music getting faster and more intricate. A swarthy, heavy-set woman in the crowd, who could easily have passed as a native, came over to our table. She was a bit tight, but seemed harmless. "How do you boys like it?" she wanted to know, swaying with the rhythm. We said we liked it. Then, without sitting down, she proceeded to fill us in on some of the details about the musicians.

We learned that the first pianist was Buddy Satan, who in two weeks would be joining Tony Pastor's band as drummer. The man now at the piano was the composer of "Music, Maestro, Please" and other such hits. He was in Key West only because one of the Broadway entertainers, who was down here for a couple of weeks trying out some new numbers, was his "chick."

Before she walked away, our informant told us that she had recently purchased one of the night spots known as "Habana Madrid" and we must be sure to come over. She was really from Miami, she said, where she owned a hotel, but it was good to come down to Key West and let her hair down; and besides, there was pretty good money to be made.

The din incredibly kept up, and to our amazement a third pianist took over. Satan left the drums and Mitchell, the composer, the piano; other musicians appeared miraculously to take their places. Mitchell and Satan sat on either side of the "chick" and the jive assumed a rhumba tempo. In a few minutes Satan, still dripping as though he had climbed out of a tub, was doing an amazingly professional rhumba with the girl friend. She, too, danced with professional ease and a little more swing to her hips than was necessary. One of the native onlookers—a pouchy, fiftyish individual—started to dance by himself in imitation, and the onlookers howled.

Finally it was time to leave and head back to the ship. I agreed with Barron's comment that we probably couldn't have found as good a show in New York; and I doubt if Hemingway ever "sat in" on a better session in that little joint.

May 18, 1944

Just made our most undramatic pickup of Buoy Zebra. How anticlimactic it seemed against the background of most of our winter arrivals!

Seas are fairly calm, but the spring haze holds a circle around us at about 3,000 yards. Without stress, with not much anticipation, with almost the casualness of routine, the walls of our circle pushed back and the insignificant stick of floating metal, so unimpressive in size, so tremendous in import, came into view. The wailing which has formerly characterized its advent was reduced to almost a spring chirp.

The heavy dullness of monotony has characterized most of this trip, brought on, no doubt, by the transfer of so many of our shipmates. We even lost Hofstra last trip. He was ordered ashore at his own request after making eight trips with us, and is now sitting somewhere out in Long Island. I miss our talks and the kidding. Once when I came aboard, he said to me in a loud voice when I entered the wardroom, "Mr. Carr, I trust you had a satisfactory sexual experience while on leave." When I grinned in reply, he added, "You know, Carr, everyone has his own way of doing it, and if it is satisfactory to the two people involved, that is all that is necessary." Then he had slapped me on the back, laughed like a Dutchman and a doctor, and we had changed the subject.

Turner is in his bunk with a bad case of amoebic dysentery, and the Captain has had a recurrence of tonsillitis. He informed me this morning that I was acting Exec.

Everyone seems only half alive. Only when I feel the reassuring solidity of the pier under me, and get to a telephone with a line to Washington, will I feel that we are really in the world again.

May 22, 1944

Three all-too-short days of leave, and a chance to get down to Washington.

Learned by way of scuttlebutt that my friend Gibbons, who I left at Conversion and Maintenance in Miami, was transferred to the frigate *Sandusky* at New Orleans, and is headed for, or has already traversed the Canal, enroute to the West Coast. Lieutenant Mintz, our good friend and mentor in the clothing locker when we first arrived at Curtis Bay, is catching another frigate, the *Grand Island*, in California, perhaps at San Diego. Bergfeld, the hero of the player-piano farce, the oldest man in our class, has taken over the clothing locker as one of the senior supply officers at the Base. And so, our classmates and faculty members are moving out into the distant theaters of the war and taking over important posts at home, which was the goal of that ninety-day pressurized indoctrination in the first place.

Weather's hot and sultry tonight and it has crept in below decks. When I got aboard I found that Turner and one of our ensigns, named Nead, were the only officers here. Everybody else is away on leave. Ramsay's gone to Boston for something.

The three of us had dinner, hot and lonesome in the wardroom, and afterward Turner went off to town to buy some railroad tickets to Colorado—he's going on trip leave this time.

May 25, 1944

Had a nasty experience last night.

Turner still had the duty, but was feeling rocky from some medicine he had taken and I volunteered to relieve him. I stretched out on my bunk to do some reading, having first told the messenger at the gangway to call me if any need arose. Then, apparently, I fell asleep.

Just before midnight I was awakened by loud noises on our mess deck and, in the time it took me to strap on my .45, grab my cap and start up the ladder, I realized some booze had been smuggled aboard.

When I strode around the big icebox and onto the mess deck, there were all the restricted characters aboard who had lost their shore liberties for one or another infraction of the regulations, sitting at one of the long tables, drinking and laughing uproariously.

Yelling, "Quiet!" with all the strength I could muster, I walked over to Nelson, sitting in the center, the ringleader in practically all hell-raising but probably the best sailor aboard ship.

When I sniffed the liquor in his glass, I delivered myself of a thunderous lecture to "Break it up and get into your bunks!"

"I'll give you ten minutes," I told them. "There are some good men here and I don't want to put you on report."

I thought I had let them off decently enough, but when I returned to the drinking fountain and leaned over it for a sip, there was suddenly a loud commotion behind me as Nelson tackled one of our gunner's mates, an Irishman, who had apparently been headed for me. Nelson wrestled with the fellow and was joined by the red-head yeoman, a very decent kid who is seldom in trouble.

The Irishman was cursing the outrage of my wearing a gun and Nelson was snarling, "You crazy bastard, you'll get us all in trouble." Obviously the gunner's mate was almost blind drunk, and he finally collapsed exhausted and sobbing against Nelson, still blustering about what he would do if I took off the .45.

Then, up the ladder came Turner, looking pale, startled and half-awake. When I told him what had happened, he took over and asked the orderly why we hadn't been called. "We thought you heard it, sir," he answered lamely, the tone of his voice indicating he didn't really think that we'd swallow that—but hoped that we might. Clearly he hadn't wanted to get in bad with the crew by calling us.

"Hell! The dock police would have been here in a minute," Turner said.

In about half an hour the place was quiet and Turner had supervised the disposal of the liquor. "I think you were right," he told me. "Let's not make out a report unless we have some more trouble."

We had no more trouble and at breakfast this morning Turner made a remark about the "Irish Mutiny."

When I saw the gunner's mate on deck this afternoon, he met my gaze directly for a moment and then dropped his glance respectfully, and I knew he was saying, "As an Irishman I am not ashamed of what happened, but I appreciate what you and Mr. Turner did for me."

Nelson, seaman extraordinary, showed me an almost mischievous deference when I encountered him a couple of times.

May 29, 1944

This is our ninth trip to Guantanamo. We are three days out of New York. This evening someone on the bridge said, "This must be the weather that tempts people in peacetime to go to sea." The surface of the ocean was untroubled. A peacefulness reminiscent of that hour back home when the robins sing and the shadows gather among the lilacs seemed to creep over us. There was no spot on all that wide ocean where a shadow might form. Broad as a plain, smooth as a desert, it reached away illimitably into the distance.

The nineteen ships of our convoy were limned like camels against the vast expanse. Under the spokes of the down-streaming sun, three escorts crawled along to the westward. Three others maneuvered on the other side of us. For the first time we have a group of seven escorts; but two of them are with us only temporarily, being scheduled for detachment and duty elsewhere after they reach Guantanamo.

The perfect repose of the evening, the extra protection of the unusual number of escorts made a feeling of security inevitable. The ocean looked as harmless as a glass of drinking water. Then came the shattering, stunning reminder that under those tranquil depths the menace still lurks. A radio message was brought up to the bridge marked Urgent. We took it below and decoded it, and there was the dispatch, BARR AND BLOCK ISLAND BOTH TORPEDOED X REQUIRE IMMEDIATE ASSISTANCE.

The position given was out of range of us to the eastward. The same message had been sent to all ships in the Atlantic area, and probably was being read by dozens of them at that moment. Some would immediately go to the rescue; others, like us, would hitch their belts, forget about the sunset and the smooth water, and turn more sternly to the business on hand.

At the core of all good weather out here at this time, there is a germ of sudden death.

May 30, 1944

Back home on this day each year, my family made their pilgrimage to the little hillside cemetery near Fairfax Courthouse, Virginia, where our forebears are buried. There is not a great deal of time out here to remember those things.

Today Stolzer took me on another kind of pilgrimage. What produced it was a casually facetious remark I had made about the lonely rigors of my job. "You feel lonesome in the wardroom decoding them messages during general quarters!" he snorted derisively. "You come with me. I'll show you what lonesome is like for the black gang," meaning, of course, the engine room crew.

"And I ain't takin' you to the engine room," he added. "There you got company!"

I had been in the roaring din and deafening confusion of the engine room on a couple of occasions, making the visits as brief as I decently could; but I had never been down to the fireroom where Stolzer now indicated he was determined to take me.

I probably could have found some way to get out of this unsought, undesired expedition; but I like Stolzer, and I am sure he likes me, and I didn't want to do anything to alter his respect for me, or to hurt his feelings. So I said, "Lead on, Mr. Stolzer. I'll take a look at your damned fireroom!"

The fireroom is reached by entering and descending an "airlock," which is located aft of the galley on the mess deck. We pass it every day, but I had never remotely considered going down there any more than I would have thought of going down in the bilges to check our keel. It involves going into the airlock and closing the outside door. An automatic klaxon starts as you open the door, and you know the door is closed when the klaxon stops its weird keening. You open the inside door (another klaxon), step onto the ladder, close the door (klaxon stops), and then begin the descent.

Stolzer had handed me a pair of gloves, and he carried some cotton waste as protection against the hot ladder rails. He led the way down into the fireroom which, he later explained, is kept under pressure by means of powerful fans, so that the danger of backfires from the burners in the boilers is minimized.

There must have been at least twenty rungs to that ladder. The place is down two decks and below the wardroom level. When you stood on the floor-plates the sound of the fans and the pressure on your ears was more than a little unnerving, as was the fury of those stiff, blue flames thrusting into the firebox. A water tender on duty down there was occupied with his tasks, and as we came down was wiping something up with a cloth. "You know Mr. Carr," Stolzer yelled above the din. "He wants to see if you're earning your pay."

I was convinced that he was earning twice his pay, but I was in no mood to debate the matter. "We've had a little dripping," the water tender said, "but I stay right after it." He had a whole basket of dirty rags beside him.

"Gudt," hollered Stolzer, reverting to his German accent. I tried to think of something to say, but the only thing coming to mind was, "Carry on," and I couldn't say it. My mental processes were not helped by the realization that this dynamic equilibrium of fire and air, in which we stood, was maintained somewhat below the level of a torpedo target.

I glanced again at the vivid blue flame and told myself that two hours would be a long watch down here. After what seemed an eternity, we were finally ascending. The first klaxon sounded, then the second, and gratefully we were on the messdeck and the suffocating turbulence was behind us.

"You've made your point," I told Stolzer. "I'll never even kid about my job again."

Stolzer grinned and grabbed me by the arm. "You're a nice man, Carr—a fine officer, but we all gotta get a look at the other fella's job sometimes."

Well, I'd gotten a look at the other fellow's job, and I remembered the water tender, who had reported aboard on one of our earlier trips, fresh from getting his training and his rating ashore. He went down to the fireroom, came back and reported to the sick bay where he stayed for the remainder of the trip. He later was discharged as a psychoneurotic. There had been a big debate in the wardroom—when is a guy crazy and when is he yellow?

Of one thing I am certain. The water tender down in that room is a brave man—perhaps braver than I am. I don't know. It is not my job to go down there. My job is to go down to the wardroom to decode messages when the crew is at battle stations. From now on, however, thanks to Stolzer, I will remember that there is a man one deck below me. Maybe a green kid from the country who has never been on a ship before. And there are other men below me, back aft, in the harried atmosphere of the engine room.

May 31, 1944

We have just about converted our forward deck to a beach club. Every afternoon at three, several of the officers gather up there to enjoy the sun. We carry blankets to spread out on the steel deck, usually dressed in shorts and a pair of sandals.

The allusion to a beach club is very apt. We have no sand, it's true, but we have the benefit of a steady breeze, sunshine consistently, regardless of the ship's heading, and a panorama of blue water and clouds. The place rides up and down just enough to prevent monotony, and by comparison to the weather we've been through, it seems positively stable. We can lean on our elbows, gossip, smoke, and pass a pleasant hour or two.

We have four visiting officers aboard again, and they are a pretty nice lot. I have gotten over any other feelings I might have had toward them. As a matter of fact, it is stimulating to exchange some new ideas with them. These particular officers are older than those in the last group. My favorite is a fellow in his forties who used to be a newspaperman in Newark.

The other day, before the rest of the loafers showed up, I took my blanket all the way forward to the bowpoint and spread it out so I could lean over the side and watch the prow cut the water. Then I discovered another pastime. As the golden globs of gulfweed came at the ship, I noticed that sometimes there was movement under them, and a closer scrutiny showed that many had little fish feeding on their particles, which detached themselves as the giant swish of our keel came along. Reminded me of a book of Dr. William Beebe's wherein he described a platform, built out from the bow of a vessel, and from which he dipped up specimens attached to this same seaweed.

I could also see the flying fish begin their lightning-swift flight under water, and travel some distance before they emerged and struck out above. Curiously enough, their progress is slower in the air than in the water, but I suppose the maneuver confounds their enemies.

Somehow, during some of our "weathery" trips we never envisioned the time when we could lie up there on the bow without getting socked on the head by a wave.

Yes, it is all very pleasant—except when we think of the *Block Island* and the *Barr*, and the men aboard them. And all those other ships and other men. "You have to go out, but you don't have to come back," is the recurring grim refrain. It seems to murmur from beneath the quiet waters, even as we sprawl lazily here in the sun.

19

"On the eve of this great
adventure, I send my best
wishes to every soldier in
the Allied team. To us is
given the honor of striking
a blow for freedom which
will live in history, and in
the better days that lie
ahead men will speak
with pride of our
doings. . . ."

Sir Bernard Law Montgomery,
message to his troops,
June 5, 1944, on the eve of
the Allied invasion of Europe.

June 6, 1944

WE RECEIVED THE NEWS OF the Invasion this morning in a very matter-of-fact manner.

The *Alacrity*, which was out practicing with us, called over the TBS to ask if we had picked up the broadcast they had just received on the news. We said we hadn't, and our operators immediately set about trying to get some further details. Up until the time we returned to port at two o'clock their efforts had been unsuccessful.

Guantanamo Base has a radio station which usually fills the air with rebroadcasts of special programs from the United States. We were certain they would give us more detailed accounts at the usual news hours of six or six-thirty on this Saturday night. Most of us didn't intend to go to the Club tonight because we are scheduled to sail early in the morning. I especially didn't intend to go, because I wanted to make up the payroll so that the crew could have a payday before they left the ship after our return trip. An additional reason was my right heel, which is swollen from some sort of fungus infection.

We turned on the radio at four-thirty and listened until seven. Not a word of news came over it in that time. Bob Hope programs,

Benny Goodman programs, Eddie Cantor shows, everything else came in bewildering succession—but not a single comment on this, a preeminent day in world history. We were almost persuaded the first report had been in error.

Then somebody suggested that the only place we could get news was at the Club; and besides, if the report proved to be correct, we ought to put on a celebration. Crippled up as I felt, and in spite of my intended paperwork, it seemed something too eventful to miss, and I agreed to go along with the rest.

At the Club we got a confirmation of sorts. Nobody knew much, but the profusion of repetitious reports argued conclusively for the validity of the main fact. The Invasion has begun and the war has entered a new phase.

We stormed the bar and assailed the waiters, with a rapid series of orders. This was something to celebrate. The sobering fact of the sacrifices that will still be demanded before the final victory escaped no one, but the important thing to all of us was that the tempo of the war has been quickened, that new forces have been set in motion that may mean changing assignments—perhaps a furlough home—and ultimately, of course, the end of the war. Small wonder then if that mahogany-paneled bar echoed with the voices of rising excitement and fresh enthusiasm.

We don't know the details and we probably won't know them for many a day—but we know that something very special in history is happening. Maybe it really is the beginning of the end.

June 8, 1944

As an aftermath of our celebration at the Club, most of us had headaches when we got to sea yesterday with our convoy. We also had a new feeling about the war and an enormous curiosity about what was going on.

"I told those radio operators to get us some news," the Captain told us at lunch, wearily rubbing his eyes, reddened from a long period on the bridge following the celebration of the night before. "And I told 'em to find out what Churchill said," he added.

That brought an enthusiastic response from all of us at the table. "Old Winnie will tell us," Cooney said. "Good or bad, he'll give it to us straight."

Although they were two days late getting to us, we finally got our bulletins this afternoon, one copy tacked up on the wardroom bulletin board, and another copy on the mess deck for the crew. Someone said our operators had gotten a rebroadcast from the BBC.

The dateline was London, June 6, 1944, and this was much more exciting than the Secretary's Christmas greeting. I have copied much of it. Churchill's influence is so profound that I think there is something to be gained from the mere writing down and repeating to oneself of his words.

> Prime Minister Churchill said Allied troops had penetrated in some cases several miles inland after effective landings on the French coast over a broad front. The Prime Minister said he had visited the various centres where latest information is received and could state that "This operation is proceeding in a thoroughly satisfactory manner."
>
> "Many dangers and difficulties which appeared at this time last night extremely formidable are behind us," the war leader reported. "Passage of the sea has been made with far less loss than we apprehended."
>
> Mr. Churchill, addressing the House of Commons after a visit to General Dwight D. Eisenhower's headquarters in company with King George, described the landing of airborne troops on the European continent as an outstanding feat "on a scale far larger than anything there has been so far in the world.
>
> "These landings took place with extremely little loss and great accuracy."
>
> Earlier he told the cheering House that the Allied liberating assault "was proceeding according to plan—and what a plan!"
>
> In tones of confidence, he reported that the Allied forces had been transported across the Channel to the shore of France by "an immense armada" of our ships with several thousand smaller craft—probably the greatest fleet ever assembled.
>
> "There are even hopes that actual tactical surprise has been attained," he continued, "and we hope to finish the enemy with a succession of surprises during the course of the fighting.
>
> "The battle which is now beginning will grow continuously in scale and in intensity for many weeks to come, and I shall not attempt to speculate upon its course."

The bulletin added that to a cheering Parliament Mr. Churchill took "formal cognizance of the liberation of Rome," stating, "American and other forces of the Fifth Army broke through the enemy's last line and entered Rome, where Allied troops have been received with joy by the population."

There was a later dispatch on our bulletin board which said "Prime Minister Churchill announced today that Allied airborne troops had captured several strategic bridges in France before they could be blown up and that 'there is even fighting proceeding in the town of Caen.'"

So there it was, bracing, wonderful, almost too good to be true. But Churchill had said it, and to me that gave it ironclad authenticity.

I think everyone aboard feels the same way. There's a change in the atmosphere. While I was reading the last bulletin, Captain Ramsay slapped me on the back. "Hell, Carr," he said, "I feel so good I think I can take a couple of games of gin away from you."

And I saw to it that he did. I played all the way for "gin," drew for the middle card of a run, or the fourth of a kind. This guy is Captain of our ship and has brought us through a helluva lot, even though—like me—a couple of years ago he was a civilian. I often wonder if some of these young commanding officers, who have attained rank so quickly out here, will be able to win comparable recognition when they get back into civilian life.

However, we are still living in the moment. The war news is incredibly good, the weather is moderate, and I am reasonably happy. We are not heroes, but we are doing our job. And we are a long way from the frightful conflict in which so many of our fellow men are engaged.

June 10, 1944

We had our own phase of a "stepped-up war" today.

We were playing gin rummy in the wardroom this afternoon when a tremendous jar shook the ship. "By God," exclaimed Stolzer, "that was a big wave!" We kept on playing and then again came this bang against our side like some giant hammer. "Must be a fish trying to get in," I said. I barely got the words out before alarms went all off over the ship, and we suddenly realized that what we were experiencing were shock waves from underwater explosions. We raced up the ladder to the mess deck, where Stolzer bolted aft and I scrambled on upwards.

On the bridge I heard the Captain saying into the phones, "I think we have a sub. A PC has made a run and dropped charges and the blimp has dropped a stick of bombs."

We were steaming over to the unprotected side of the convoy. The PC was running wildly around in circles trying to establish contact and the blimp was hovering overhead.

Almost immediately our sound man said, "Check bearing 045."

"Bearing is foul—it is a merchant ship," was the reply.

Then a moment later, "Check bearing 270."

"Bearing clear," from the Captain. Here we go! This is what we have been waiting for!

"Man the hedgehog," came the command, and the number one gun crew jump to their stations round the awkward-looking monster. Contacts are coming in a steady stream. This is too perfect, I think. What will go wrong?

At 1200 yards the hedgehog is manned and ready. We call the PC to stand clear. We are coming in on a contact.

One thousand yards, nine hundred, eight hundred. How the seconds drag. At seven hundred we take a lead. Right on in we come.

"Stand by to fire." The damn blimp is almost in line of fire. Will he turn in or out? It is too late to warn him. After two seconds that seem like hours he does turn slightly away.

"Fire!"

The stream of projectiles from the hedgehog roar upward like angry hornets. The blimp is running now, straining, rudder hard over, to get out of there.

Then in a few moments our K-guns throw the ashcans out from our sides like giant frogs jumping from a steep bank. Finally, we roll the heavy, deep-set cans off the stern. The pattern is complete.

Suddenly there is an enormous explosion that seems to rip the sea asunder. Then a gigantean bubble of air, fully thirty feet across, appeared. "My God," shouted a man in the gun crew, "he's surfacing!" But nothing like that happened. A large oil slick starts to form. We swing in a wide circle and come around for another run, but cannot regain contact.

We are smitten with both disappointment and relief. We cannot pick it up again. We make another run, crossing and recrossing our previous track. God! How can they have gotten away so quickly!

Finally the CTU decides we should be back with the convoy and we leave the PC and the blimp to continue the search. Reluctantly we steam back toward our station, uncertain as ever as to what we may have hit or damaged below the waves.

June 11, 1944

This morning the PC rejoined our screen, having been relieved by other ships sent out as a result of our messages. No further action was reported. Once more, apparently, we will not be entitled to wear a star on our American Theater campaign ribbons, nor have a scalp painted on our stack.

Sighted a drifting life raft this morning and ran in close. It was the Merchant Marine type with two air tanks, one of which seemed to have been punctured—rusted through, Ramsay surmised.

The only sign that there had been any human presence was the fact that the locker containing the emergency rations was open and empty. The thing must have been in the water a long time, because it had collected moss on the under side and a number of sizable fish were feeding on it.

We circled it twice, trying to find some identification, then went on. The drifting derelicts of the war—with their often unknown tragic stories—will be floating about the seas for a long time.

The news from Europe continues good, but according to the bulletins catching up with us, Churchill sounded a note of caution in the House of Commons on Thursday, warning against over-optimism in the Battle of Europe and against "the idea that things are going to be settled in a rush."

"Although great dangers lie behind us," the bulletin quotes him, "enormous exertions lie before us. . . ."

I think that's probably something all of us had better remember.

Today's date reminds me that a year ago I reported in at Coast Guard Headquarters in the Customs House in Boston. Things could have been a lot worse and, in spite of a bit of wear and tear, we have managed to get through the year, which is, as Churchill might say, "more than I apprehended" a year ago.

Going to play some more gin with Stolzer tonight. He plays like we're betting blood. On one of our earlier trips he was playing with Doc Hofstra and, slamming his cards down violently. When he "ginned" after drawing only about three cards, he said, "Doc, I'm gonna hit you with a blivvet!" And when Doc, red-faced, with a handful of face cards, inquired hotly, "What in hell is this blivvet?"

Stolzer had jumped with glee and said in effect it was "twelve pounds of manure in a ten-pound bag!"

Today has been uneventful. Seas moderate.

June 12, 1944

I had just climbed up to the bridge this morning when another explosion shook the ship, followed by columns of water over by a PC on the starboard side.

"I have a contact," he says.

"Sink it," we say with the new found bravado gathered from our day-before-yesterday exploit.

In the next hour he continues making runs and dropping charges until he is out of sight astern. But he never asks for assistance.

Two tankers over on the starboard side, who have been stragglers all trip and have caught hell from us for "smoking up" before dark, are suddenly catching up with the formation. You can almost see them turn up another knot every time a charge goes off.

June 13, 1944

We saw several "black fish" this morning, and, as far as I'm concerned, they are small, dark-colored whales. I actually spotted three of them, and one was blowing. But the oldtimers who peered in their direction insisted, "They're black fish—you often see 'em around here, off Norfolk."

Our final Invasion bulletin was sobering and gave detailed losses on ships sunk or damaged. An ominous note was the information that the enemy were concentrating their submarines against Allied cross-Channel lifelines.

Despite this news and the realization that the Germans were being kept very busy on the other side, we are standing extra watches.

This has been quite a trip!

June 14, 1944

This morning the commodore's ship gives the word a gun crew member on one of the freighters is sick. The usual symptoms including pain in stomach.

The doctor asks if the man has had his appendix out. No. Well, it looks bad. The doctor goes aboard her. Very shortly the word comes back, "Acute appendicitis. Imperative to operate as soon as possible."

At least we are nearing port. Some hurried calculations show one of the PC's could reach a base in twenty-four hours on a force run. Too risky to pick up a plane in this bumpy sea.

So the PC is ordered alongside the freighter to take the doctor and patient aboard. We return to our screening station. An hour later the PC cuts a pretty figure as she steams at full speed on her new mission.

All sailors are going to have to have their appendix out before they go to sea, or a breed without the offending organ is going to have to be discovered.

June 16, 1944

We went up to the Officers' Club at Staten Island to celebrate after we got in. It was good coming in this time. For some reason there were quite a few spectators around Pier Eight. Our maneuvers were perfect; we hit the tide right and didn't get crosswise of the slip. Our lines went through the air like professionally-thrown lassos, and dropped right into the proper spots and hands. Back aft I was barking my commands officiously, and we settled against the pier as gently as a canoe.

Then came the final command of all voyages, like putting a period at the end of a log, "Double up and secure." Meaning, of course, to put out duplicate lines and to fasten them securely.

Mr. Ramsay came down from the bridge, followed by Cooney, both obviously pleased by our performance, and doubtless enjoying the added feeling of well-being from the "payday" I had passed out to all hands while we were coming up the channel.

"Carr," the Captain said, "let's get a drink."

At the Club he met some friends and introduced me, saying, "This is my finance officer who used to be an officer of a bank back in Washington, D.C."

If he wanted to tack on that part of it, it was all right with me. I felt at the moment salty, tough, and experienced, and the bank once again was something far removed from the immediate present.

The drink was delicious. And suddenly I had a deepened sense of belonging in that atmosphere of seagoing characters.

20

| "Refrain from peering too far."
| *Olympian Ode*
| Pindar (518-438 B.C.)

June 23, 1944

TURNER IS BACK FROM HIS trip to Denver. He loves the West and his eyes shine when he talks of seeing the mountains again and breathing that wonderful air.

During my hurried visit to Washington, I found that "the little man" is toddling all over the apartment now, and has cleared—or caused to be cleared—all the tables and shelves within his reach. He did a complete wrecking job on one of my Guatemalan pigs before the message got across. Dee was very apologetic about it, but after coming from our practice at "wrecking things" it seemed a very unimportant bit of depredation.

We had dinner tonight, Turner and I, in the large, gleaming Grill Room of the Hotel Commodore, with its immense oval bar that exudes a cheery elegance, along with an Irish brand of New York hospitality. Had sparkling burgundy as a reminder of Guantanamo. Smiled at some Spar and Wave officers, whose principal duty, I think, is to look pretty, as well as efficient.

Bought a copy of the *Times* and caught the subway downtown. The war news is good, except for the casualty figures from the Invasion which are now coming in. Four thousand dead and 11,000 wounded. Way back when I was a kid in Southwest Washington, I learned, "In Flanders' fields the poppies blow between the crosses, row on row. . . ." I wonder what verse this war will produce.

There was something a bit puzzling about Captain Ramsay's self-satisfied expression when he and Cooney came back aboard a few minutes ago from their convoy briefing.

I have a feeling that something is up, but they didn't say anything except that they were going to the Club for a quick drink and officers' liberty would expire at midnight.

Cooney takes a sight with a sextant

Our mess attendant culprit just came clinking and clanking to the door of the Pay Office to ask for some fountain pen ink. He went over the hill for the second time the other day, but was immediately caught by Shore Patrolmen. Now we have him securely fettered in leg irons. I didn't look around as I handed him the ink, but I wondered for a brief instant if I would feel a crack on my head.

June 24, 1944

The reason for Ramsay's elation is the size of our convoy—forty-eight ships (our largest)—including two ammunition ships bound for the Pacific. He attempts to cover up his gratification at this considerable responsibility by fussing about on the bridge.

"Wouldn't you know," he complained this morning, "that it would 'haze up' just when we have those two big pregnant bitches back there!"

There is quite a surface mist but the seas are moderate, and we appear to be moving into formation without difficulty. Coming down the channel this morning there was a haunting nostalgia in hearing the familiar command to "Set sea watches."

June 25, 1944

We learned from Ramsay at lunch that the *Block Island*, torpedoed during our last trip, was one of the converted carriers that has been the nemesis of subs in the Atlantic for the past year or more. She had a brilliant record and did her share of knocking off many of the undersea craft. The *Barr* was one of her screening destroyer escorts. The Germans were no doubt especially anxious to get her.

June 26, 1944

Somewhere opposite the Carolina coast tonight, with the moon throwing a languorous track. The air is soft and scented, and already the temperature below deck is oppressive.

Back in the moon haze our forty-eight ships dip along. They say the ammunition ships would blow up the whole convoy if they ever went off, but we don't worry about it much. Their position is in the center of the group.

Our old friend and shakedown partner, the *Intensity*, is running with us this trip. The *Alacrity* is in drydock getting her new sound gear. The *Intensity* has already been converted and we will be going in soon.

Oh, lovely prospect of shore leave!

June 27, 1944

Sighted another pitiful floating symbol of somebody's last hope. Just before dark we went to general quarters with a small target on the horizon. Turned out to be a lifeboat floating perpendicularly with only its nose out of water. We put our searchlights on it, but again there was no identification. Only the silent bobbing reminder that sometime, somewhere, an unknown number of souls had been forced to commit themselves to its too-frail protection.

June 28, 1944

If I ever attempt to write a formal history of the *Haste*, I shall probably call it something like "Twenty Times Past San Salvador."

There are few spots as significant in world history, yet few are passed with less ceremony than occurs when we traverse this stage of our voyage. To most of us, by now, it is but a friendly strip of land marking our entrance into the islands, which is the way we speak of this portion of the sea. If a strong wind is blowing, it diminishes; if the weather is bad in the higher latitudes, we know beforehand that when we enter this shelter the sun will shine warmly, the ocean burn with a magic blue, and a sense of well-being pervade the atmosphere.

The strain of convoying is not only physical, but psychological. The greater part of our work consists in waiting and searching for a fight that very rarely, if ever, takes place. And yet, every escort or patrol ship is supposed to be completely alert from the time she passes the sea buoy until she returns to harbor. Our efforts, for the most part, are unknown to the general public. There is nothing heroic in unfought battles. So, despite the need for constant alertness, the searches, the false alarms, and frequent exasperations with the vagaries of the ships we are escorting, there are still long hours of excruciating boredom and frustration.

Consequently, a holiday spirit descends on the *Haste* when we enter these waters. Suddenly our downward journey is almost complete. Men smile more easily and speak in a friendlier manner to each other. In the evening, under the magnificent skies of this area, they lounge on the bridge and fantail, and a sense of good fellowship prevails. The petty bickerings and quarrels, which strain and boredom produce, are forgotten. The ship becomes one again, welded by the common phenomenon of lifted spirits.

Undoubtedly the same thing happened in greater measure among Columbus' crew. After days of fear and uncertainty and disappointment, suddenly the low-lying shadow of land spread an unguent upon their souls that led them to give thanks for their salvation, and to name the island appropriately, San Salvador.

June 29, 1944

In brilliant blue weather, the tropic birds wheeling and darting above us, we broke off from the convoy and headed for Guantanamo. Stolzer, standing next to me on the bridge, watching the departing convoy with its new escorts, observed, "I'm glad to see them floozies go," meaning, of course, the ammunition ships.

Cooney, nearby, looked at Stolzer, who—like all of us—was bare to the waist, and remarked with a detached expression, "When the hairs on your chest turn gray, I guess you're really getting old."

Stolzer pretended to burn, but before he could say anything Cooney went on, "Mr. Carr has a lot of gray hair at his temples but not on his chest."

Stolzer had come from a tough school, and in a sense so had Cooney. In his previous nine months on the *Modoc*, in the North Atlantic, Cooney had said he was ribbed, galled, hazed, and derided by wardroom mates who taught him to give back as good as he got. "You can imagine," he told me, "what a regular C. G. Academy graduate officer would say to a landlubber Reserve kid like the one I was when I came from civilian life direct to deck duty!"

Now, aboard the *Haste*, Cooney and Stolzer were well matched and often put on a great show of apparently virulent exchanges. Cooney had ribbed Stolzer before about the full-rigged ship tattooed across the same gray-haired chest. Today, continuing the exchange, Stolzer regarded the younger man in the manner of one about to pose a question to which he already knew the answer. "Mr. Cooney," he shot out, "how much of a living did you make before you came out here?"

"None," said Cooney blandly. "I never worked before. I was in school."

"Well, I want to see you, sonny boy, when you're my age and

have three kids," Stolzer snorted. "Maybe you couldn't even come out here at forty!"

"Okay, Adolph," grinned Cooney, using Stolzer's first name, which most of us avoided. "I wasn't casting any aspersions on your virility or ability."

"You see what kind of brass they send us out here?" Stolzer addressed the rest of us. "This Mr. Education who never made a dime!"

Having heard enough, or being merely bored, Mr. Ramsay looked toward the shore and said, "Gents, the first jackpot of any kind gets a buck from each of us."

There was a general chorus of "Agreed!" The shore tower was already blinking admittance to us with the steadying promise that before long we would feel land under our feet again.

July 1, 1944

Turner and I left the ship together this afternoon, headed for the Club. We saluted the Chief on duty at the gangway, walked a couple of steps down the contraption, and turned to salute the flag on our stern. We perform this little ceremony routinely now, but it is one that we like.

I recall going aboard the ship for the first time in Boston with Adams. "We stop and salute, you know," Adams had said. I didn't know, so I dropped behind him a couple of steps. He started up the gangway, then turned to salute the fluttering ensign astern. Then, saluting the man on watch, he sang out, "Ensign Adams reporting aboard." I followed suit, feeling a little awkward and self-conscious and wishing I could bawl it out as well as Adams did in his heavy drawl.

We have come aboard and gone ashore hundreds of times since then, and saluted the flag on the stern in all kinds of weather and in all kinds of spirits. Few of the routines we perform are more inspiring than this simple salute to one's ship and one's flag.

After dinner we went to the movies and saw Betty Grable in "Pin-Up Girl," with Martha Raye, John Harvey, and Joe E. Brown. Not bad. Betty was greeted almost as if she were making a personal appearance as soon as her form was flashed on the screen.

July 4, 1944

Another Independence Day. We were firing outside again. Mr.

Ramsay does a lot of drinking at the club, but he gets us out here early in the morning for practice. And he looks as well as any of us, and perhaps a little better. He has enormous energy and he is determined to be a good Skipper.

"These kids are getting so damned tired of practicing," said Turner, "I bet they can shoot a star-shell in their sleep."

July 6, 1944

We almost cut the *Intensity* in two this afternoon. We were returning from another practice session and were scheduled to tie up outboard of her.

We came in fast, banking on the wind which suddenly cut out entirely. In a flash, we were pointed for our sister ship amidships.

From my position back aft, I heard the engine room bells and the throttleman yell, "Two thirds astern," then immediately "Full astern," and the old *Haste* "rared back," shaking and shuddering with all her might. But it was too late to avoid the crash. Our bow rode up on the *Intensity's* deck, snapping off a steel davit, then crumpled two life rafts into pulp and kindling. The steel plates of the two ships carried on a noisy war of their own, with much screeching and groaning, but fortunately nothing else gave way. When we dropped our lines over, we literally threw them around the necks of the *Intensity's* gang, so high were we sitting over them.

The Skipper looked mightily chagrined when he came down from the bridge. But by midnight tonight the yard workmen had repaired and replaced much of the damage.

Stolzer, our machinist, emerging from the engine room hatch after this afternoon's accident, was livid with anger, but still cautious enough to make sure the Skipper was not within earshot before vehemently exclaiming to me, "If we go 'full astern' like that many more times, them engines will be goin' out into the bay by themselves!"

That was a regal blast from a regal little engineer with a very regal name, Adolph Heinrich Wilhelm Stolzer. "I really got 'em all," he shyly confessed to me when we were making out some forms in connection with a promotion he received after Pangle's transfer. Hitler had poisoned his first name, Himmler, his second, and the Kaiser hadn't helped him much with his third. Small wonder that years before he had opted for the nickname, "Dutch."

249

July 7, 1944

I suppose the way we feel about anything depends upon our immediate mood. We are always glad to get here—but equally glad to depart. At the moment, I shall be very glad to get out of this place. Heard it referred to the other day as a "bastard base," and the term seems appropriate enough, probably because it has become a sort of backwater of the war. They've had seventy-four accident victims here in the past few weeks, most of them airplane casualties.

One plane hit a mountain in broad daylight. Another ran down a crash boat in a daytime takeoff. A Lieutenant Commander drove a jeep into a truck—and so on. Some people say the heavy drinking is having its effect; others, that the mishaps are all a result of boredom and carelessness.

Apropos of the drinking, Brownie told me the other day that the "ration" per officer in the package store was three bottles of rum and one bottle of whiskey per day. When I protested that the term "ration" implied some restriction, he explained, "Why, hell—they'd drink ten bottles a day if we'd sell it to 'em!"

However, at the moment, my main and very personal reason for wanting to get away is the fact that my foot has been acting up again down here in the heat—just as I had been afraid it might, but hoped it wouldn't. Our decks are hot, the roadways and walkways are hot when we go ashore, and the damned infection just doesn't clear up. I have tried several medications at the suggestion of Doc Randall (who replaced Hofstra), but without success.

July 11, 1944

Three long days and nights at the bottom of the ship, seeing neither sun, nor stars, nor blue sea. Like living in a submarine.

The "tropical fungus" in my heel brought me down flat in my bunk. My ankle grew to look like a coconut, and shades that seemed no part of human pigmentation spread over it. Doc and the pharmacist mate went to work valiantly and did battle as best they could with the vicious micro-organisms. Whatever it was that brought me down has not been diagnosed or identified beyond "a combination of things, beginning with the skin infection." Meanwhile I was engulfed in some of the minor apsects of misery and loneliness.

The only way I knew daylight had arrived was by the advent of the faithful mess boy, who brought me a glass of ice water at seven.

The pharmacist mate bathed and tended my foot at nine every evening, then put out the lights and retired topside. Between those two events there was a void of almost complete blackness, heat, and partial sleeplessness.

Our new room (Turner's and mine) is forward of our former room, contains only two bunks, and is partially closed off from the wardroom lobby by the bulkhead of the gyro room, which leaves only a narrow passage to the entrance. When the lights are put out, the room is stygian at first, then a faint glow is reflected on our metal cabinet from the crimson blackout bulbs outside. If anyone with claustrophobia woke up in this room, he'd tear himself to pieces. If he were an ardent student of Dante's *Inferno*, he might think he had finally arrived.

On our way down I was not fully aware of how utterly bleak and isolated it was. But during the three days and nights just past, the fine details of its loneliness and detachment have etched their way into my consciousness.

During my incarceration, the Captain came down and looked at my foot and sardonically inquired if I was malingering. Some of the officers would stop in to visit me during the day and bring whatever news there might be. Most of the time I thought about home and listened to the water gurgling within six inches of my ear.

Turner was most helpful, and when he crawled out for his four-to-eight watch he always had a cheery word, or came up with some kidding remark about how some people could stay "flaked out" in their bunks. And somehow the time passed till I could hobble up and breathe a restoring lungful of sea air.

Today I spent a couple of hours in a cot on deck. The foot is much better; still swollen, but more human-looking. I have hopes that it will be nearly well by the time we reach New York.

July 12, 1944

Yesterday, toward the end of the day, the thing happened that I have not permitted myself to think about in definite terms. The alarm sounded! Never had it seemed noisier.

I threw myself off the bunk. There was a sudden fracturing explosion of little lights in my head and a sickening sensation of pain. The thought surfaced, "This is it—the thing has hit!" I was anticipating the inrush of water and the secondary explosions, but then distantly I heard the alarm again, stridently, urgently, "Come out!" it seemed to say.

I found myself crawling to my feet in the crimson light near the door to the gyro room, moisture streaming down my face as quickly, miraculously I had hold of the ladder and was pulling, pushing, hauling myself upward. "I fell!" I said to myself. "That goddamned foot was asleep. I've got blood running down my face." Without having looked, I felt it and could see it on my hand.

I crossed the deserted mess deck and threw myself, almost gasping aloud, at the second ladder. "Those bastards came out of there." I found myself cursing. "I heard their goddamned feet on the ladder as I went down. They didn't even wait for me!" And I was totally and immeasurably angry at having been left behind.

Then suddenly, very suddenly and very wonderfully, I was out on deck and the sky was still burnished with the sunset colors. The good air flowed into my lungs and I stumbled over to a stanchion.

Our black attack flag was up and we were coming hard to starboard. Behind me at the machine gun crew, I heard someone say the lookouts had spotted a torpedo. From my position on the main deck, I could interpret little more from the action around me, but one thing was certain—I was not going to engage in the ignominy of struggling up that ladder to the bridge in my barefoot, bloodied condition, and stand there like a wounded jackass. The hell with it! I would wait it out down here.

The minutes stretched out and the antique gold sky faded. We never made contact. Perhaps the first sighting had been in error—a big fish, a shark, or a sail, they suggested later. And just before word came to secure from general quarters, the leveling, balancing thought came to me, "Don't be angry at those guys—the reactions, the orders, the training, is 'get out and get ready to fight.' You would have done the same thing." In its starkness this evolved itself into a piece of almost Old Testament-like philosophy that proclaimed, "Nobody runs your ladders for you; it's you and your own efforts against the hatchways of this world."

Afterward, when Doc came down to check my foot and apply a disinfectant and coagulant to my forehead, he said, "Mr. Carr, I guess you thought you'd had it, coming out of there."

"Doc," I answered thoughtfully, thankfully, remembering that favorite phrase of Levendoski, whom Doc had never even known. "You ain't just a-bird-turdin'!"

July 13, 1944

This may be my last night at sea. At least for the present. Captain Ramsay fired off a message to Headquarters requesting my transfer. This was not at all to Turner's liking, who thought I should try a "trip leave." However, Ramsay said, "You scared me back there. I thought you had blood poisoning. I think we'd better have a little survey to find out what's wrong with that foot."

Cooney, who stood grinning behind the Skipper, couldn't resist his habitual needling and contributed, "You're too old to be out here anyway, Carr." The broad, rascally smile was inviting a flare-back from me, but I was not going to argue about going ashore and Cooney knew it.

Anyhow, as far as I'm concerned, I've picked up the philosophy found among the majority of naval personnel of doing the job as best I can, taking my chances, volunteering for nothing, and leaving the rest to Headquarters and the fates.

We are slipping along easily and quietly on our way up Ambrose Channel toward the harbor. The twinkling flakes of phosphorus from our bow waves seem to wink at me as they go by.

I wonder if it is really my last night at sea.

July 18, 1944

Red lights, stemmed like flowers by the masts of ships here at Staten Island. All kinds of ships. Frigates, corvettes, PC's, SC's, members of general classes, yet each different in its own way. Like individuals, people almost, with special characteristics and quirks.

The *Haste* is outboard of the *Intensity* at Pier Number Eight. Across from us is a frigate, the *Natchez*, one of the first to come off the ways, and our partner on the hunter-killer mission back in September. Something about this night reminds me of Boston a year ago, when I was first becoming acquainted with sea duty. The same ship between us and the dock, workmen busy on interminable jobs, singing ventilators and, over all, the same sense of urgency and haste.

This is my next to last night aboard.

July 19, 1944

Well, I guess tonight is the last, incredible as it seems. I have finished up my accounts and the ship is sailing in the morning with a new pay officer aboard.

In vain I have tried to fall into something of a commemorative mood, but there doesn't seem to be anything to spark it. I feel nothing except confusion at getting off the ship, and wondering where my next job will be, and where I'll sleep tomorrow night. A year ago I would have thought such a feeling would be impossible. There would have been nothing but unmitigated relief at getting ashore again. But time and circumstances still wield their subtle magic. And a man, it seems, puts down roots even on an uncomfortable, crowded little vessel like this one.

Climbed up on the bridge awhile ago and peered around the harbor. A strong wind is blowing outside and whitecaps are visible out in the stream behind us. The *Haste* has been bucking and pulling at her lines like a show horse and we had to put out some steel cables. The cane fenders groan and squeak as she crowds up against the *Intensity*. Across from us now are four rusty Canadian corvettes, two of them having slipped in last night. A small vessel which was astern of us had to be hauled away because she was taking such a battering up against the pier.

A year of my life is gone—a confused, lonesome, often desolate year. One or two of the friendships I made will stick for a long time. The others have probably started to go already. I saw far more of the sea than I ever dreamed of as a kid; yet somehow most of the magic of the dream was gone. The romance and the glamour and the excitement I might have seen in it fifteen years ago were not there. Perhaps it was the war and the state of our nerves. Or perhaps it was just that I am fifteen years older and my interests have too long been elsewhere.

I wonder how it will all seem ten years from now.

21

> "And this day shall be unto
> you for a memorial. . . ."
>
> Exodus 12:14

July 20, 1944

CROSSED THE HARBOR THIS MORNING on the spacious Staten Island ferry, thoroughly enjoying the early morning view of the skyscrapers of lower Manhattan and the new and optimistic—even if uncertain—angle of circumstances from which I viewed them.

Afterward I passed one whole hour lounging on a bench in Bowling Green beside the statue of one Abraham De Peyster, who must have been one of the early town fathers of the little Dutch village of New Amsterdam. The finance officer at nearby Coast Guard Headquarters, 42 Broadway, would return after ten-thirty and I was to talk with him about my next assignment.

A sense of ecstatic relief at being ashore was tempered by the realization that there was nothing very heroic about my reason for being there, which was not as a result of the usual rotation-in-duty assignments but because of what Turner referred to as "a tropical disturbance in my foot." I wondered what attitude the finance officer would take toward my situation. He very quickly set me at ease.

Commander Sponburgh was a regular, perhaps a few years my senior in age, who turned out to be a quick, forceful and likable officer. Looking over my orders, he said, "Thirteen months. That's quite a while to serve on one of those things."

That was almost like a citation! So it had indeed been a long while; and perhaps, after all, I need not feel too abashed at being shunted ashore.

"There are still some men around here who haven't been out at all," he added, his eyes considering me closely for a moment, as though divining my thoughts. "We'll find a place for you around the harbor, and give you a few months to rest and get that foot back into shape."

When I started to say a word of thanks he stood up, and calling to a smiling blond Spar officer told her, "Take Mr. Carr to Transportation and tell them to find him a room uptown for a few days until we can make some arrangements for him." Then, holding out his hand, he said pleasantly, "There'll be another day—if the war lasts long enough. But, in the meantime," he concluded, using the customary Navy greeting for all personnel reporting to new posts at sea or ashore, "Welcome aboard."

Dee was almost unbelieving when I finally phoned the good news. Must write her a letter tonight, and make some closing entries in my diary.

July 21, 1944

Working temporarily at the District Office, 42 Broadway. It appears that I exchanged the masts of the *Haste* for another kind of spars. (A very bad pun.) Today I saw as many as three "two-stripers" with skirts on. The office must be at least fifty percent female now.

The Chief in Transportation contacted the Officers Service Committee at the Hotel Commodore where they have a listing agency for rooms. We got a list of four places—three for eight dollars a week, and one for nine dollars a week. Naturally, all of the eight-dollar ones were gone, but I was a little glad because the nine-dollar proved to be superior. My address is 179 East 80th Street.

This is an old brownstone house and my room on the third floor is what used to be termed a "hall bedroom." Small and scrupulously clean, it possesses a large window that looks out on the back yard. You can't see the yard without getting close to the window because there are several trees out there, but there is a wonderful view of their green leaves.

That window sold me the room. When the landlady showed it to me yesterday, I saw those leaves through the window almost immediately and said, a little unbelievingly, "Trees! Leaves!" "Oh, yes," the woman agreed pleasantly, "It really has quite a country atmosphere." That was for me. A country atmosphere on East 80th Street!

I seem to be sensitive now to anything green. I don't know whether it is the color itself, or the association with things that are rooted and stable. Perhaps it is all centered around the remark of Captain Boyce that the best cure for seasickness is to "sit under a tree and read a book." At any rate, after weeks of gray water and gray ships I find the color most attractive.

After taking the room, one of the first things I decided to do was to take a bath. Perhaps it was the bathroom itself that intrigued me. The wallpaper, in this supposedly utilitarian room down the hall, creates an effect like a trellis of roses. Little panels of pink flowers, that are really not roses at all, but only hybrids from some designer's imagination, run up the walls and extend across the ceiling. Soaking in the tub, the surprising thing to me was the extension of the design up there; it was such a radical departure from the usual practice of covering that portion of the room with mottled white paper. The space occupied by the skylight is the only imperfection in the arbor-like design.

The skylight shows that the house is old, especially the fact that it is a "deep" skylight with a peaked top covered with dirty glass. The bathtub shows that the house is old, too. It is narrow and lean, with painted sides, and you get the feeling that lots of bodies have been in it.

To me, there in the tub, the room was comfortable, almost cheery. I stretched, and sank deeper into the cool water. Even my foot, swollen and discolored, felt better. Merely being ashore, I discovered, is in itself a natural unguent. Finally, I splashed myself upright, climbed out and grabbed a towel. As I leisurely prepared to shave, the whole business seemed like a game—and the *Haste* was something I could forget for awhile.

Later, in my room, I unpacked my things and piled them neatly behind the draperies on the set of shelves that serve as a dresser.

After I emptied my suitcase, I stretched out on the chenille spread. My feet overhung the small bed, but I didn't mind; it was better than banging them against the wooden foot of the coffin-like bunk I occupied on the *Haste*.

A breeze was coming through the window. I knew it must be nearly seven-thirty. High up over the treetops there was a sense of brightness as of reflected sunlight, but the shadows were gathering in the yard. From the backs of the houses across the open space I could hear the sound of dishes. It was hard to believe that this was

New York City. For the first time in weeks, a day was going out with the proper sounds of people and homes, the way a day should go out. How different from the lonely, miserable dying of a day at sea in a blacked-out convoy.

July 22, 1944

Mist in the stone cliffs of lower Broadway this morning. You can smell the sea here, but how much better it smells here than aboard the *Haste!*

At the moment I have a new awareness of how wonderful land can be. Nerves that were thin as gossamer have a new feeling of strength and resilience. My foot has continued to improve. The Doc who looked at it said he thought I was allergic to one of the treatments Randall had tried. All in all, I am beginning to feel like a human being again instead of a mechanically functioning part of the *Haste.* But, as I look back, I realize that the real finale for me was on Thursday when she sailed.

Even in my eagerness to be ashore I found it difficult to leave. I suspect it is always like that. The things we long for, plan for, suddenly become in their realization a problem in readjustment and good-byes. I'd had an excellent excuse to remain until the last minute; the officer replacing me had failed to show up. For the first time, it began to appear the *Haste* would sail without a pay officer attached to her.

This was especially galling to me. Ever since her commissioning I had paid her in good weather and in bad, and I felt a responsiblity for her present plight. But in all the goodbyes, although the crew felt it and the officers felt it, there was not one word of reproach concerning the fact that the *Haste* would be facing a "moneyless" voyage.

At last the time came when the Captain said, "I guess we go without him," and giving me a last handshake, he headed up the outside ladder to the bridge. In the excitement of getting my bags together and crossing our sister corvette, the *Intensity,* moored inboard of us, I saw none of the other officers except Turner. That seemed fitting because it was with Turner I had bult up the warmest friendship. But, even here, we said very little in farewell.

At six-forty-five I was on the dock and the *Haste* was ready to get under way. The tugs worked her stern out, and then with a resounding blast of her whistle, she backed away under her own power. I walked from behind the *Intensity* to watch her. Out in the stream the ship looked pitifully small. I could see the caps of Cooney and the Captain on the bridge. Somebody waved from the forward deck and I waved back. It made no difference who it was. It was my farewell to them all. Turner, was there, but he didn't wave.

She slowed down, stopped, and then churned up a froth as the props started again. The *PG-92* was on her way—out to the gray water and the white foam and the perpetual, oppressive restlessness of the sea.

From the bridge of the *Intensity* they yelled, "Take in all lines." Suddenly I found that I was alone by the bollard where the Number Four line was fast. The seamen at that position on the *Intensity* looked at me somewhat quizzically, not daring to request my help, but I took three quick steps and threw the line off. I felt a strange warmth of satisfaction in making that small move, like doing a last favor for a friend. The tug towed them out, and they, too, were on their way.

Mechanically I walked to the center of the covered pier to see if the new pay officer was running up the dock; but he was nowhere to be seen. It seemed quite incredible to me. Under the circumstances almost any officer would have been aboard a couple of hours ago, since the sailing time of an escort could not be gauged with split-second accuracy, as anyone in this service must surely be aware.

I returned to my baggage and suddenly stopped short. The gap beside the pier held me transfixed. There, a few moments before, had been the two ships. Now, there were only the peaks of little clashing wavelets, struggling back to tranquility, and, across the slip, a view of the rusty Canadian corvettes. I had seen the ships go, and yet there was, in their absence, a suddenness and mystery—almost like the disappearance of life itself.

At seven-thirty my young, pink-cheeked relief climbed out of a cab, with his briefcase under his arm. He couldn't believe it when I told him he'd missed the ship. Later in the morning, Coast Guard Headquarters in New York sent him down the bay in a crashboat in a futile attempt to catch the *Haste*.

It bothered me perhaps more than it bothered him to think of the *Haste* sailing without a pay officer. The whole thing still seemed an almost unbelievable set of circumstances. The young officer had gone aboard the *Haste* two days before, with a reputed $25,000 for the *Haste's* payroll and expenses. He had deposited it in the safe and changed the safe's combination. Now the money and the *Haste* were at sea—and he was not.

But there was nothing I could do about it. All that bound me to the *Haste* had been severed. I turned my face toward shore, but I knew that later that night, as I walked the garden of this good earth, I would think of them out there. "After this day (I found myself saying the words aloud) I doubt if it will ever seem real again."